IMAGES
of America

PRAIRIE COUNTY

I0806218

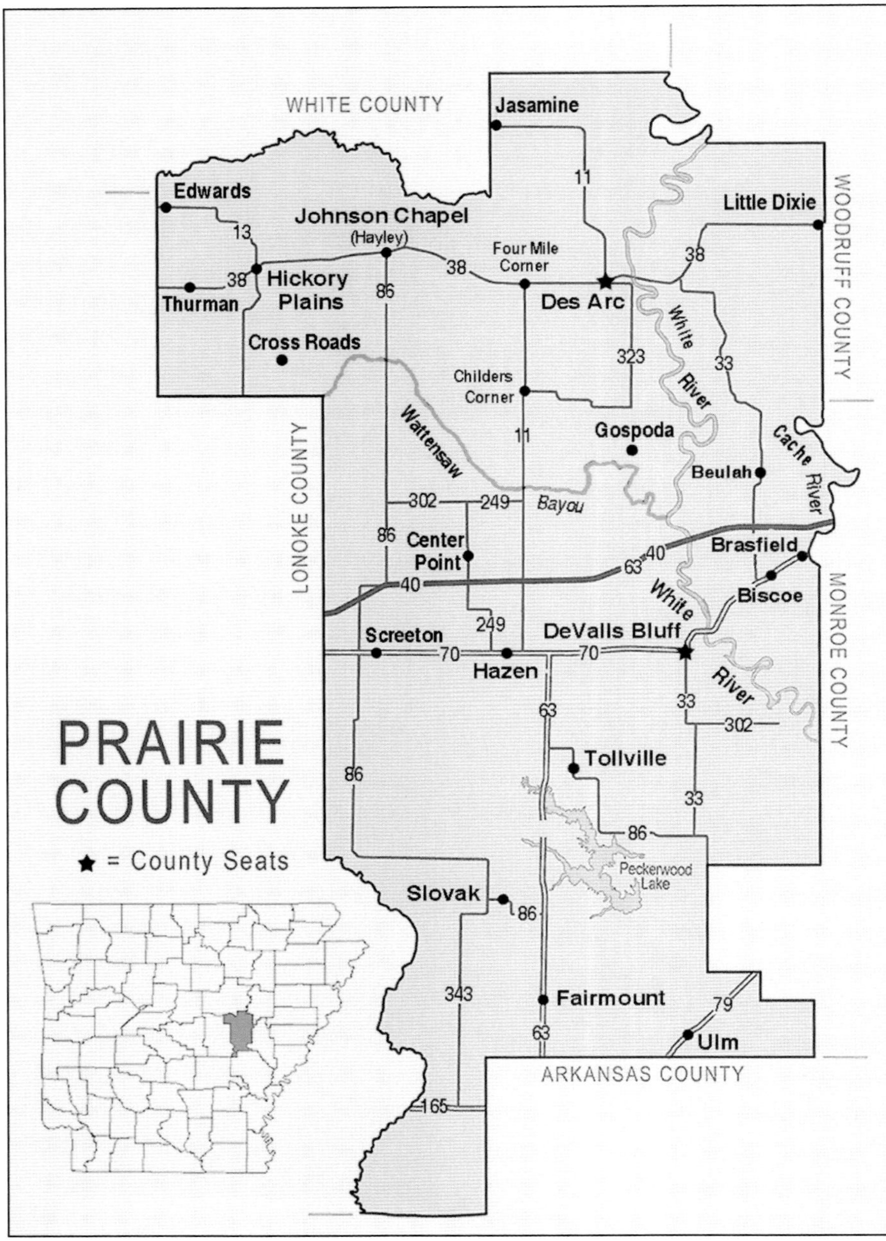

In 1885, Prairie County was divided into two districts, Northern and Southern, and DeValls Bluff was again made a county seat of government. It is believed the chief reason for the division was because it was difficult for those in the southern end to reach Des Arc when Wattensaw Bayou flooded. (Courtesy of Arkansas Highway and Transportation Department.)

On the Cover: DeValls Bluff's population had swelled to about 900 when this c. 1915–1920 photograph was taken on Main Street. Among the passengers in the car driven by Robe Mason are A.K. Johnson Sr., J.C. Morrill, and Paul Swinney. Sitting on the bench, order not known, are Bosy Nicholson, Dosy or Dosey Robinson, and ? Armstrong. All others are unidentified. (Courtesy of Harry Mason Jr.)

IMAGES
of America

PRAIRIE COUNTY

Bill Sayger

ARCADIA
PUBLISHING

ISBN 978-1-4671-1032-7

Published by Arcadia Publishing
Charleston, South Carolina

Printed in the United States of America

Library of Congress Control Number: 2013932259

For all general information, please contact Arcadia Publishing:
Telephone 843-853-2070
Fax 843-853-0044
E-mail sales@arcadiapublishing.com
For customer service and orders:
Toll-Free 1-888-313-2665

Visit us on the Internet at www.arcadiapublishing.com

This book is dedicated to the memory of Mike M. Anzaldua, my friend and a great humanitarian.

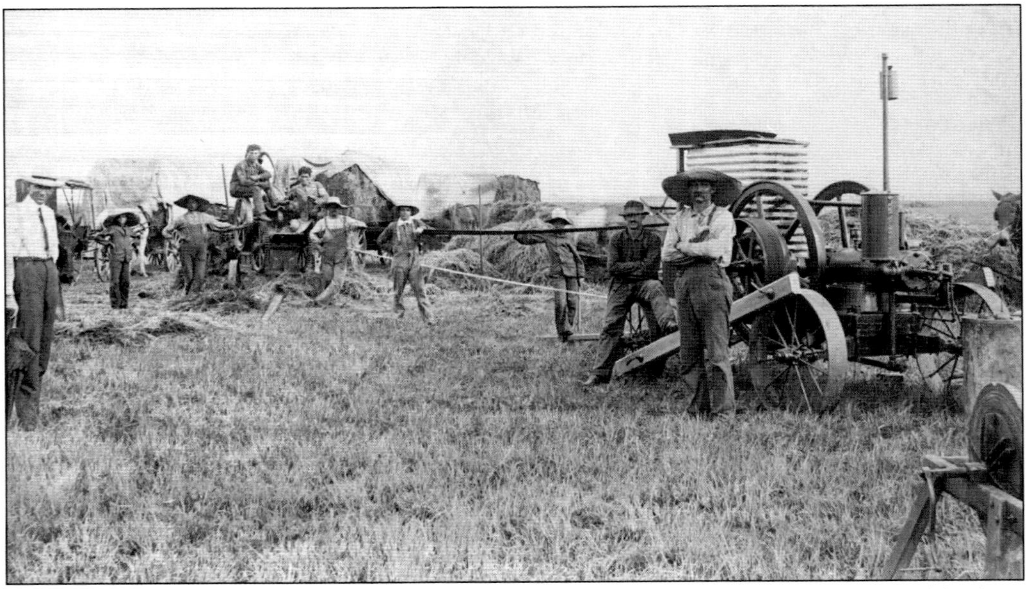

The workers are harvesting hay around 1905 on the farm of E. Wilkins, located roughly three miles southwest of Hazen on the Grand Prairie. The gasoline-powered hay press could produce 100 bales of hay per hour. (Courtesy of the late Ruth Carlley Austin.)

Contents

Acknowledgments

My thanks first to the Bill and Sharon Arnold Foundation for its financial support of the book's preparation. The Arnolds consider this an educational tool, and it is an extension of their mission and faith in God. Judy Toll-Booher's work, scanning the many photographs considered for the book as well as handling other tasks, was indispensable. A good number of pictures in her collection were selected. My friend Debbie Robinson Cook and I had a great time traveling the county in search of photographs. Debbie was a former county assessor. She and Carrie Acrey of Lonoke were typists for the project. The staffs at the Lower White River Museum, the Stuttgart Public Library, and the Museum of the Arkansas Grand Prairie, especially Gina Seidenschwarz, were very helpful and also provided pictures. Many photographs were obtained from the archives of the University of Arkansas at Little Rock, the Butler Center at the Central Arkansas Library, the Arkansas History Commission, and Torreyson Library at the University of Central Arkansas. We are also grateful for the many individuals in the county who shared their photographs with us.

INTRODUCTION

In 1846, a portion of Pulaski County was taken to form Prairie County. Its first settlers were more interested in hunting wild game and raising cattle and hogs than in cultivating the land. The 1850s saw the blossoming of the cotton culture and, with it, the importation of many more slaves.
Des Arc was the first white settlement in present-day Prairie County. Some consider 1845 its founding date, when W.L. Scroggs and James Erwin established a trading post there. The *Arkansas Gazette* announced in May 1848 that town lots were being sold.

Settlement of the Hickory Plains area began about 1845. In 1860, W.A. Garner and his wife opened the Hickory Plains Male and Female Institute, a private subscription school. Public schools would not appear in the county until after the Civil War.

In 1862, the Memphis & Little Rock Railroad was completed from the capital city to the bluff on White River, named for Jacob DeVall and his son Chappel. Large numbers of Union soldiers were stationed there from 1863 to the end of the Civil War and later, to protect the railhead and port there. The town grew rapidly. In 1871, the last of the rails were laid connecting Little Rock to Memphis.

The east side of the county was fertile delta land that was suitable for growing cotton. It included Biscoe, Beulah (Upper Hill), and Brasfield, which was annexed from Monroe County in 1869.

Hazen was surveyed and laid out in 1873. It was named for the William C. Hazen family members, slave owners who settled there in the 1850s. The St. Louis Southwestern Railway (Cotton Belt) laid a branch rail line from Stuttgart to the town in 1911.

The early farmers had little interest in settling on the prairie land, and malaria was a problem in river bottoms and along streams. They preferred to settle on the rolling land with its mixture of prairie and timber. However, around 1880, a scattered community called Fairmount started forming on the southern end of the county on the Grand Prairie.

In 1880, the Payers, Kornbaums, and Packebush families moved from Illinois and settled near the present site of Ulm (first called Payer). In 1889, Henry Kerksieck, formerly a Union soldier stationed in Prairie County during the Civil War, arrived on a Cotton Belt train along with livestock, household goods, and eight children. Most of the early settlers there were German and Lutheran.

In 1888, Burgess Toll and his older sons purchased land at the present site of Tollville, where he and his family built their homestead and engaged in farming. They also worked in timber, as they had their own sawmill, along with other business ventures. In 1912, the Rock Island Railroad laid a branch line from Stuttgart to Mesa, passing through Tollville. The Rock Island (the 1902 successor of the Memphis & Little Rock Railroad) and Cotton Belt Railway advertised in midwestern and northern states urging people to come settle on the rich farmland of Prairie County.

Slovaktown was founded in 1894 by the Slovak Colonization Company, which purchased the townsite and surrounding land that same year. Many Eastern Europeans had immigrated from Slovakia, Hungary, Poland, and Moravia to this country in the 1880s and 1890s. Some of the men worked in the coal mines and steel mills in Illinois, Ohio, and Pennsylvania. Migrating to Slovak, families of Eastern European descent, among them the John Bednar family, bought town lots and farms.

W.H. Fuller of Carlisle is credited with introducing rice as a viable commercial crop on the Grand Prairie. People in the Hazen and Carlisle area offered Fuller $1,000 to raise a crop in 1904, with no less than 35 bushels per acre on 70 acres. He managed to raise 5,225 bushels on the acreage that year at a cost of $3,147.50. He received his $1,000 "thanks to the good people of Hazen, Carlisle, and vicinity," to use his words. The rest is history. Arkansas is now the largest producer of rice in the nation.

One

First Settlements
Des Arc and Hickory Plains

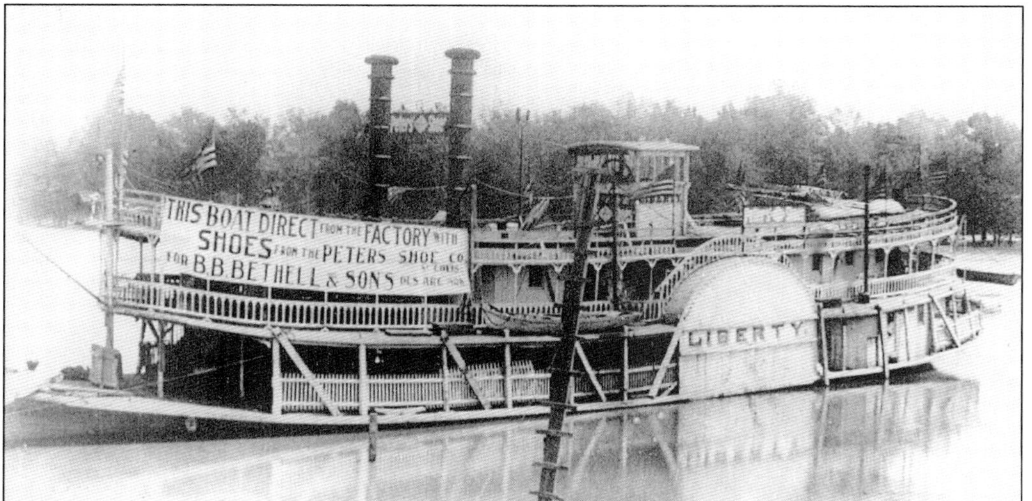

The steamboat *Liberty* is shown delivering shoes to the B.B. Bethel & Son's store at Des Arc. The *Des Arc Citizen* announced, on December 2, 1854, that the *National Sangomon*, *Naomi*, *Luella*, and *Julia Dear* were operating between Memphis and points on the White River. (Courtesy of Ralph DuPae and the Murphy Library, University of Wisconsin at La Crosse.)

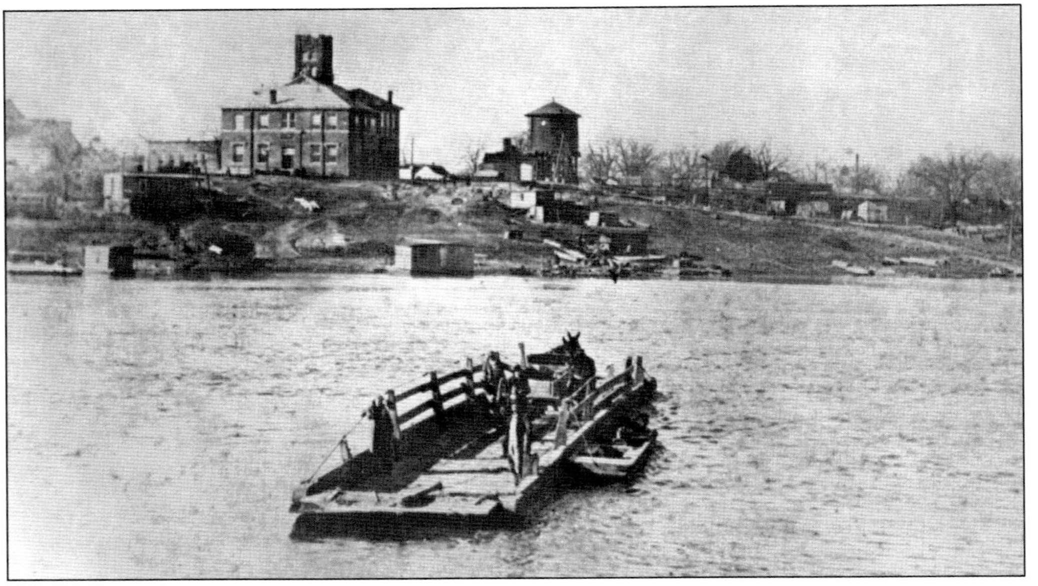

The White River ferry at Des Arc, with the county courthouse in the background, appears in this 1920 photograph. George M. Daniels operated the boat for many years. He once had to dive into the cold water to rescue a young girl who was kicked off the ferry by a wild mule. (Courtesy of Dean Walls.)

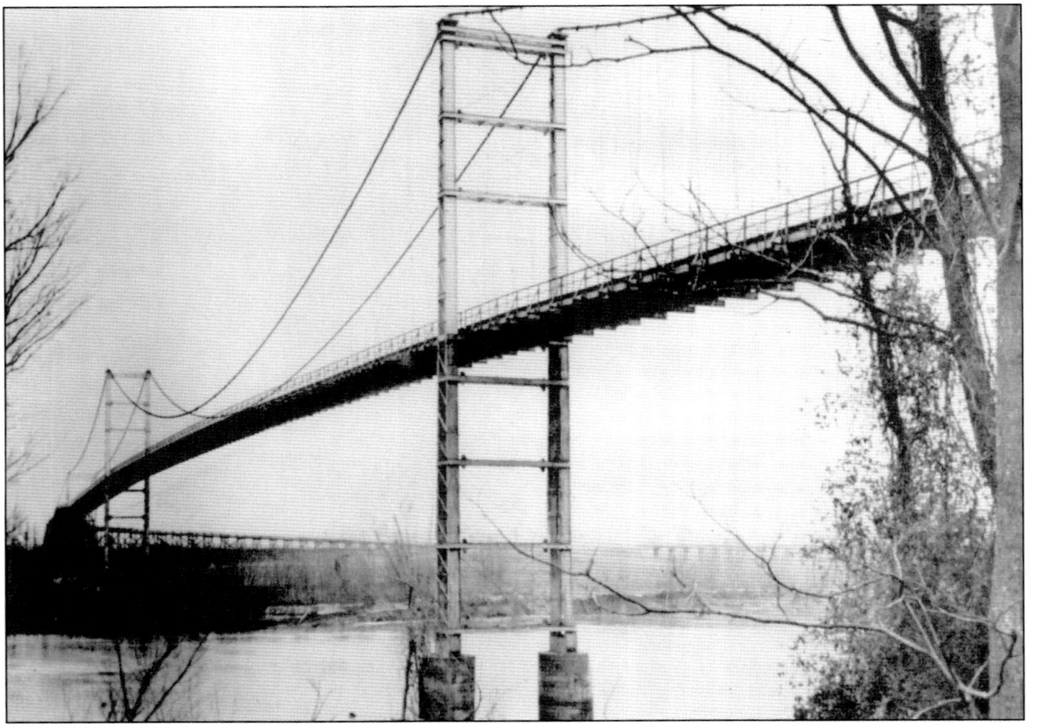

The Des Arc and Powhatan Bridge Company built the suspension bridge at Des Arc in 1927–1928; it was a toll bridge until 1940. Several people lost their lives failing to navigate the curve on the eastern approach. The bridge was taken down in the early 1980s. (Courtesy of Harvey Joe Sanner.)

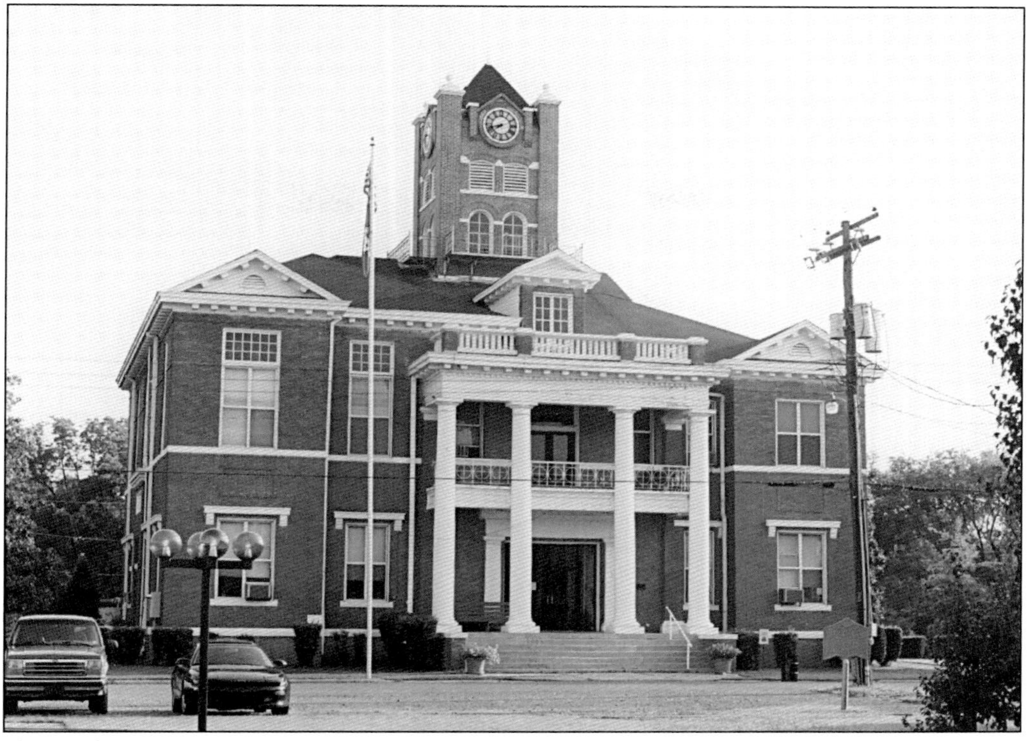

Shown above, the present courthouse at Des Arc, built in 1913, is listed in the National Register of Historic Places. The first Prairie County Courthouse was built in 1846 in Brownsville, the year of the county's creation. In 1868, the county seat was moved to DeValls Bluff. Part of old Prairie County, which included Brownsville and part of old Pulaski County, was annexed in 1873 to form Lonoke County. In 1875, the courthouse was moved to Des Arc. In 1885, the county was split into two districts, Northern District and Southern District. The old courthouse at Des Arc, pictured at right, was burned in the fall of 1911. Newspaper accounts intimate that it was destroyed due to continuing political differences. (Above, author's collection; right, courtesy of the Lower White River Museum.)

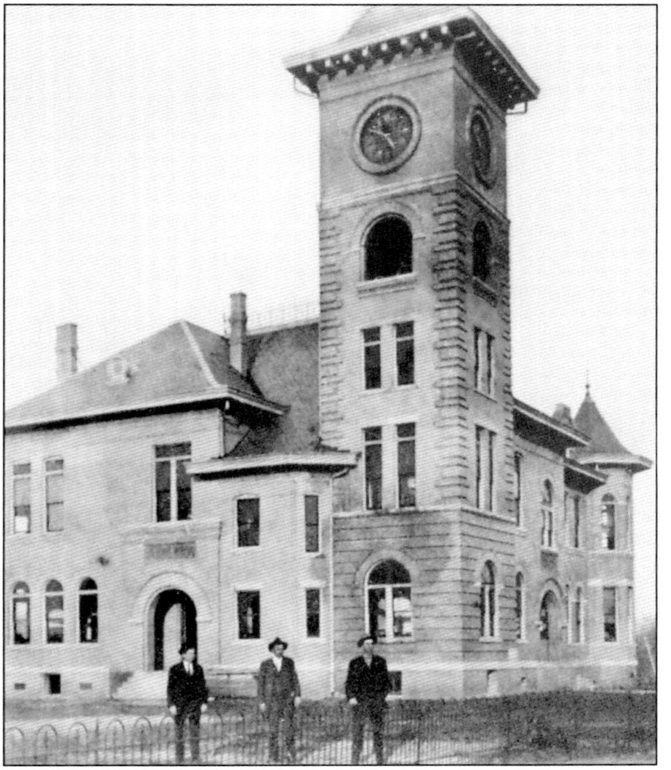

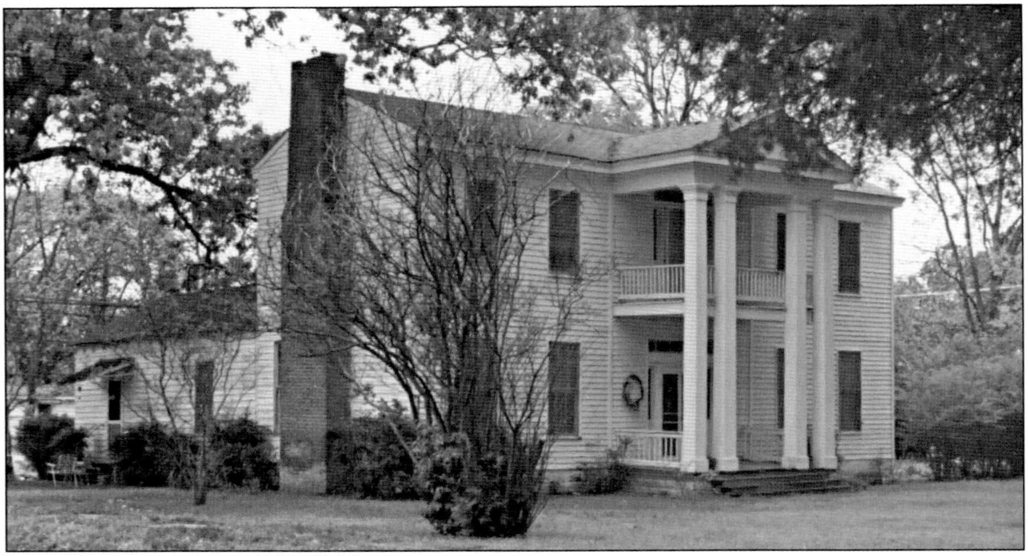

The Plunkett House is located on Main Street in Des Arc, across from the former Presbyterian church. The antebellum home, constructed around 1847, is listed in the National Register of Historic Places and in the Arkansas Register of Historic Places and reflects the prosperity of the era (1850–1862). William A. Plunkett (born 1834) was elected Prairie County sheriff in 1860 and served the Confederate cause as captain of Company C of the 25th Arkansas Infantry. After the war, he entered the mercantile business. His son William B. owned the Plunkett farm on Upper Hill, which later passed to his daughter and son-in-law William Bond. Gilbert Purvis managed the farm for many years. (Author's collection.)

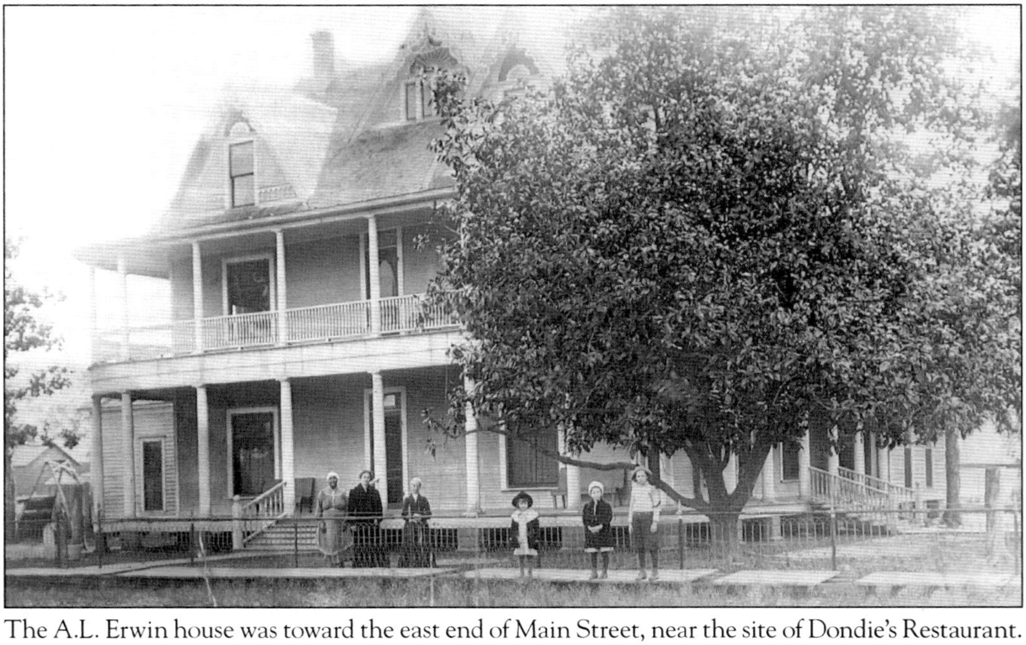

The A.L. Erwin house was toward the east end of Main Street, near the site of Dondie's Restaurant. From left to right are Sally Vance, Sue Sutcliffe (Mrs. Ambrose L. Erwin), Natalie Walt (married a Childress), Gladys Erwin, unidentified, and Brough Erwin. In its day, the house was the largest in Des Arc. (Courtesy of Sarah Berry Ward and Sue Kirkwood Berry.)

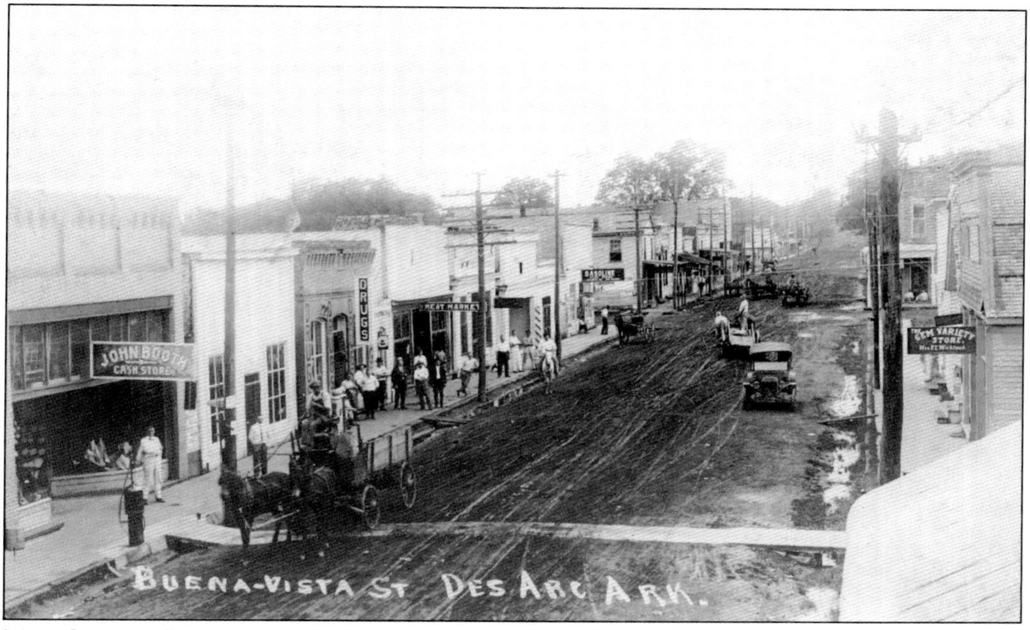

Main Street in Des Arc was first known as Buena Vista Street. Only one automobile is in view in this 1916 photograph. On the left side of the street at a distance can be seen a sign for gasoline; however, there is no standing gas pump visible. (Courtesy of Dean Walls.)

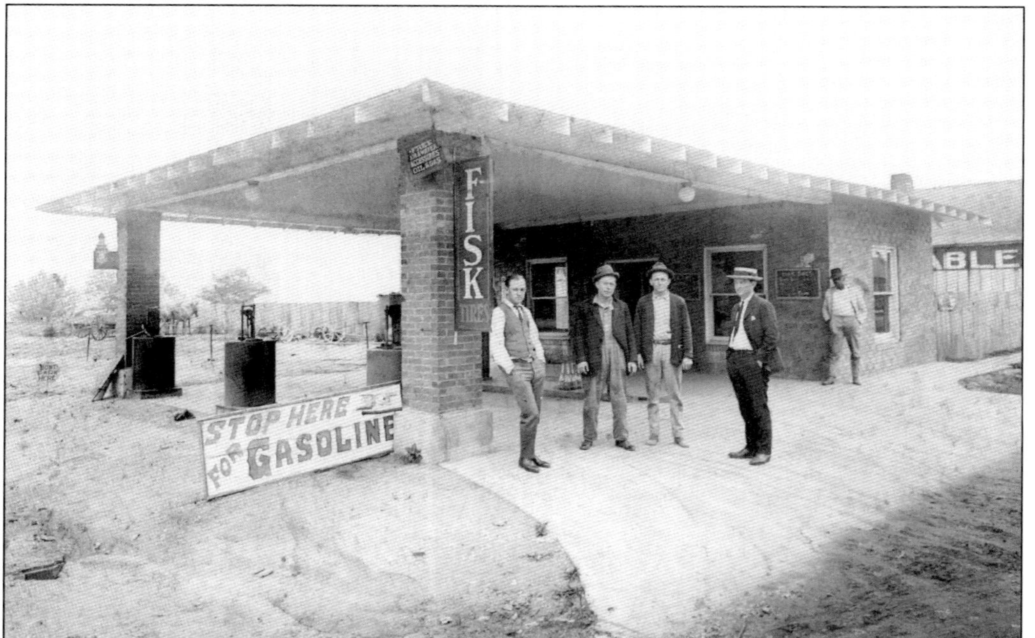

The gas station and garage at Second and Main Streets marketed Fisk tires. The building later housed the Farrish Oil Company. A horse stable was located behind the station. (Courtesy of Emily Fetters.)

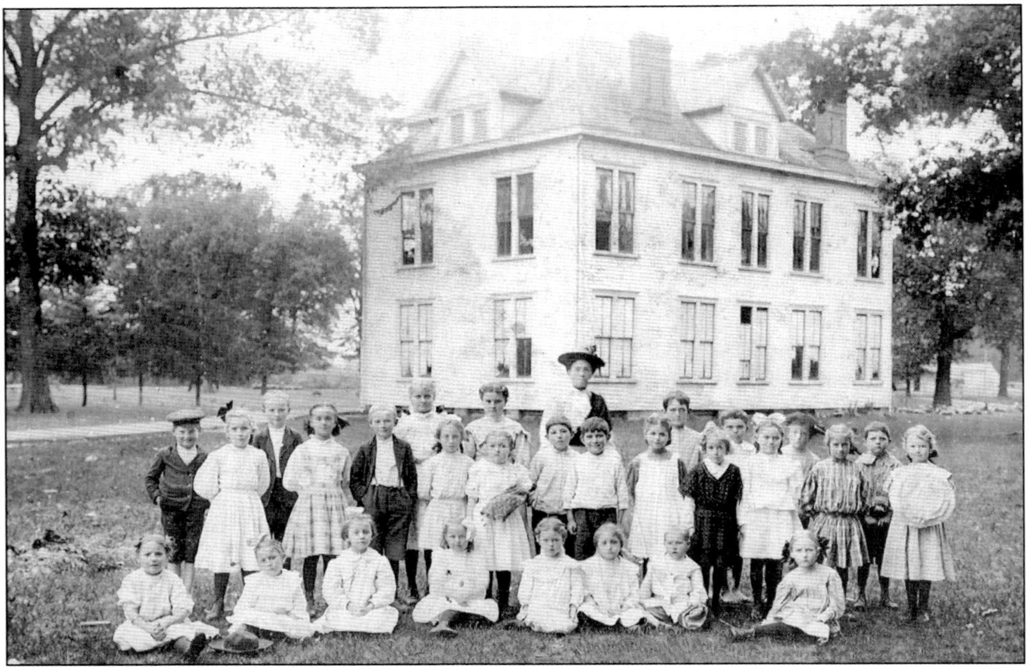

This four-room school was erected in 1892. Maggie West was the teacher and her granddaughter Marguerite Riley is seated on the far left. This photograph was taken in 1903. (Courtesy of Joe Anderson.)

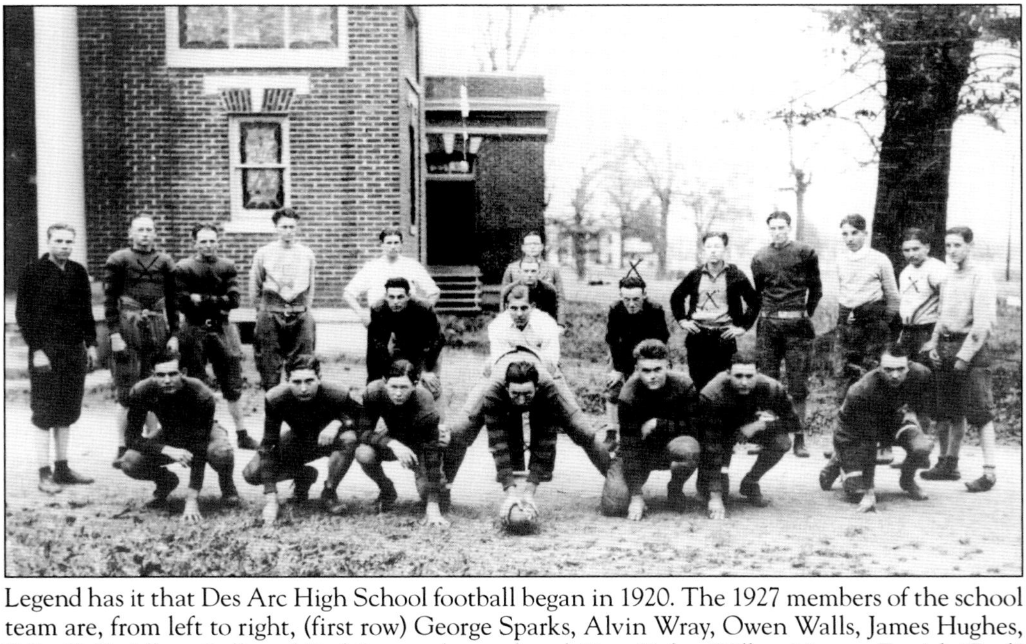

Legend has it that Des Arc High School football began in 1920. The 1927 members of the school team are, from left to right, (first row) George Sparks, Alvin Wray, Owen Walls, James Hughes, Felix Hall, Albert Ball, and Earl Ragon; (second row) Troy Hoke, Wilbur Meyers, Farrish "Red" Williams, and Marvin Dickson; (third row) Duke Morton, Bill Walls, Bruce Pearce, Eugene Lumpkin, Carlos Andrews, coach Earle Fisher, Ben Erwin, Elizie Berry, Howard Ford, Dallas Webb, and Charles Sparks. (Courtesy of Paul Lumpkin and Paula Presley.)

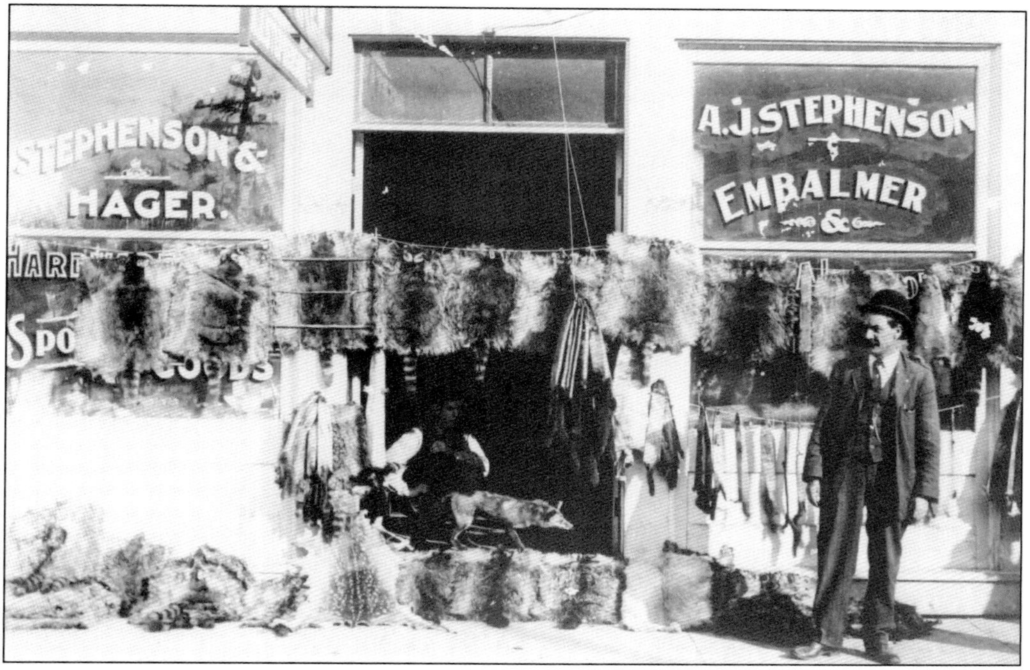

As early as 1898, Amos J. Stephenson was listed as an undertaker in a Des Arc business directory and was apparently also a fur dealer. (Courtesy of Emily Fetters.)

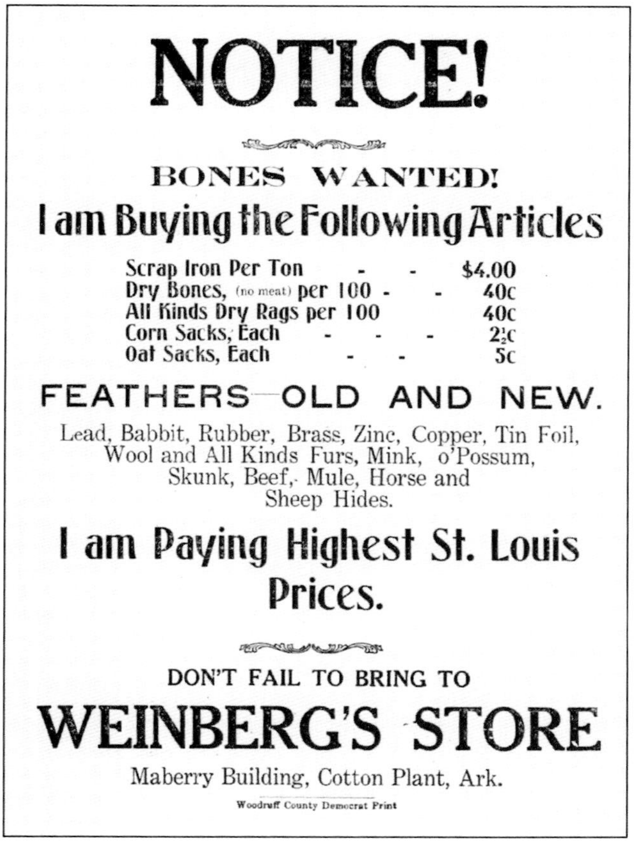

NOTICE!

BONES WANTED!

I am Buying the Following Articles

Scrap Iron Per Ton - -	$4.00
Dry Bones, (no meat) per 100 - -	40c
All Kinds Dry Rags per 100	40c
Corn Sacks, Each - - -	$2\frac{1}{2}$c
Oat Sacks, Each - -	5c

FEATHERS—OLD AND NEW.

Lead, Babbit, Rubber, Brass, Zinc, Copper, Tin Foil, Wool and All Kinds Furs, Mink, o'Possum, Skunk, Beef, Mule, Horse and Sheep Hides.

I am Paying Highest St. Louis Prices.

DON'T FAIL TO BRING TO

WEINBERG'S STORE

Maberry Building, Cotton Plant, Ark.

Woodruff County Democrat Print

The Woodruff County town of Cotton Plant is only six miles east of the Prairie County line. Years ago, before the town's decline, many people in northeastern Prairie County shopped and transacted other business there. Some men made their living hunting and trapping mink, raccoon, and otter. Sharecroppers could supplement their meager income in the winter that way. In the last few decades, there has been a big decline in the market for Arkansas native fur. This c. 1910 poster shows other items that were sold and bought. (Courtesy of Angela Wiesle Hinton.)

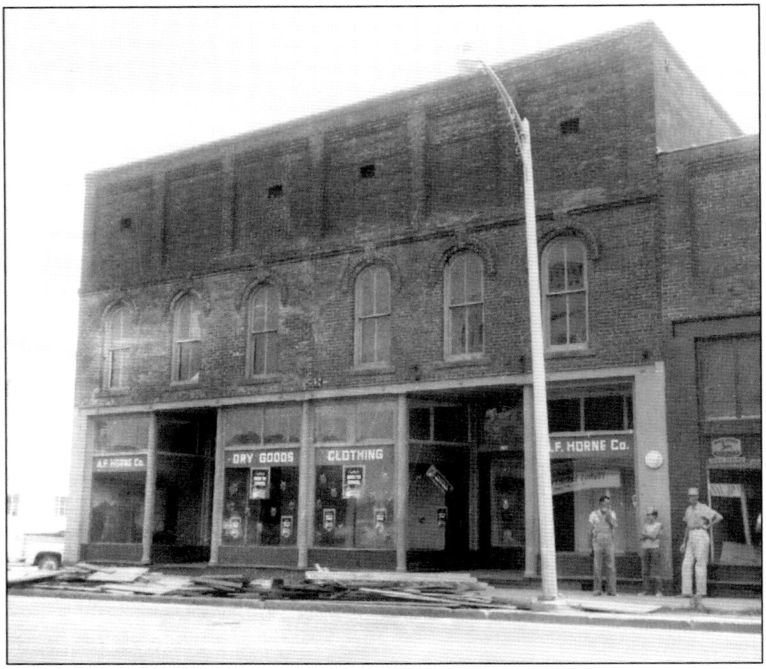

The A.F. Horne Company store on Main Street, shown here in August 1962, was built in 1878 by Bedford Brown Bethel, who operated a general mercantile store for 56 years. Bethel was one of the men who rode with the Confederate guerilla Howell A. "Doc" Rayburn. (Courtesy of Matilda and Gene Horne.)

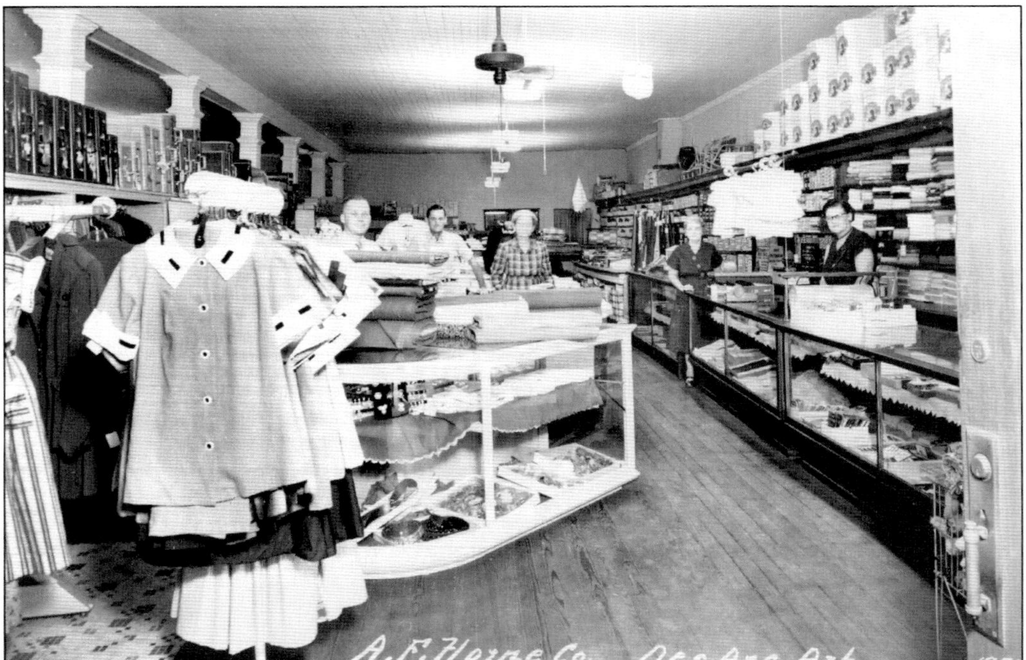

Appearing in this 1954 view of the interior of the A.F. Horne Company store are, from left to right, Gene Horne, Ralph Weatherly, Carilla Flynn, Edna Horne, and Clara Gillispie. (Courtesy of Matilda and Gene Horne.)

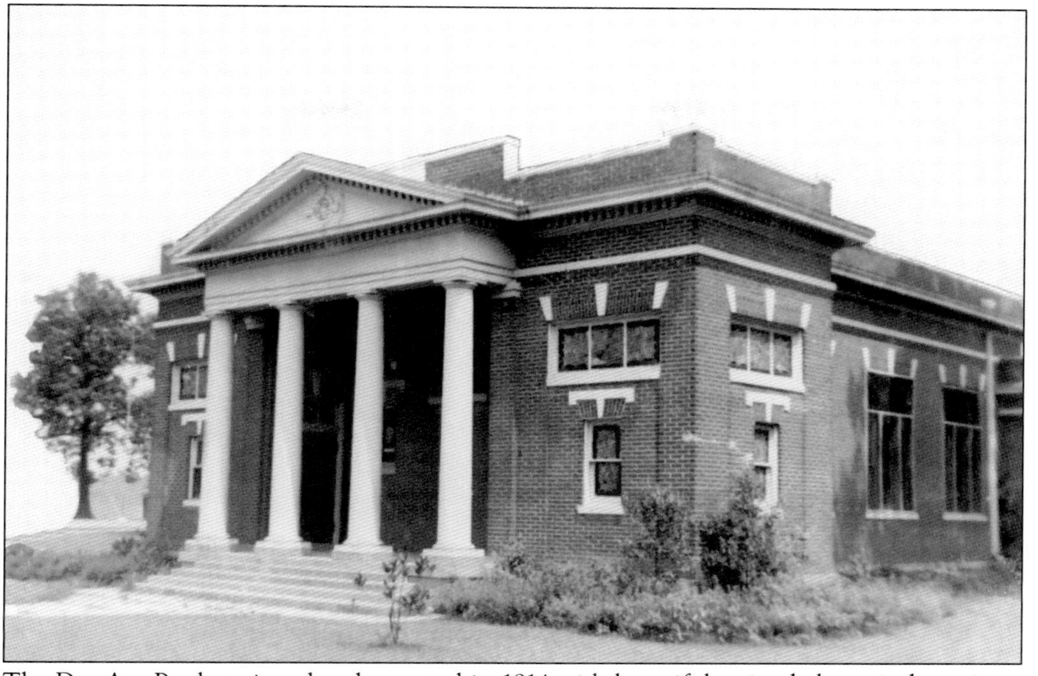

The Des Arc Presbyterian church, erected in 1914 with beautiful stained-glass windows, is no longer used as a sanctuary and has recently been donated to the town to be used as a public county library. (Courtesy of Dean Walls.)

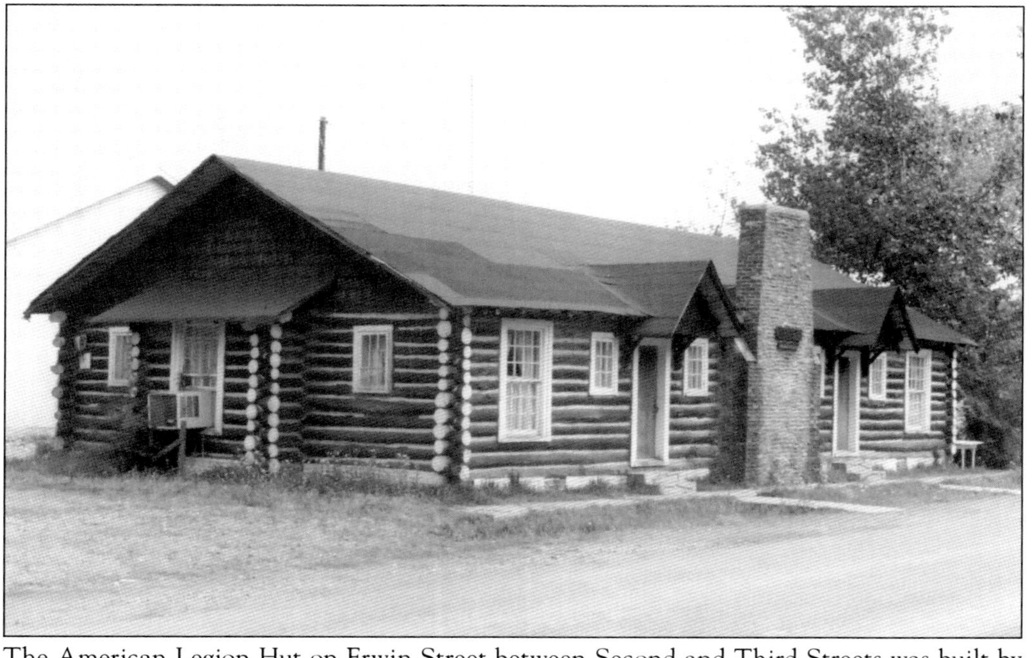

The American Legion Hut on Erwin Street between Second and Third Streets was built by the Works Progress Administration workers in either 1934 or 1935 and still serves as a place for veterans to meet, socialize, and dance. Similar structures for veterans were built in other Arkansas communities. (Courtesy of Emily Fetters.)

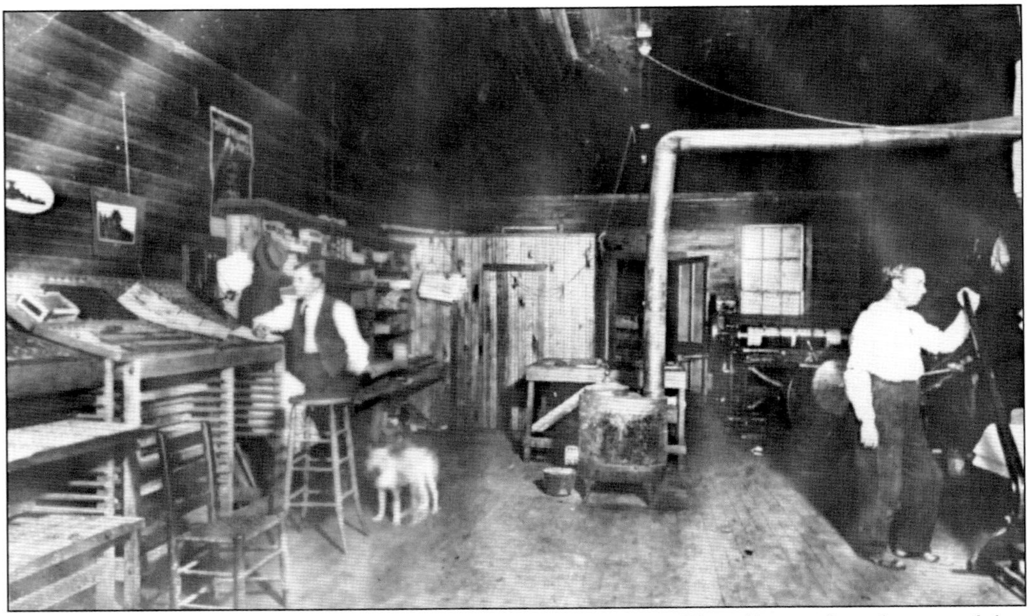

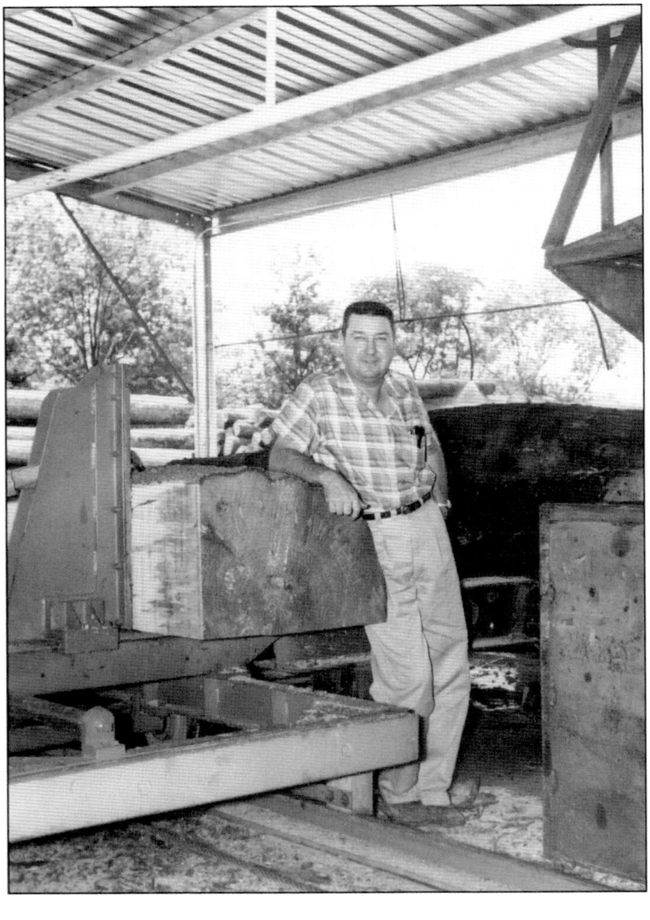

The office and workroom of the *White River Journal* newspaper at Des Arc, photographed about 1915, was on Buena Vista (Main) Street. From left to right are Charles Alfred Walls and Troy Hoke. Charles founded the paper in 1907, which passed to his son Charles. The second Charles's widow, Dean Walls, now publishes the paper. In 2007, the newspaper entered its second century of publication guided by Dean with her more than 60 years of service. (Courtesy of Dean Walls.)

The Miller Patterson Lumber and Timber Company Inc. began operating in Des Arc in 1962. Archie Patterson, shown here, died in 1973, and Jack Miller sold his interest to the Patterson family in the 1990s. Ardie's son Rodger Patterson now operates the sawmill, which manufactures hardwood lumber and cross ties. (Courtesy of Roger Patterson and Marilyn Burnett.)

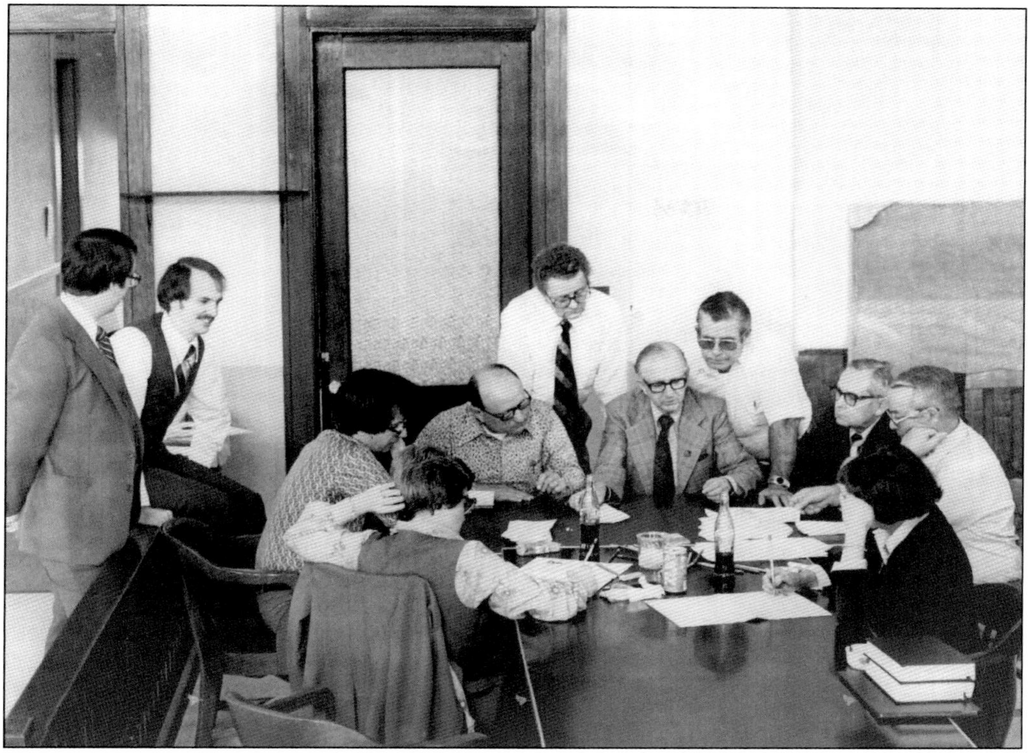

Members of the Prairie County Election Commission are shown tabulating the votes at the Des Arc Courthouse, possibly for the 1980 election. The women are unidentified. The men are, from left to right, Buster Guthrie, Randy Gammill, John Stevens, Pete Sickel, Jim Bain, Billy Garth, Jimmy Lee, Leo Simmons, and Conway George. (Courtesy of Liz Hampton.)

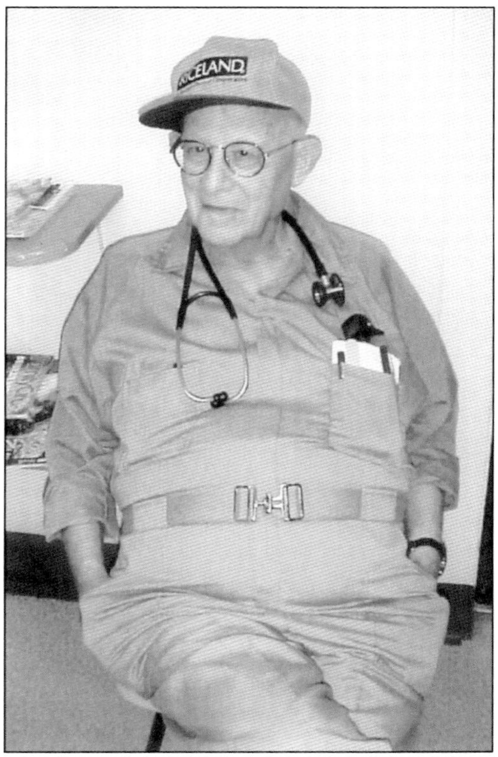

Dr. Gerald Schumann (1909–2006) served the Des Arc community as a family doctor for over 50 years. His first residence and office was in the hotel, but he later purchased a two-story building on Main Street, making the upper floor his residence with his clinic and patient rooms downstairs. He was beloved by the citizens of the town and area. (Courtesy of Dean Walls.)

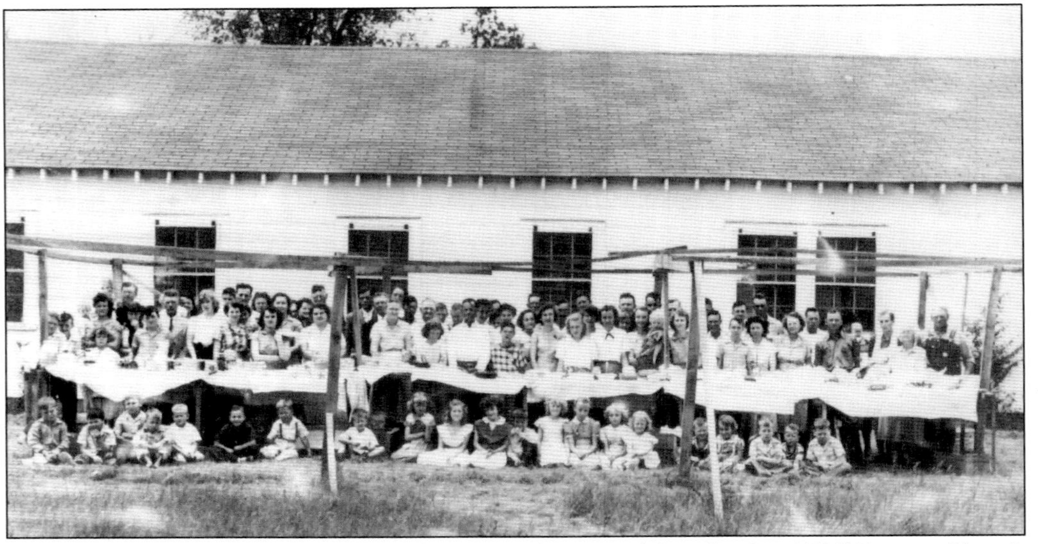

Some of those enjoying this c. 1953 "dinner on the grounds" at the Sand Hill Baptist Church are Harvey Joe, Steve, Jim, Henry Otis, Joe, and Hattie Sanner; Freda and Hattie Mae Jenkins; and Mrs. Gant Rogers. Tenth from the right is Louise Sanner Jenkins holding her daughter Gail Jenkins Rye. The wood frame over the table was used to support a brush arbor at times. (Courtesy of Gail Jenkins Rye.)

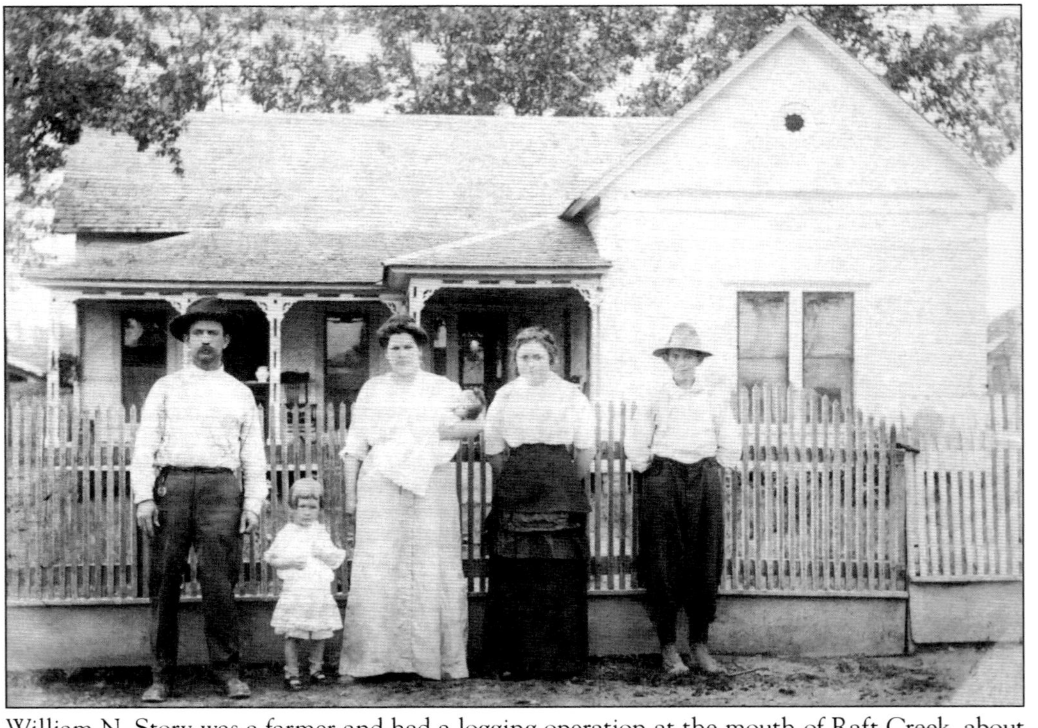

William N. Story was a farmer and had a logging operation at the mouth of Raft Creek, about five miles north of Des Arc. Shown in this c. 1913 photograph are, from left to right, William N. Story, Eunice Story Hamilton, Stella Story (holding baby Stella), Lilly Story, and Robert Story. (Courtesy of the Lower White River Museum.)

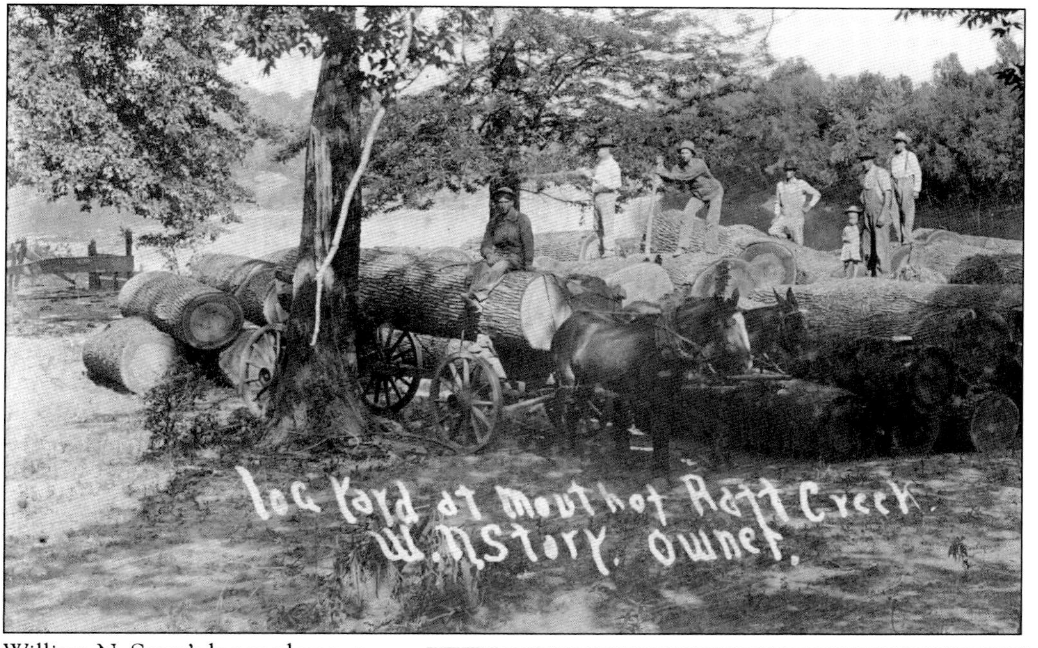

William N. Story's log yard was at the mouth of Raft Creek, which flows into the White River. Des Arc in 1916 had a large hoop and lumber mill, three veneer mills, one banana crate factory, one spoke and hub factory, and two sawmills. (Courtesy of the Lower White Museum.)

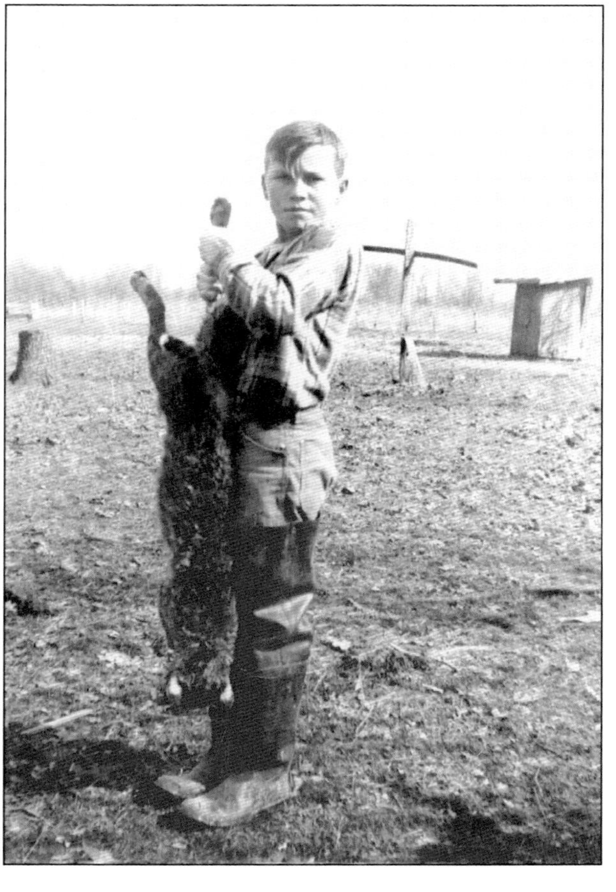

Jim Boggan, William N. Story's grandson, is standing tall and holding a bobcat, common to the region at that time, in this 1949 photograph. (Courtesy of the Lower White River Museum.)

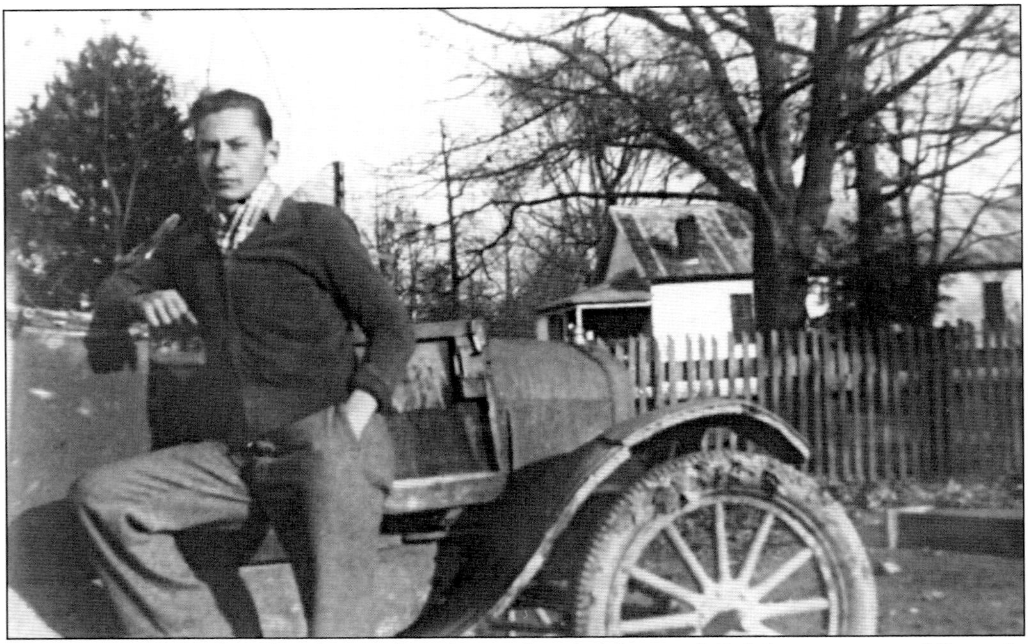

Mateusz Lucyan Buczkowski, who was from Russia, founded the mostly Polish community of Gospoda about 1910. The community was located about five miles south of Des Arc on Rock Island's Mesa-to-Searcy branch rail line. Ed Buczkowski, the son of Mateusz and his wife, Stephania, appears in this 1944 photograph with his first car, for which he paid $10. (Courtesy of Ed Buczkowski.)

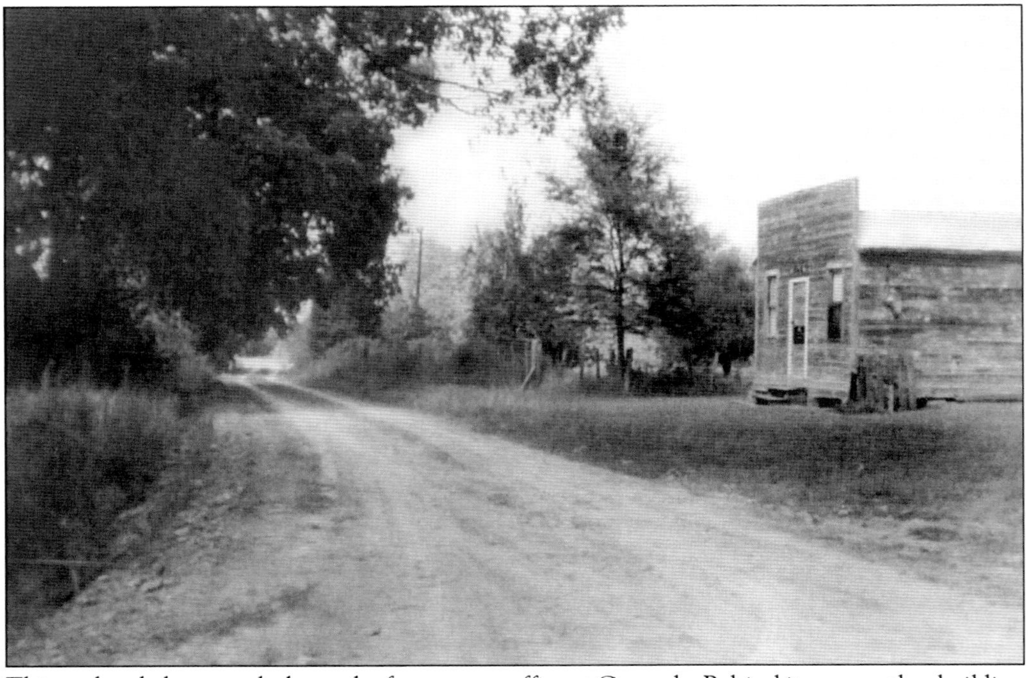

This undated photograph shows the former post office at Gospoda. Behind it was another building where dances were held. The community also had a mercantile store. After the Depression, many people left Gospoda to find other means of making a living. (Courtesy of Ed Buczkowski.)

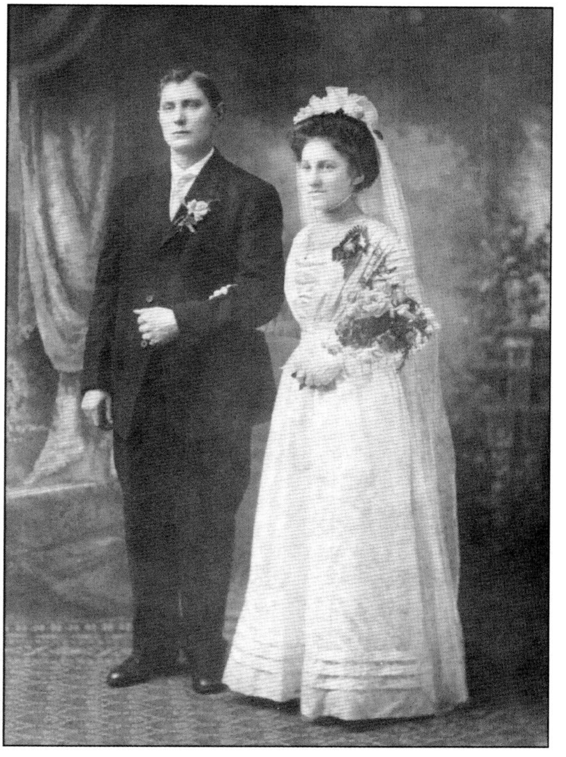

Edna Agnes Nowak (1891–1987) appears here with her husband, Bronislow Walicki, in an undated photograph on their wedding day. Edna was a midwife and also served as interpreter for the Polish at Gospoda who could not speak English. (Courtesy of Janelle Taylor.)

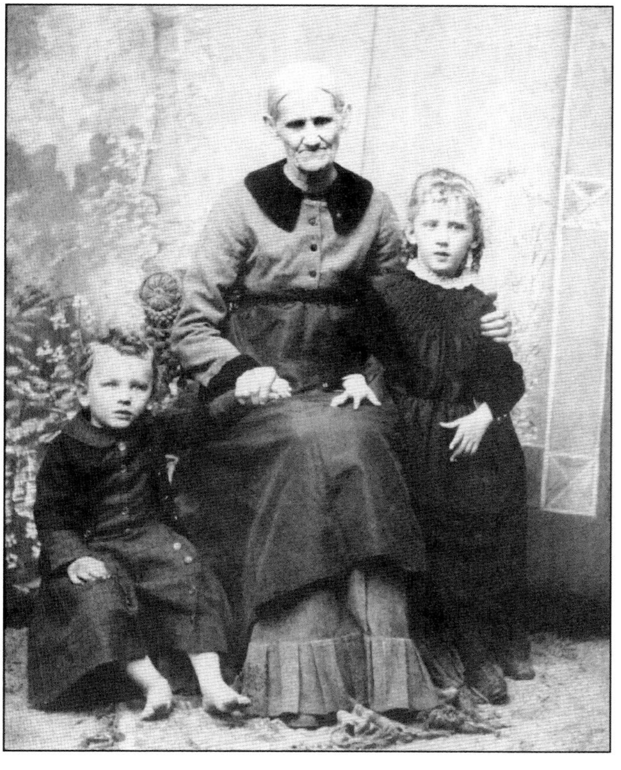

Emily Edwards (1816–1893) was the wife of Asa. O. Edwards, who, on May 8, 1861, led a procession at Des Arc celebrating the secession of Arkansas and Tennessee from the Union. Although he did not serve in the Confederate service, he was a member of Prairie County's home guard. Emily and Asa were part of the Stringtown community, located a few miles south of Des Arc. Emily is pictured here with her nephew Hugh Morrow and niece Ellen Morrow. (Courtesy of Troy Tacker.)

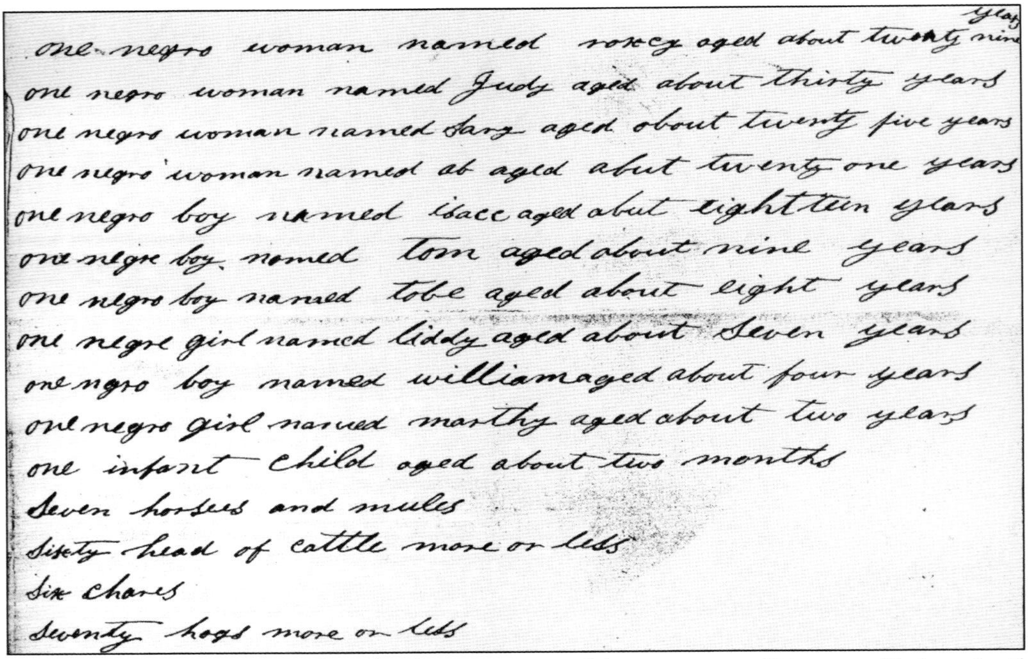

one negro woman named roxcy aged about twenty nine years
one negro woman named Judy aged about thirty years
one negro woman named Sary aged obout twenty five years
one negro woman named ab aged abut twenty one years
one negro boy named isacc aged abut eightteen ylars
one negro boy named tom aged about nine years
one negro boy named tobe aged about eight years
one negro girl named liddy aged about seven years
one negro boy named william aged about four years
one negro girl named marthy aged about two years
one infant child aged about two months
seven horses and mules
sixty head of cattle more or less
six chares
seventy hogs more or less

This list of the late Asa O. Edwards's slaves was part of the inventory of his estate filed on April 14, 1862, at the county courthouse. While slavery was an inhumane and unjustifiable institution, some probate files before and during the Civil War contain vouchers and other items that refer to medical care for slaves and other signs of caring, either out of a personal concern for their welfare or for cold economic reasons. (Courtesy of the County and Circuit Clerk's Office, Des Arc.)

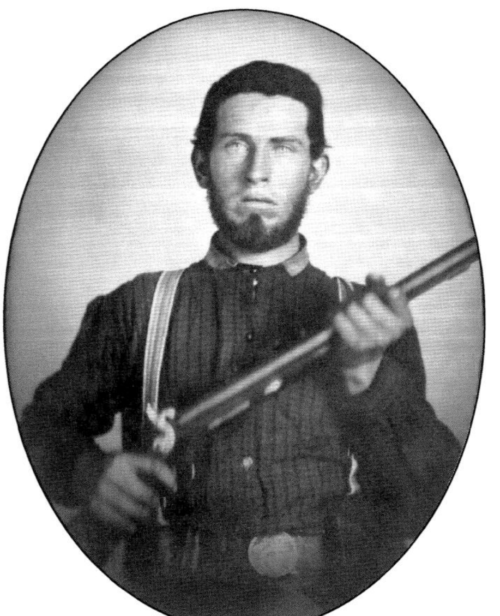

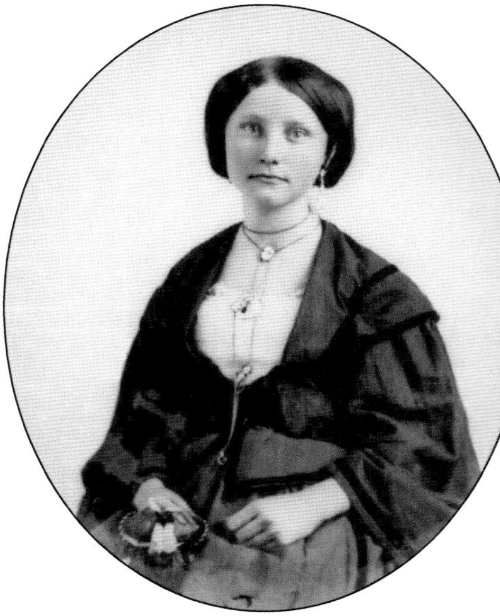

Francis M. Haley (left) joined the Confederate army from Prairie County and served in the battles of Murfreesboro and Chickamauga. After the war, he returned to farming at what has become known as the Johnson Chapel community, about six miles west of Des Arc. Born in 1840, Laura Ford (right) became the wife of Francis on August 11, 1858. (Courtesy of Mary Hayley Roe.)

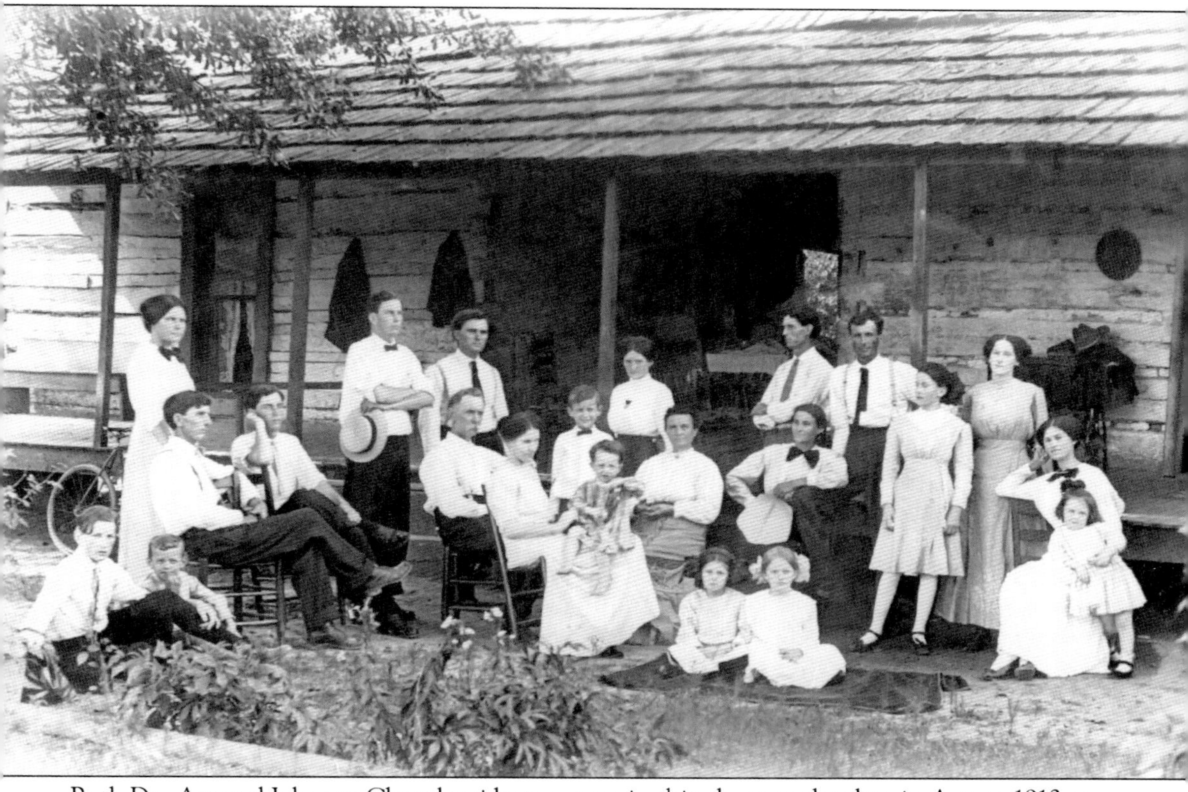

Both Des Arc and Johnson Chapel residents appear in this photograph taken in August 1913 at James Franklin Hayley's home at Johnson chapel, a dogtrot log house built in the late 1850s for his parents, Francis M. and Laura Ford Hayley. Seated on the ground are, from left to right, Schuyler Hayley, Vernon Berry, Flossie Landers, and Bessie Stevens; seated in chairs are, from left to right, A. Keener Thompson, Talmadge Hayley, James Franklin Haley, Eva Hayley Hart with her son Amon on her lap, Sallie Rochelle Hayley, Minnie Berry, and Ethel Wesson Langford with little Pauline Hart; standing are, from left to right, Laura "Lollie" Hayley Thompson, Eugene Hayley, ? Stevens (Nazarene preacher), Elmer Berry, Mrs. ? Stevens, Wilbert Langford, Lonnie Berry, Willard Baker, and Mable Hayley Curry. (Courtesy of Sarah Berry Ward and Sue Kirkwood Berry.)

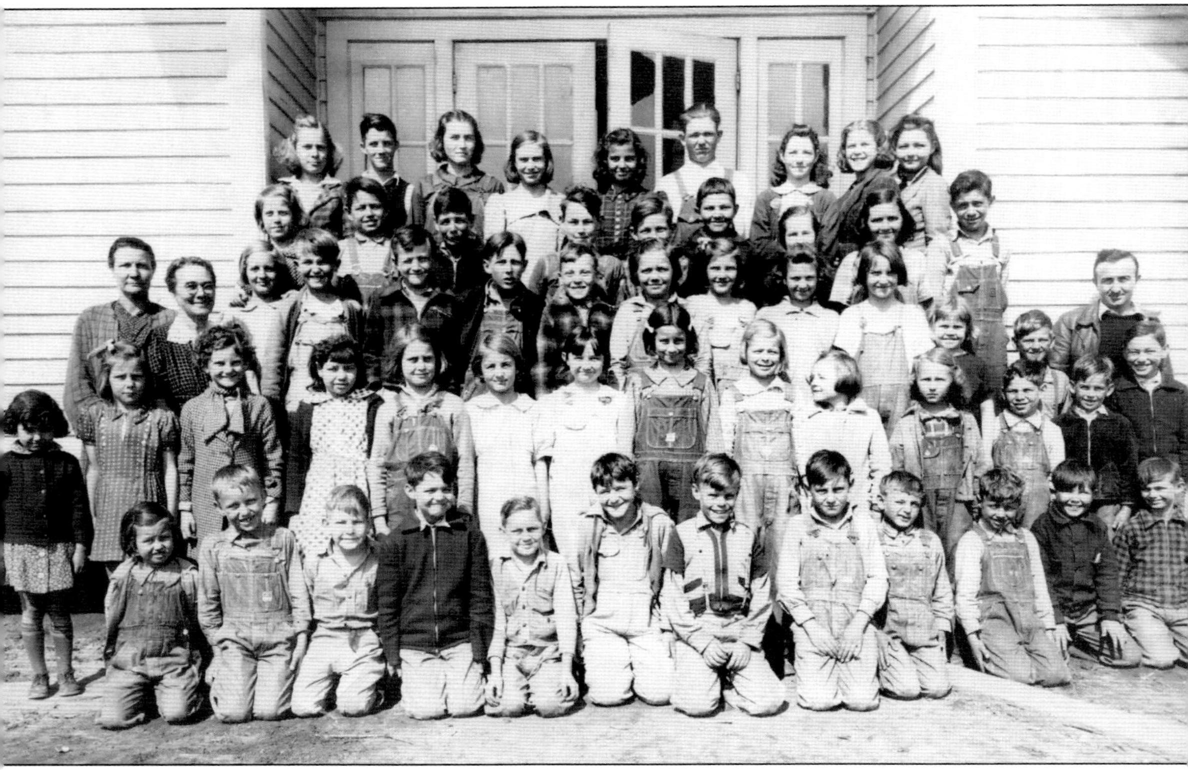

These children attended the Johnson Chapel School in 1938–1939. Pictured are, from left to right, (first row) Mary Ellen Terry, Alfred Eddins, Richard Cox, Kenny Jones, Eugene Hughes, "Jack" Barlow, John Howell, "Buddy" Odle, William Bone, J.B. Jones, Vernon Dean Gage, and Palmer Shepherd; (second row) Sue White, Francis Hayley, Ruby Weatherly, Louise Kirk, Helen Maye, Odene Bone, Dora May Hayley, Janice Curry, Christine Chrisel, Mary Jane Cate, Allie Terry, Tommy Gene Kirk, Clarence Jolly Jr., and Otho Lionel Hayley; (third row) Pearl Sanders (teacher), Mrs. William Reinhardt (teacher), Clolene Bone, Brook Gage, James Hayley, Bruce Marshal, J.C. Love, Geraldine Parchman, Patsy Lou Marshall, Joyce Shepherd, Rena Mae Lenderman, Dot Maye, and Gerald Weatherly; (fourth row) Faye Maye, Lowell Jones, Joe Kirk, David White, "Billy" Fite, Ellis Throap, Collean Love, Marceline Wilson, Gene Horne, and Elmer Kirk (teacher); (fifth row) Ada Mae Hayley, Ray Langford, Lorene Montgomery, Lucille Barlow, Helen Jones, "Sonny" Walter Gage, Louise Kirk, Rachel Mae, and Juanita Terry. (Courtesy of Mary Hayley Roe.)

This fragment of the 1892 Prairie County map compiled by Joseph Gustavus Thweatt shows the locations of the school, churches, and businesses in Hickory Plains. The location of Joseph Gustavus Thweatt's father Nicholas Thweatt's farm is indicated to the right. The map also indicates the Crossroads community south of Hickory Plains. (Courtesy of the Library of Congress.)

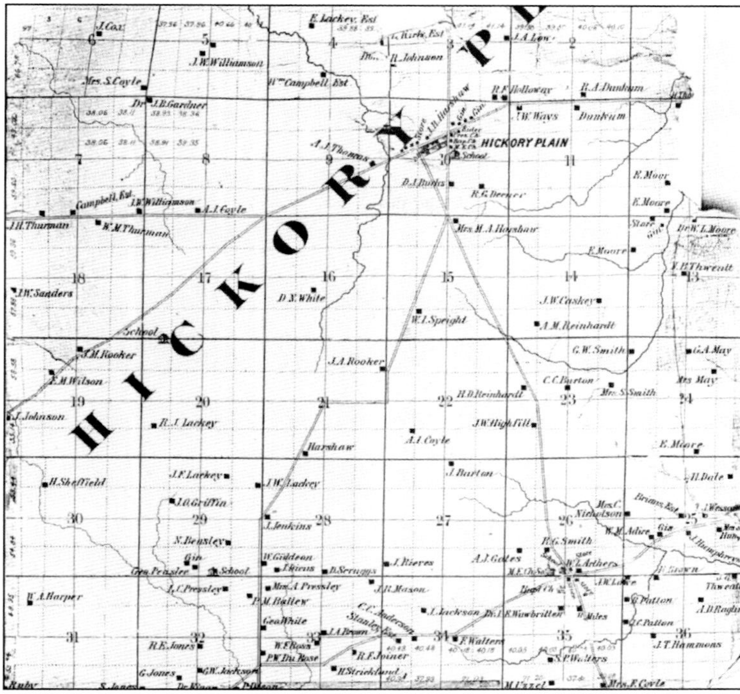

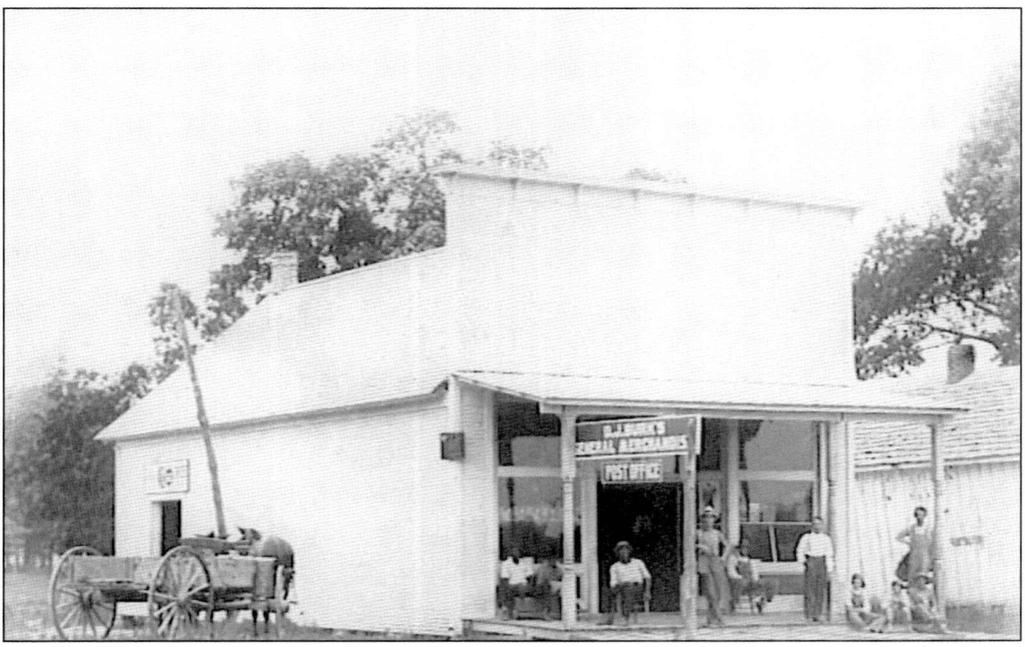

The Hickory Plains post office was at one time located in the D.J. Burks General Merchandise Store, pictured here about 1920. The people on the porch are unidentified. (Courtesy of Doyne Turner.)

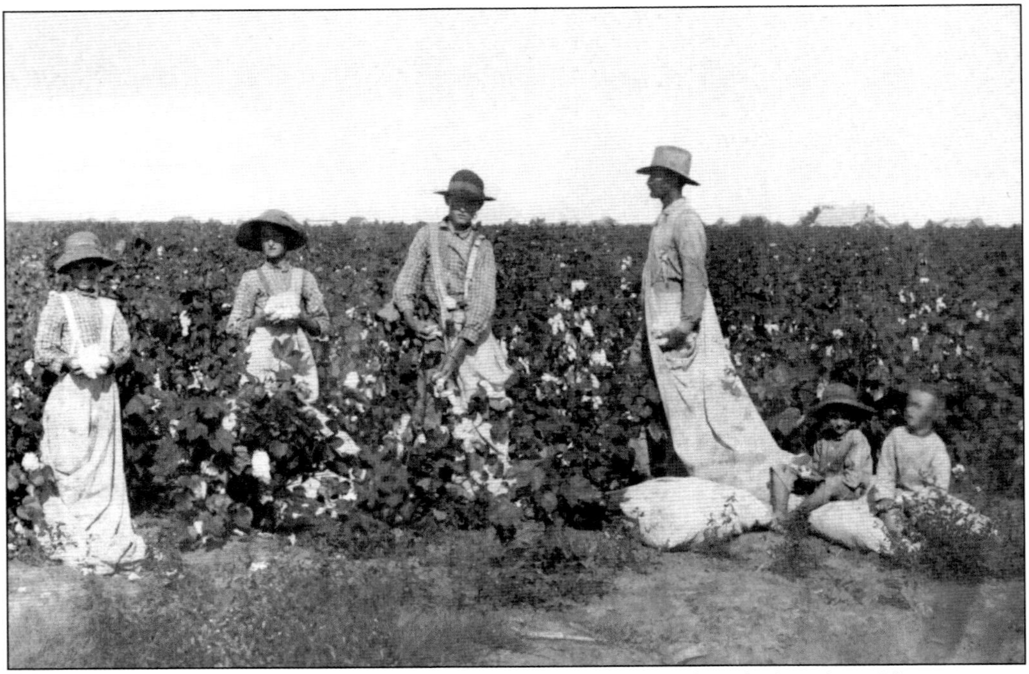

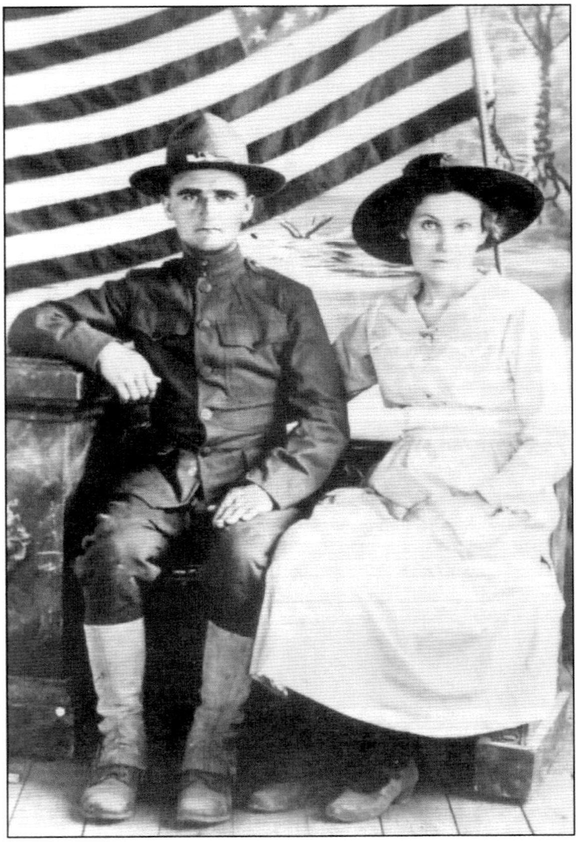

An unidentified Hickory Plains area family is shown harvesting their cotton crop. An exodus of people from eastern Arkansas in the late 1940s and the 1950s forced landowners to start using mechanical cotton pickers. Still, in the 1950s, most of the cotton was harvested by hand; by the 1960s, cotton was picked mostly by machine. (Courtesy of David Smith.)

Pictured in 1918, Jessie Robert Covington (born 1896) and his wife, Athea Loraine Covington, moved from Romance, Arkansas, to near Hickory Plains in 1936. Their furniture was transported by truck, but the horses, cows, hogs, and one goat were herded down through Beebe and the Cypress Bayou bottoms to their new home. They raised cotton and corn and had a dairy for several years. The Covingtons had 13 children. (Courtesy of Robbie Covington Veazey.)

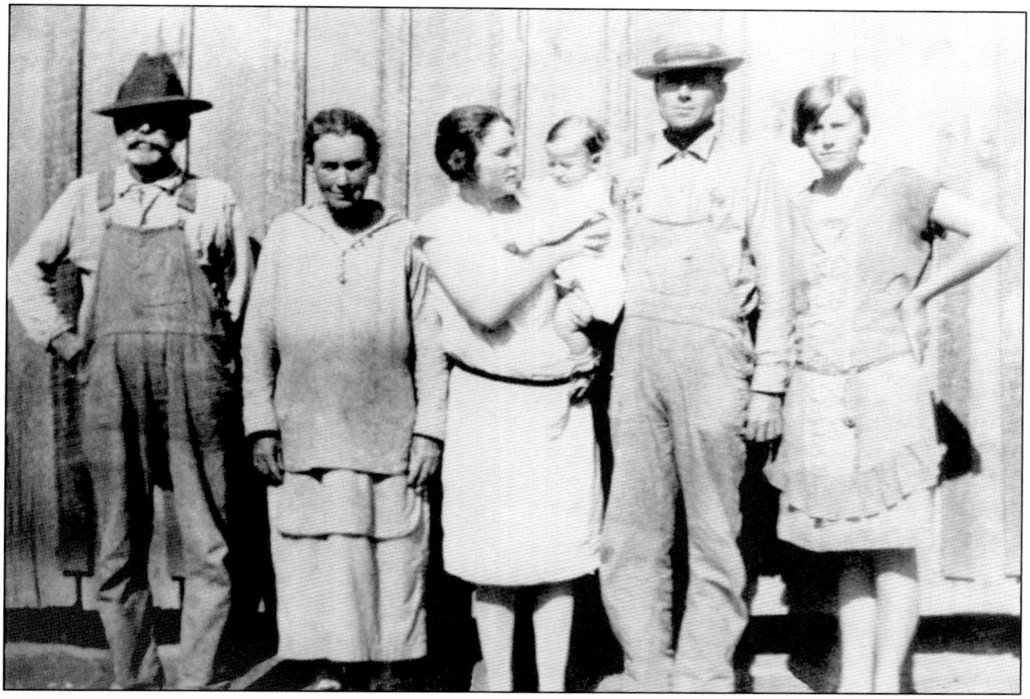

Ollie and John Bill Smith of the Hodge community were one of 52 couples from Prairie County and elsewhere to purchase and move onto farms in the Biscoe area as part of a Farm Security Administration resettlement project in the 1930s. From left to right are Thomas F. and Mollie Wyman Smith (John Bill's Parents), Ollie holding an unidentified child, John Bill, and his sister Eula Smith. (Courtesy of David Smith.)

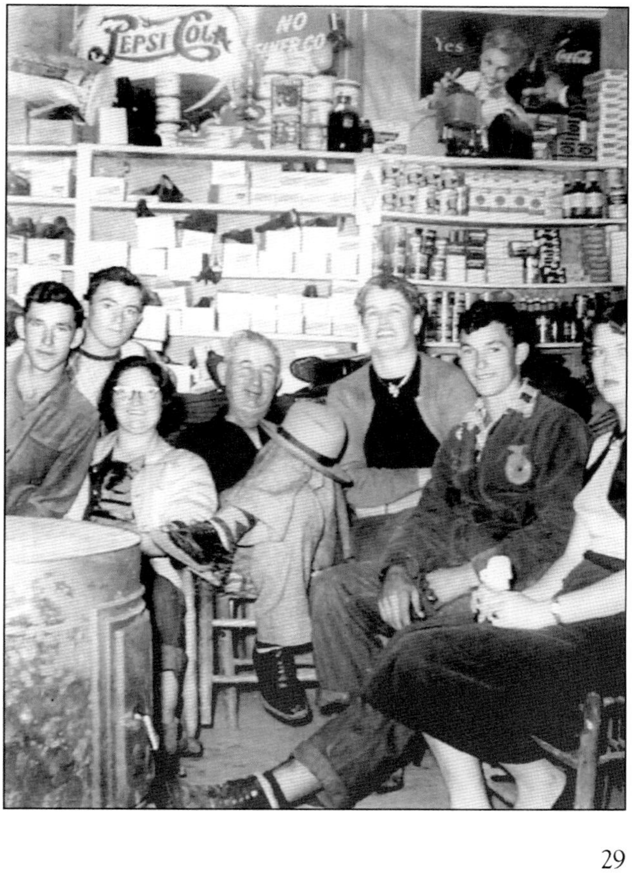

T.R. Adams is shown in a gathering of townspeople at his general store in Hickory Plains about 1950. Though he was not licensed to sell it, he sold beer stored in his icehouse next door. From left to right are Charles Price, Doyne Turner, Callie Marie Gunter, T.R. Adams and his wife, Bobby Dean Price, and Imogene McWhorter. (Courtesy of Doyne Turner.)

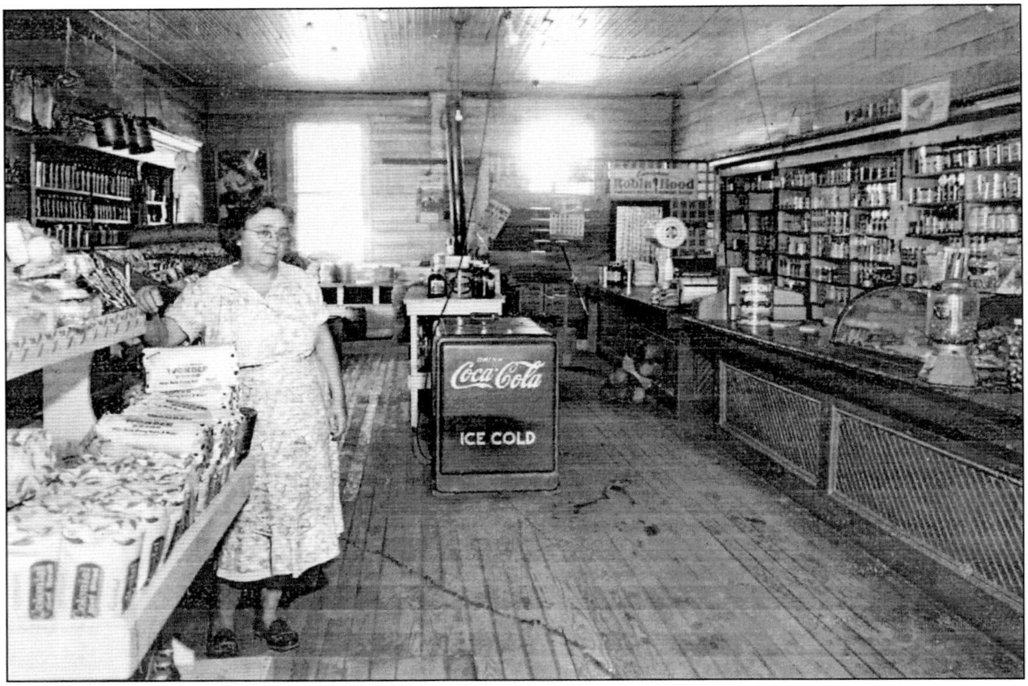

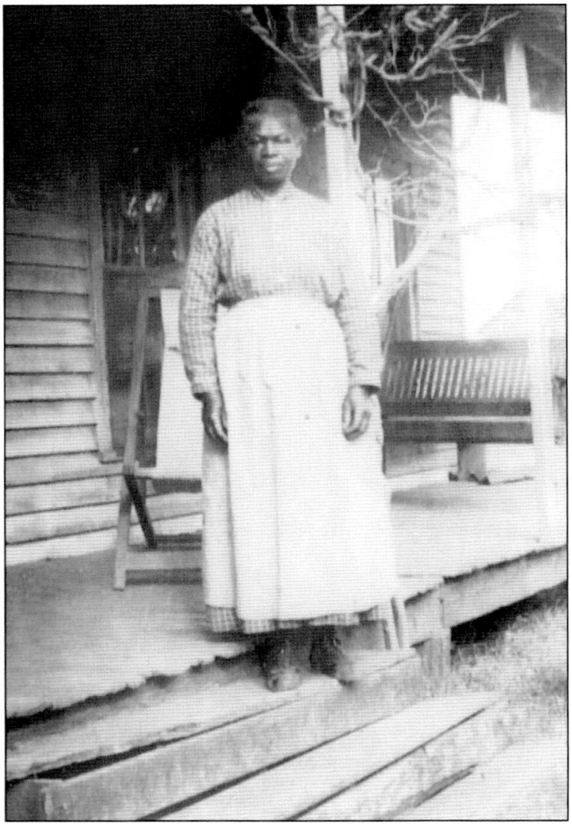

Tennie Morris, shown around 1950–1952, and her husband, Floyd, had this store at the southwest intersection of Highways 38 and 13, across from the present-day Bell family's quick-stop store. (Courtesy of Doyne Turner.)

Charles A. and Nancy Burton, who had been slave owners, moved to Butlerville in 1867 at the end of the Civil War. They cared for the abandoned slave child Ann Burton. She continued to live with the Burtons' son Thomas, who established a store at Butlerville. Thomas and his wife, Cora, moved to Hickory Plains and opened a store there around 1900. Ann lived with the Burtons until her death. (Courtesy of Bill Sayger.)

Two

The Railroad and Civil War Arrive

DeValls Bluff

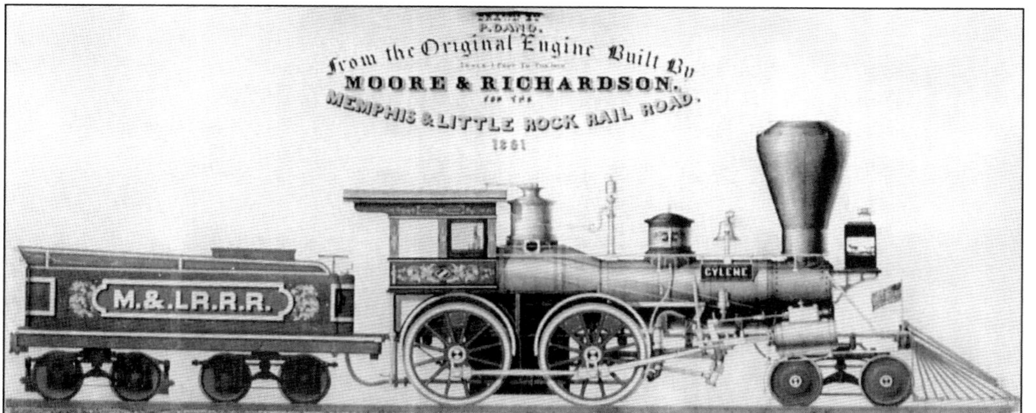

The *Cylene* locomotive, shown here in an 1861 ink-and-watercolor rendering, was one of at least four built by the Cincinnati Locomotive Works (a.k.a. Moore & Richardson) for the Memphis & Little Rock Railroad. The rail line was completed from Memphis to Madison in 1858 and from Little Rock to DeValls Bluff in 1862, and the connecting link was opened in 1871. The locomotives were transported by steamboats from Cincinnati and unloaded at Memphis and Little Rock. (Courtesy of Bruce Peterson.)

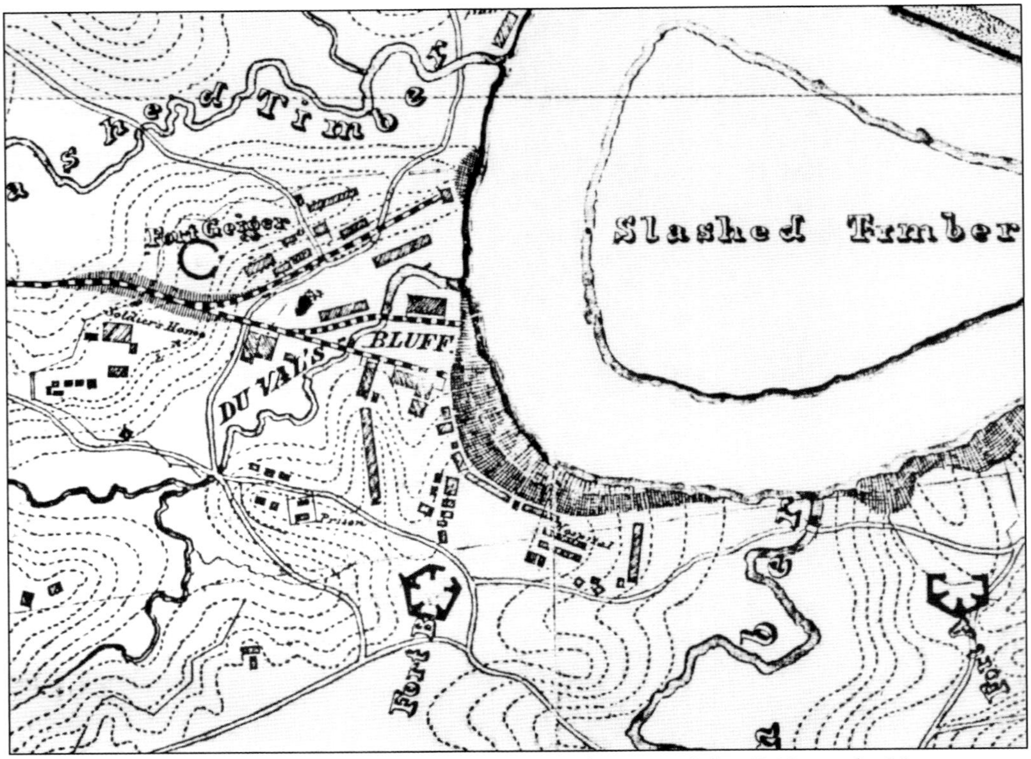

This part of the 1864 map by Union captain J.L. Sanders shows the western section of the Memphis & Little Rock Railroad ending at White River. When the water was low, Federal steamboats could not navigate the Arkansas River to reach occupied Little Rock but they could come up the White River to DeValls Bluff where soldiers and supplies would then be transported to the capital city by rail line. (Courtesy of the National Archives.)

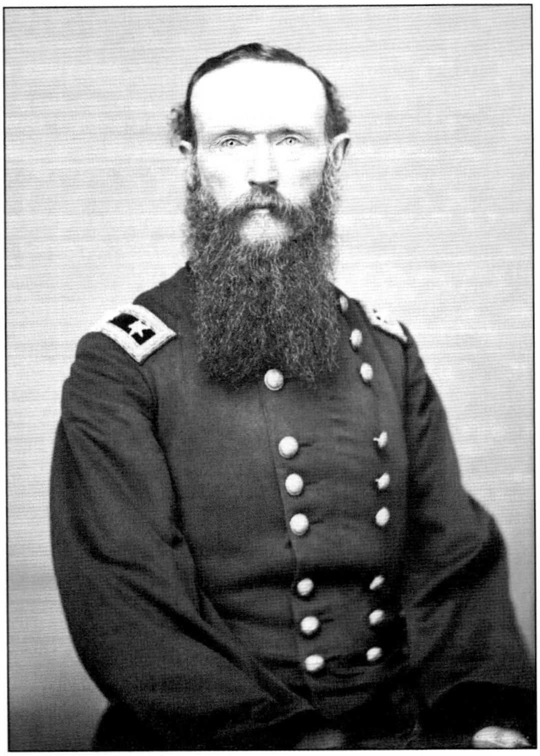

Union general Frederick Steel's forces moved out of Helena in August 1863. He created a base of operations at DeValls Bluff, and in September, his men marched westward over the Military Road, capturing Little Rock on September 10. (Courtesy of the University of Arkansas Photograph Collection, University of Arkansas at Little Rock Center for Arkansas History and Culture.)

Brig. Gen. Christopher C. Andrews had black union troops build one of the fortifications at DeValls Bluff known as Fort A. In a November 3, 1864, letter to his friend Pres. Abraham Lincoln, Andrews wrote that he promised his men that if they made a good job of it, "we should call it Fort Lincoln." (Courtesy of the Wisconsin State Historical Society.)

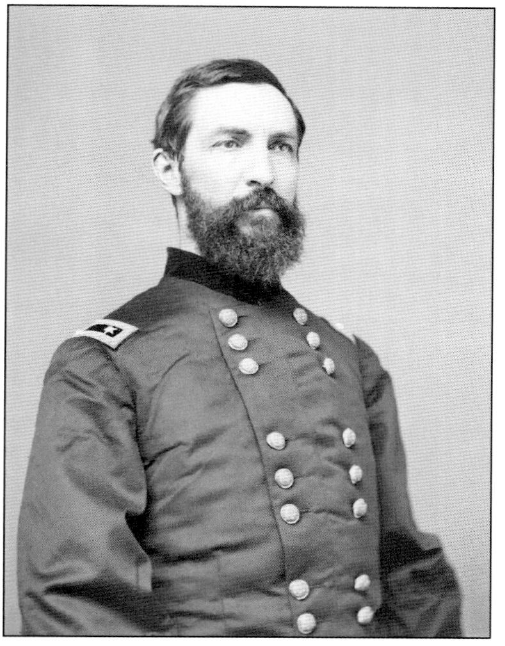

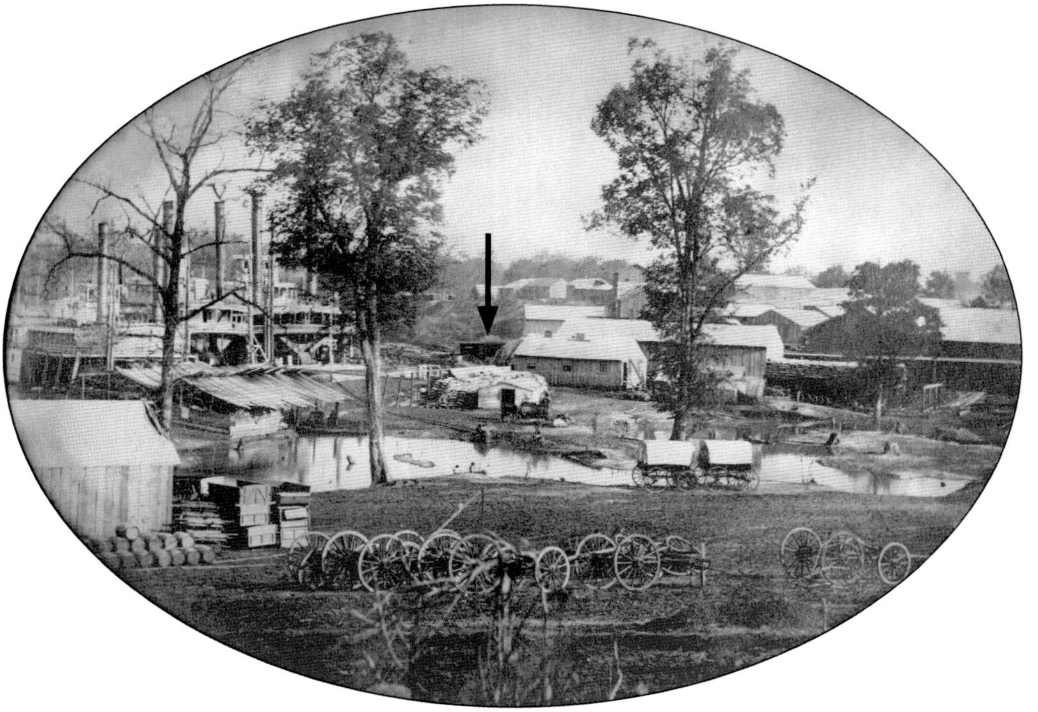

An 1864 view of the port of DeValls Bluff shows boats in dock, the warehouses used by the Federal forces, and also business houses. The arrow indicates a freight car of the Memphis & Little Rock Railroad. In 1918, water broke through the neck in the loop in this section of the river, and the channel changed, creating a body of water called the White River Basin. (Courtesy of the Little Rock Photograph Collection, University of Arkansas at Little Rock Center for Arkansas History and Culture.)

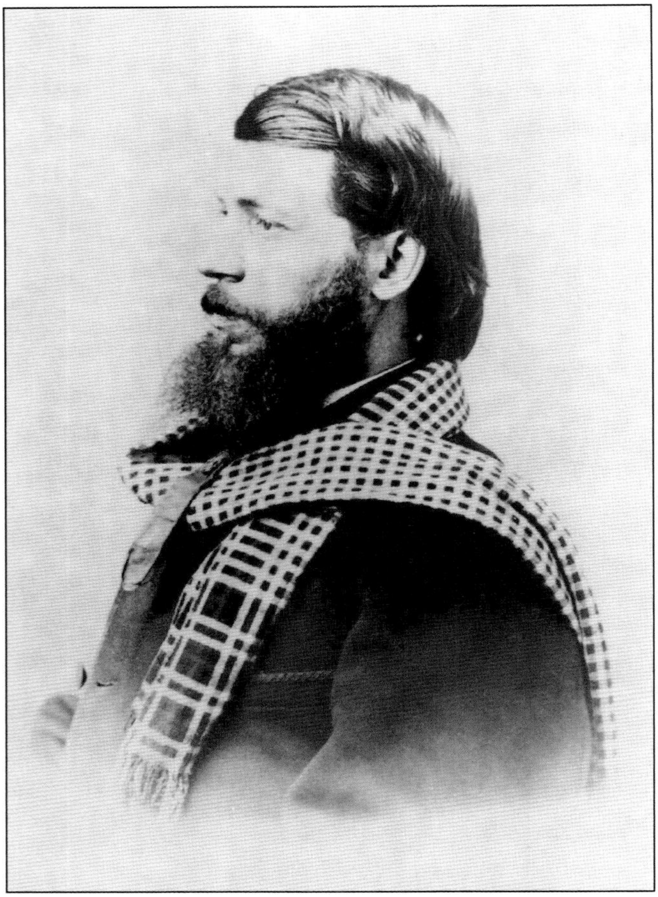

R.H. White, who probably came from the midwest with the Union army, opened a photography studio in DeValls Bluff in 1863 or 1864. He was the most prolific of Arkansas's wartime photographers. Sometime in 1864, he moved his studio to Little Rock. (Courtesy of the Arkansas History Commission.)

Aaron Harvey of the 57th US Colored Infantry is holding the side drum in this photograph, taken most likely after the war when the unit was mustered out on December 1, 1866. In the latter part of the war, the unit was assigned to defend the Memphis & Little Rock Railroad. Gloster (or Gloss) Barnett, the prized slave of Thomas Barnett, joined the 57th and later settled at DeValls Bluff. (Courtesy of the Arkansas History Commission.)

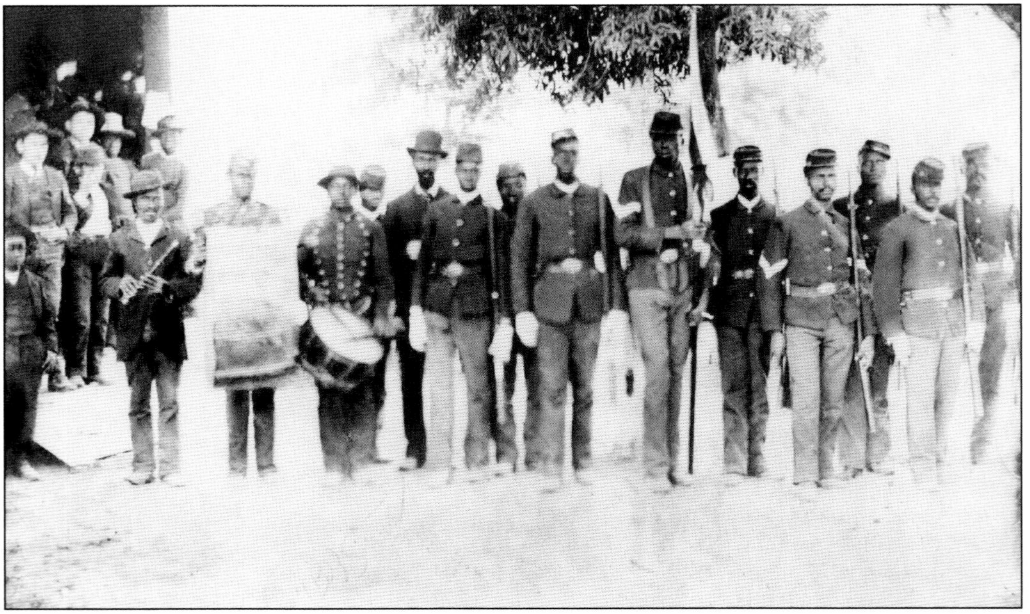

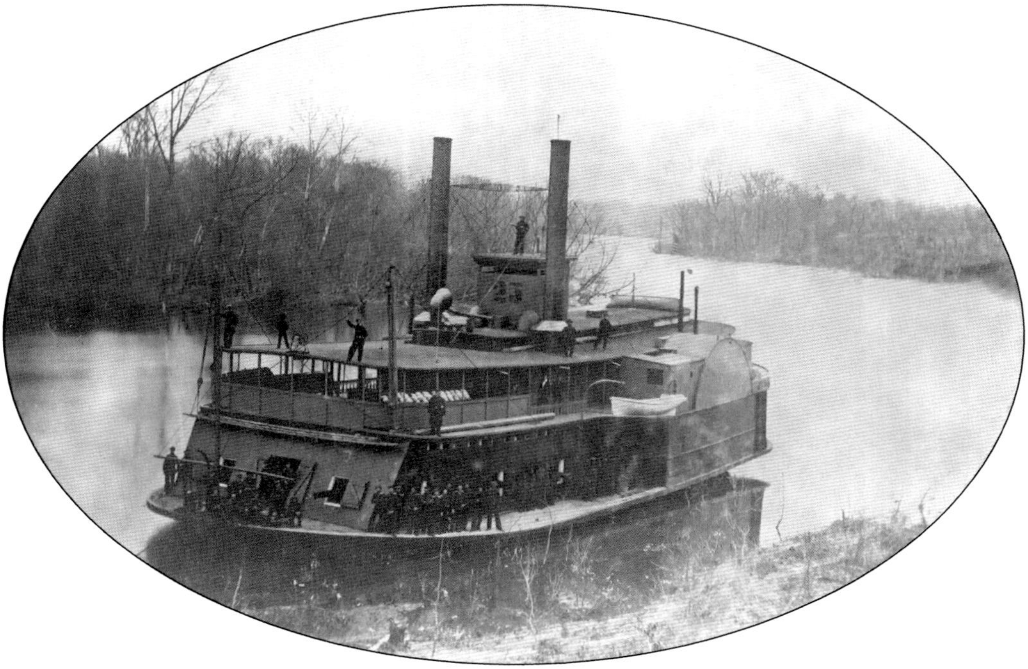

The *Signal*, photographed at DeValls Bluff, was one of the gunboats used on the White River by the Union forces. (Courtesy of the Arkansas History Commission.)

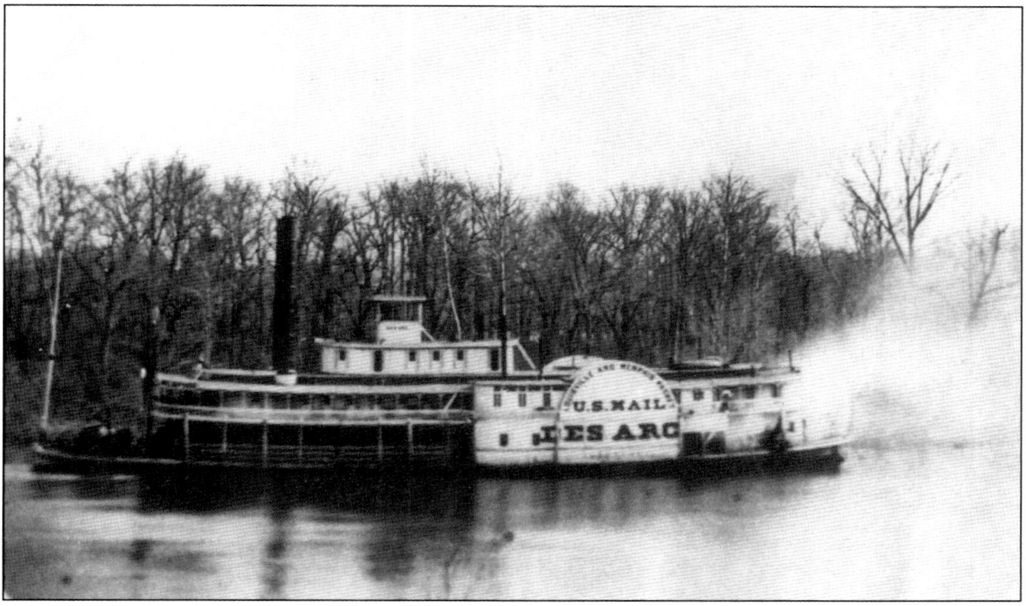

The *Des Arc* was one of the steamboats used by the Union army to move troops and supplies on the White and other rivers. Such boats were favorite targets of Confederate guerillas. The *Des Arc* was deliberately sunk to prevent total loss at DeValls Bluff on March 22, 1864, when cotton in its hold caught fire. (Courtesy of the University of Arkansas Photograph Collection, University of Arkansas at Little Rock Center for Arkansas History and Culture.)

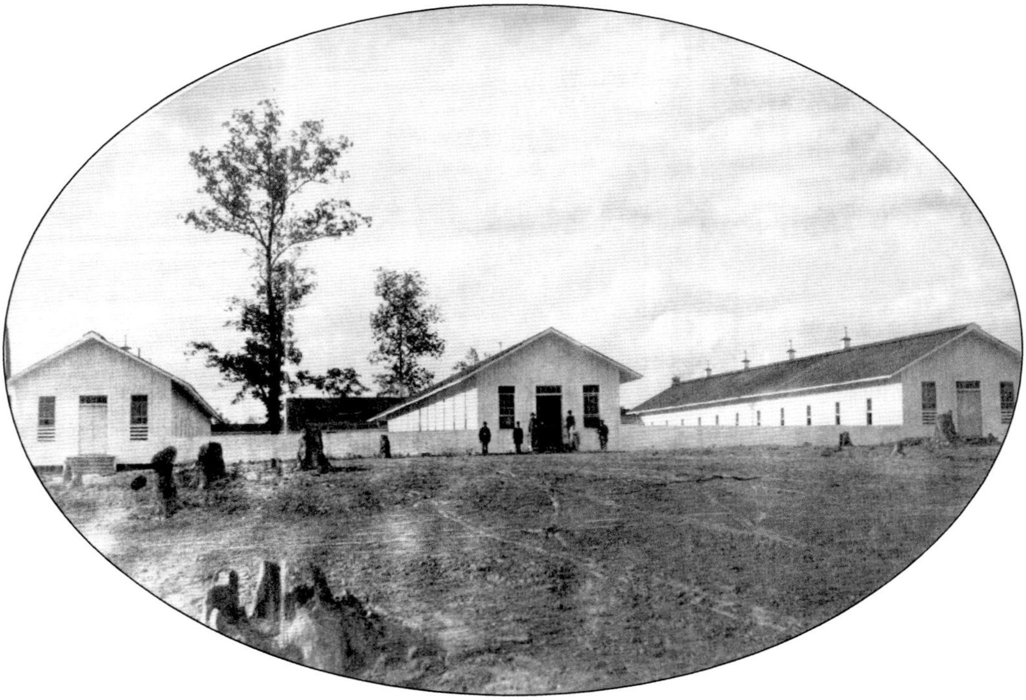

The "Clarendon shakes" and other illnesses were common at the DeValls Bluff post, and many of the enlisted men were treated in these buildings. Over an 18-month period, 153 Minnesota infantrymen died of fever. (Courtesy of the National Archives.)

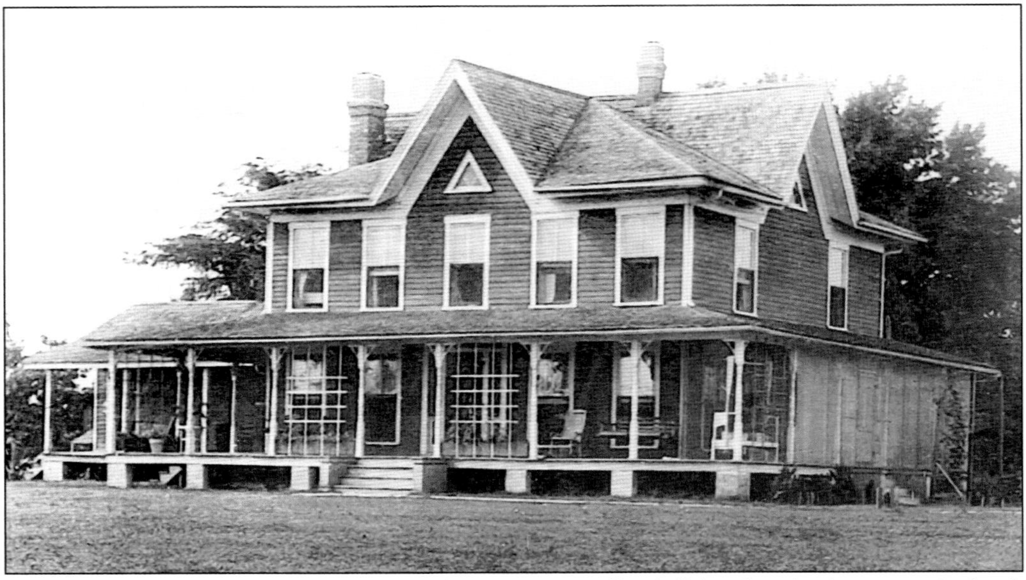

Gen. Alexander Shaler, a commander of the post at DeValls Bluff, lived in this house on the bank of the White River (later the Basin). According to Miss Jennie Pickard, an early town resident, it housed Union officers and their wives. Later, it served as the home of some of the Wells family, who opened a mill and boat oar factory in town in 1884 or 1885, which reinvigorated the town's economy. (Courtesy of the Torreyson Library, University of Central Arkansas.)

On August 24, 1864, Confederate general Joseph O. Shelby led a successful raid against Union fortifications at Ashley's Station on the Memphis & Little Rock Railroad between Hazen and Carlisle. Civilian contractors were cutting hay for the thousands of horses and mules at the Union military base in DeValls Bluff and other bases in Arkansas. (Courtesy of Wilson's Creek National Battlefield Collection, National Park Service.)

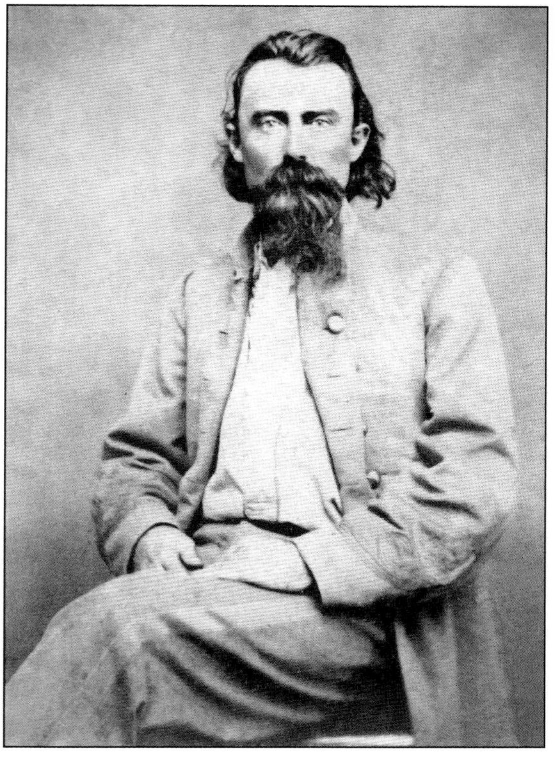

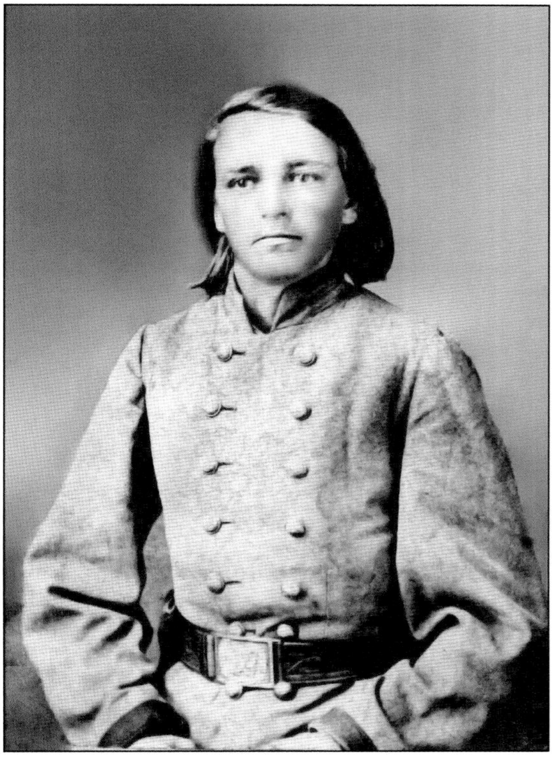

Howell A. "Doc" Rayburn was a Confederate guerilla fighter who pestered the Union forces in White and Prairie Counties. One tradition maintains that he once gained entry to a ball being given for the Federal forces stationed at DeValls Bluff by dressing as a woman. He managed to escape late in the night with several of their horses. One of the men who rode with him was John Pinkney Bethell. (Courtesy of Lawrence T. Jones Collection, Southern Methodist University.)

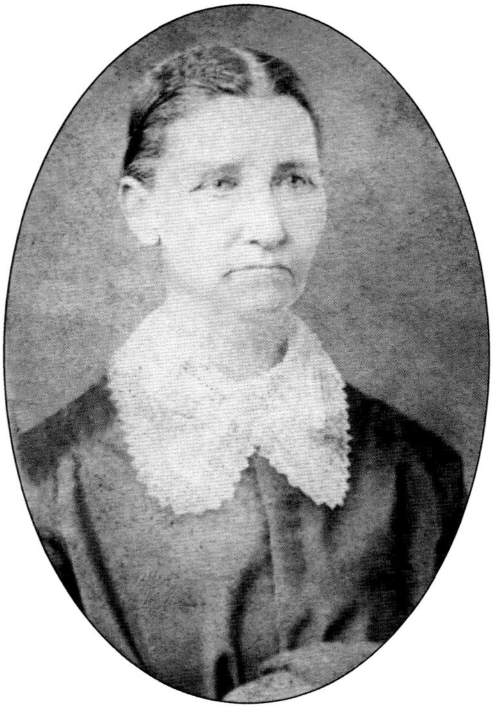

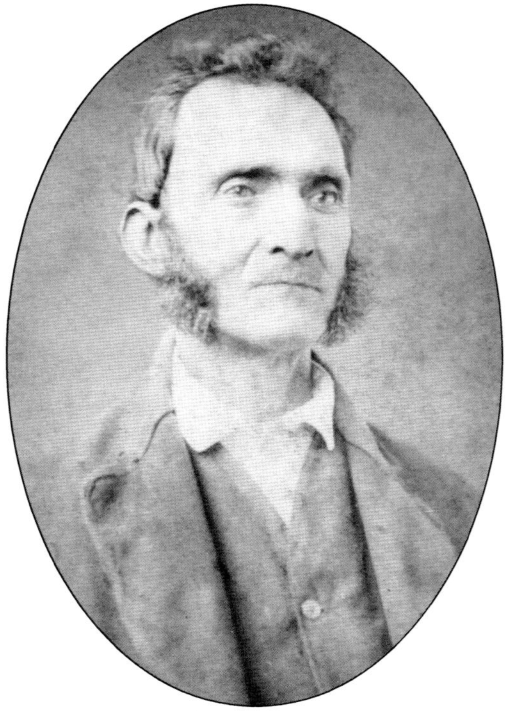

To the left is an albumen photograph of Nancy, wife of H.A. Balch. The man is assumed to be her husband. Written on the backs of both images is "H.A. Balch Artist." Balch was born about 1827 in Ohio, took daguerreotypes in Joliet, Illinois, in the 1840s, and later moved to Arkansas. He appears in DeValls Bluff on the 1870 US census. (Courtesy of Henry Wilks.)

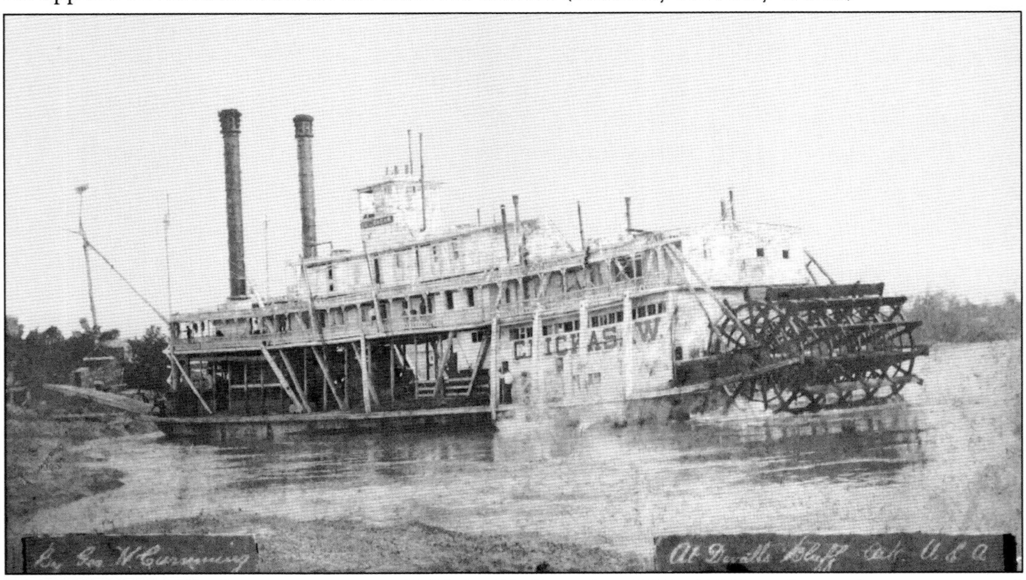

The steamboat *Chickasaw* appears at DeValls Bluff in the 1890s. Ed Postal was the captain, and brothers Joe and Charlie were the clerks. Captain Rice was first mate, and Green Snow was head pilot. The *Chickasaw* was a fine showboat and the first to have electric lights, which frightened some people living along the White River when they first saw it. (Courtesy of Jo Claire English.)

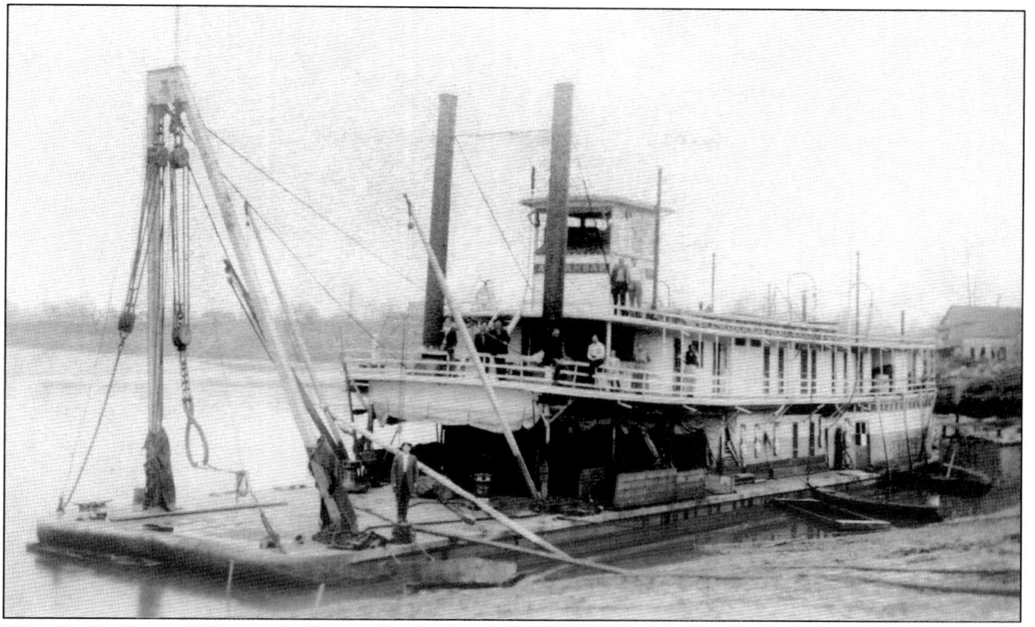

The dredge boat *Arkansas* is shown docked at DeValls Bluff. Newt Parks said there were two boats named *Arkansas* that looked somewhat alike. L.C. Holloway worked on one of them. (Courtesy of Henry Wilks.)

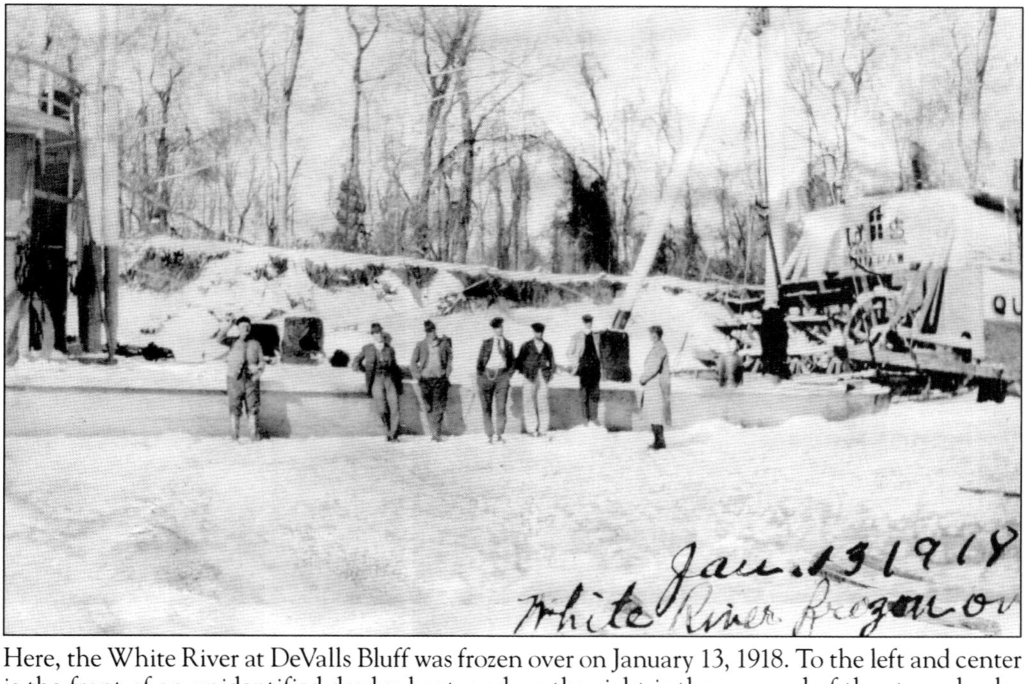

Here, the White River at DeValls Bluff was frozen over on January 13, 1918. To the left and center is the front of an unidentified dredge boat, and on the right is the rear end of the sternwheeler *Quapaw*. (Courtesy of Harry Mason Jr.)

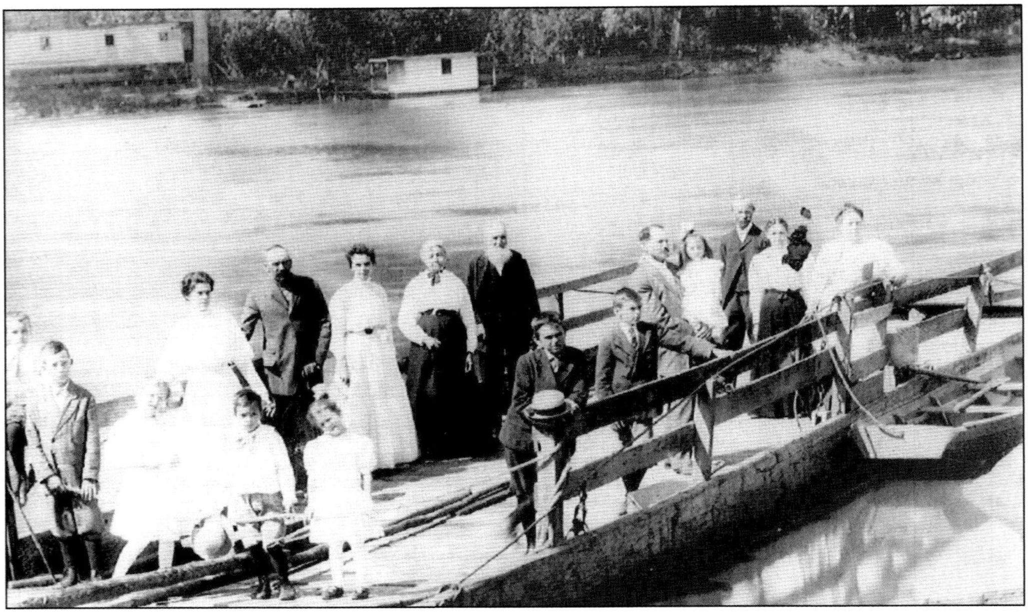

When this White River ferry photograph was taken about 1910 at DeValls Bluff, the crossing was over what is now known as the White River Basin. The river channel changed in 1918, and the operation was moved a short distance upstream. The boy in front with the white shirt, holding his hat, is William Herman Whitcomb. Behind him are his parents, William H. and Ida Whitcomb. (Courtesy of the late Ray Whitcomb.)

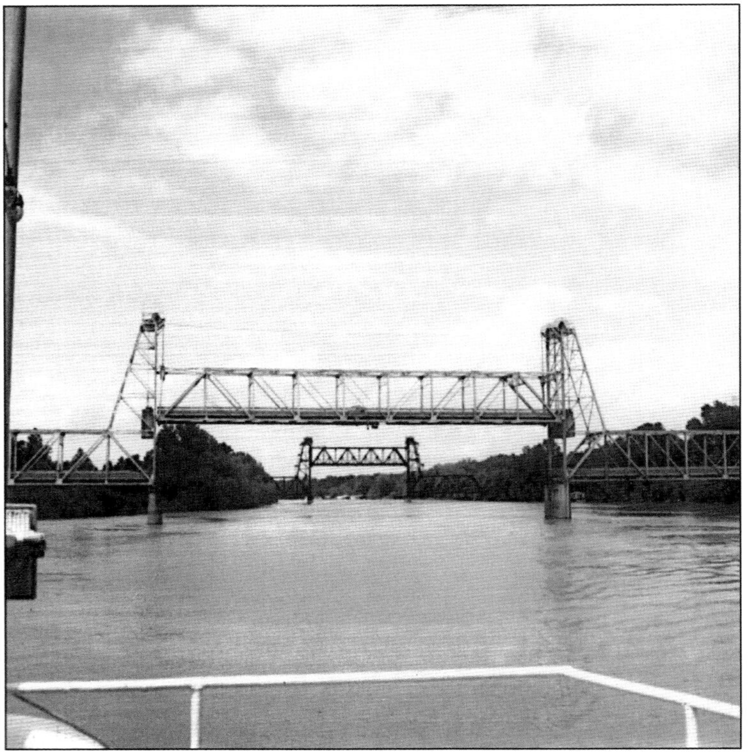

The vehicular and pedestrian lift bridge in the foreground was opened in 1925 over the White River at DeValls Bluff and was a toll bridge for several years. The Rock Island railroad bridge in the background was built in 1927. The Memphis & Little Rock Railroad first spanned the river at this point in 1871. (Courtesy of Judith Toll-Booher.)

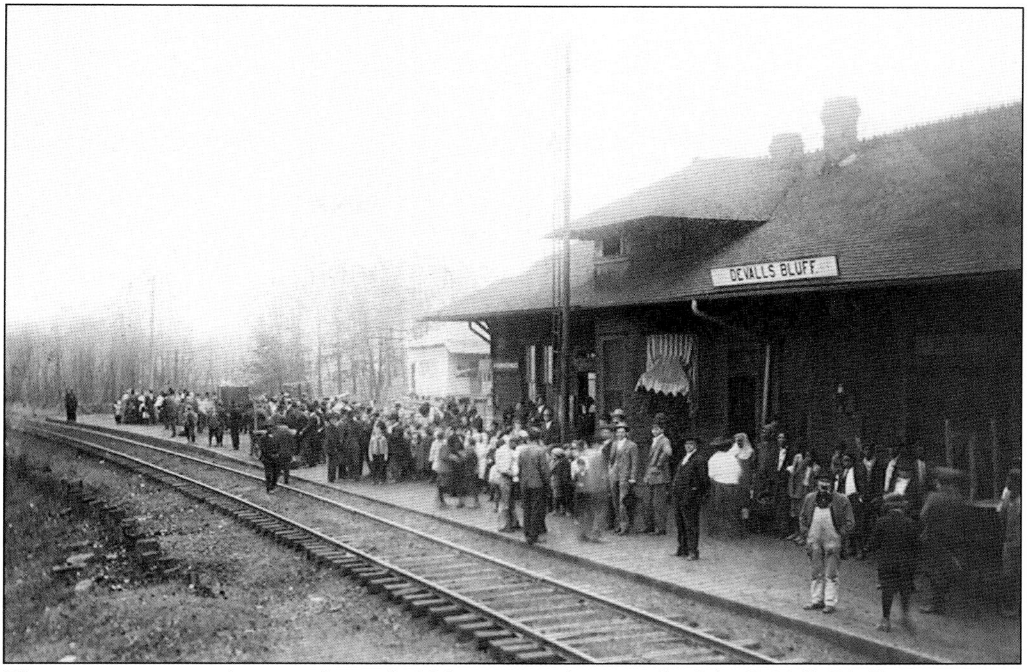

The camera is pointed east in this early 20th century photograph of the DeValls Bluff train station. (Courtesy of the late Ray Whitcomb.)

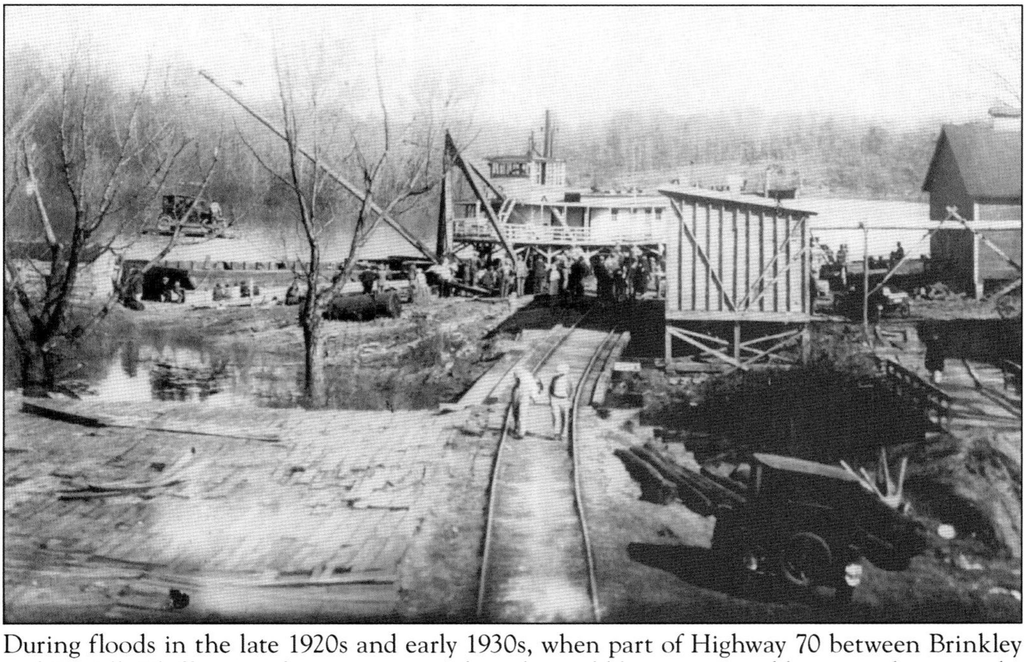
During floods in the late 1920s and early 1930s, when part of Highway 70 between Brinkley and DeValls Bluff was underwater, cars and trucks could be transported between the towns by means of barges. Here, a car is being loaded onto a barge at the DeValls Bluff White River port to be moved downriver to Clarendon. From there, motorists could drive over the "high-and-dry" Military Road to Brinkley. (Courtesy of the late Mary Louise Hill.)

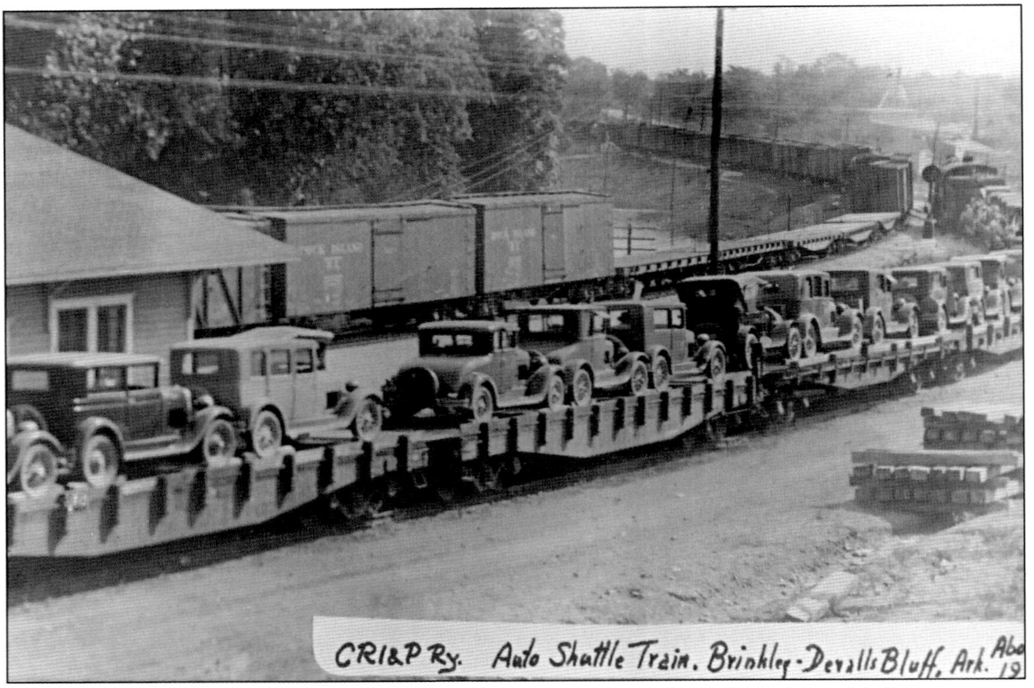

Rock Island provided an alternative for motorists traveling between Brinkley and DeValls Bluff when Highway 70 was flooded. The shuttle train was no longer needed when a higher roadbed was opened in 1934. (Courtesy of John P. Ascher.)

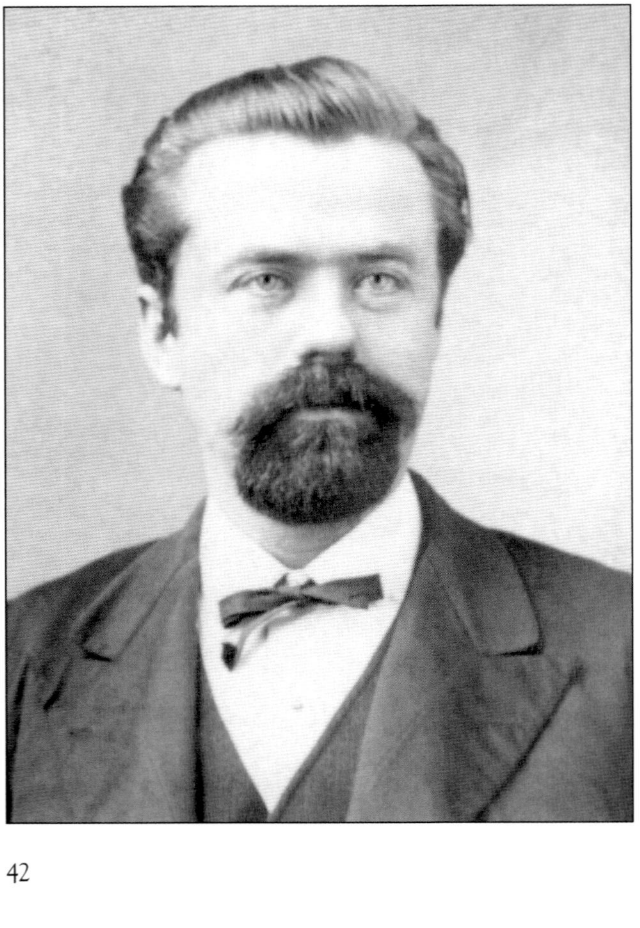

Joseph Gustavus Thweatt was born near Hickory Plains. He became an attorney and established a law practice in DeValls Bluff in 1888. His son John Dale also practiced for many years in the same office, which still stands in DeValls Bluff. Both Judge J.G. Thweatt and Monroe County judge Clarence F. Greenlee in Brinkley were credited for having DeValls Bluff and Brinkley placed on the route for Highway 70. (Courtesy of the Arkansas History Commission.)

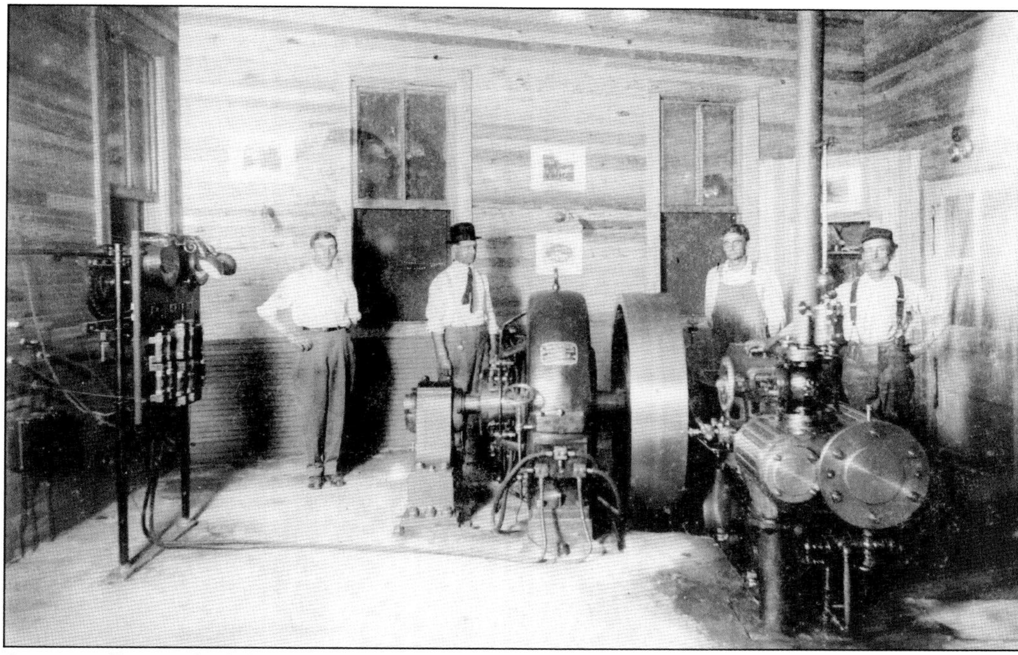

Some small towns had their own electric power plants before the appearance of Arkansas Power and Light Company and the cooperative associations, such as this one at DeValls Bluff, photographed about 1910–1920. Leander K. Armstrong was the owner, and James G. Hendricks was the light plant engineer in 1920. (Courtesy of Harry Mason Jr.)

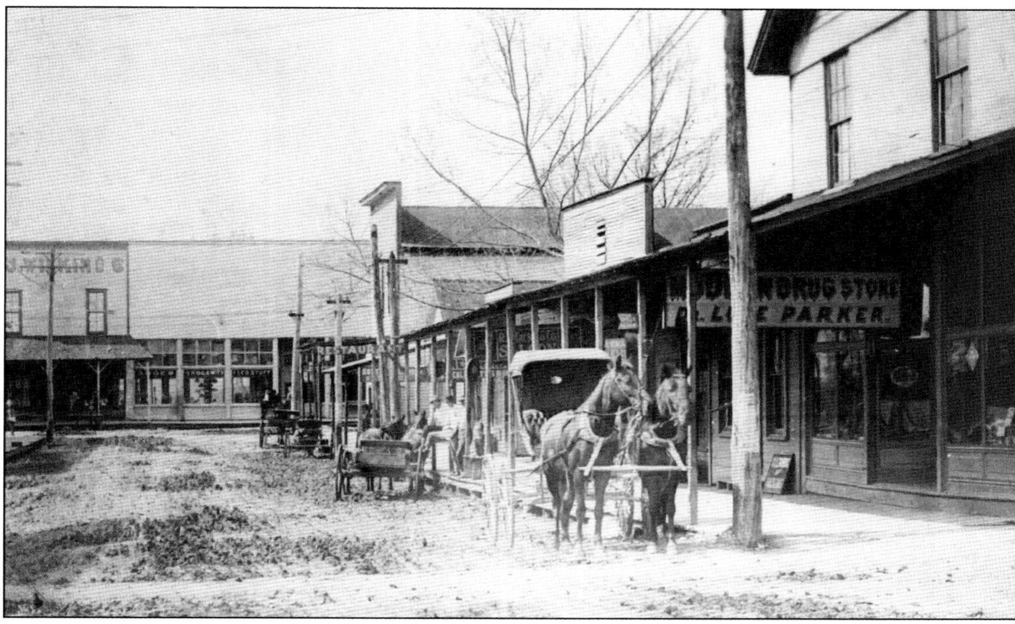

Part of DeValls Bluff's Main Street structures, shown here, burned in 1912 but were rebuilt with bricks. Elias Brooks Robinson's mercantile store was erected in 1913, located where the Luke Parker drugstore is seen on the right, on the southwest corner of Main and Brinkley Streets. (Courtesy of Jackie Adcock.)

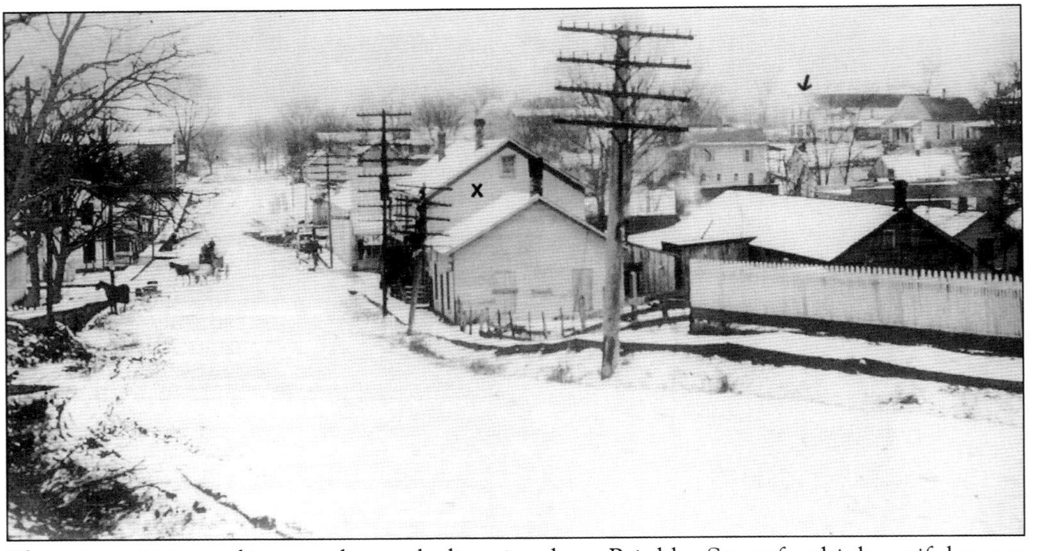

The camera is pointed in a southeasterly direction down Brinkley Street for this beautiful snowy scene. The arrow indicates the old Gates mercantile store, and the "x" identifies the Planters Supply building, which burned in 1912; it was replaced by the E.B. Robinson brick store building in 1913. (Courtesy of Steven Hanley.)

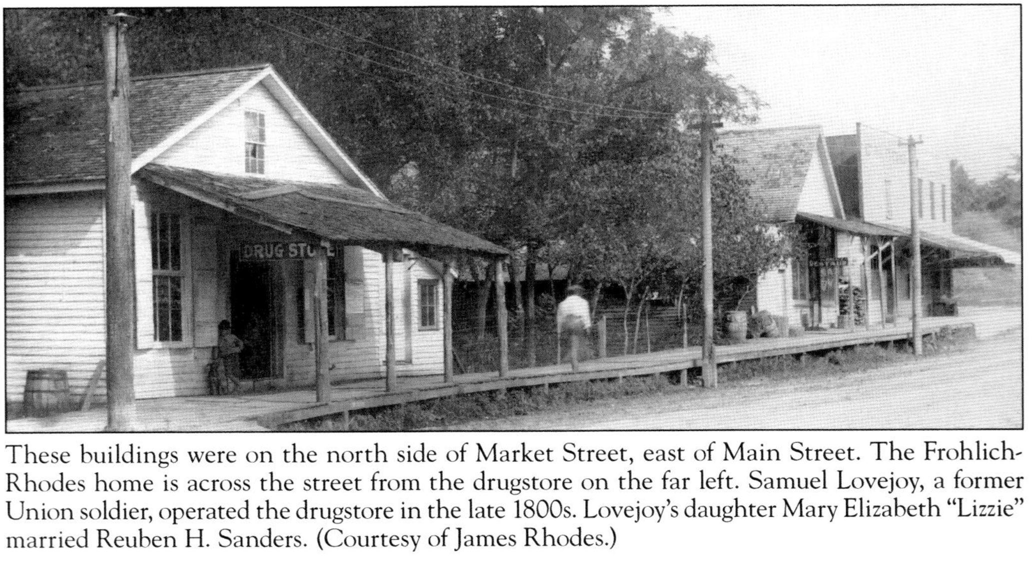

These buildings were on the north side of Market Street, east of Main Street. The Frohlich-Rhodes home is across the street from the drugstore on the far left. Samuel Lovejoy, a former Union soldier, operated the drugstore in the late 1800s. Lovejoy's daughter Mary Elizabeth "Lizzie" married Reuben H. Sanders. (Courtesy of James Rhodes.)

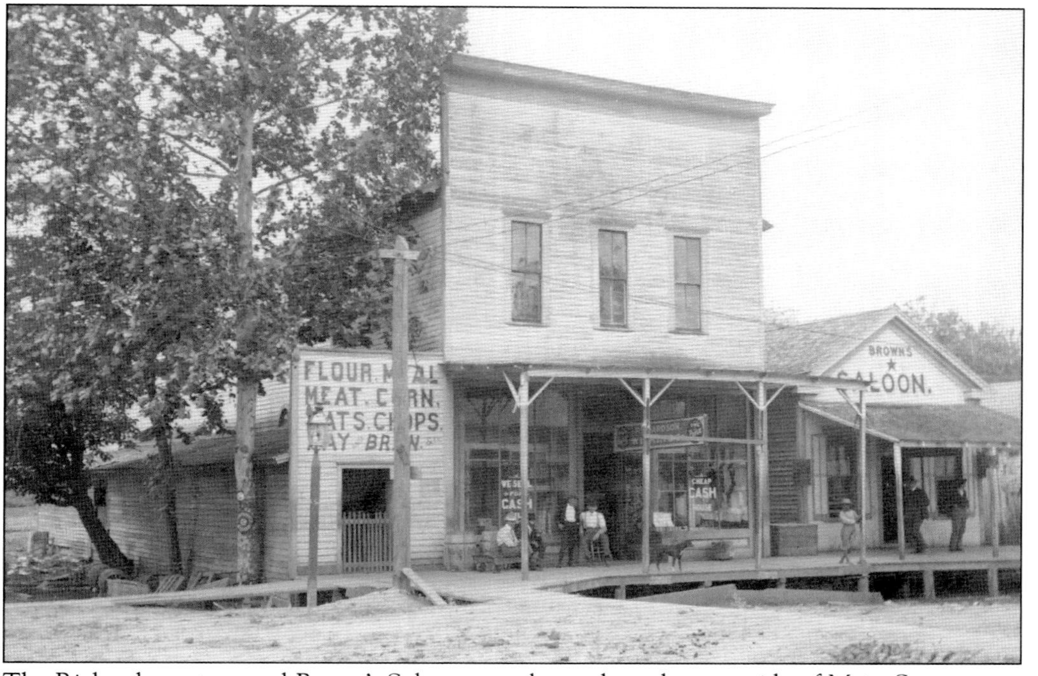

The Richardson store and Brown's Saloon were located on the west side of Main Street, near Market Street. In 1882, Robert E. and James M. Richardson moved to DeValls Bluff and bought out the mercantile firm of R.P. Watt (or Walt) and Company. (Courtesy of James Rhodes.)

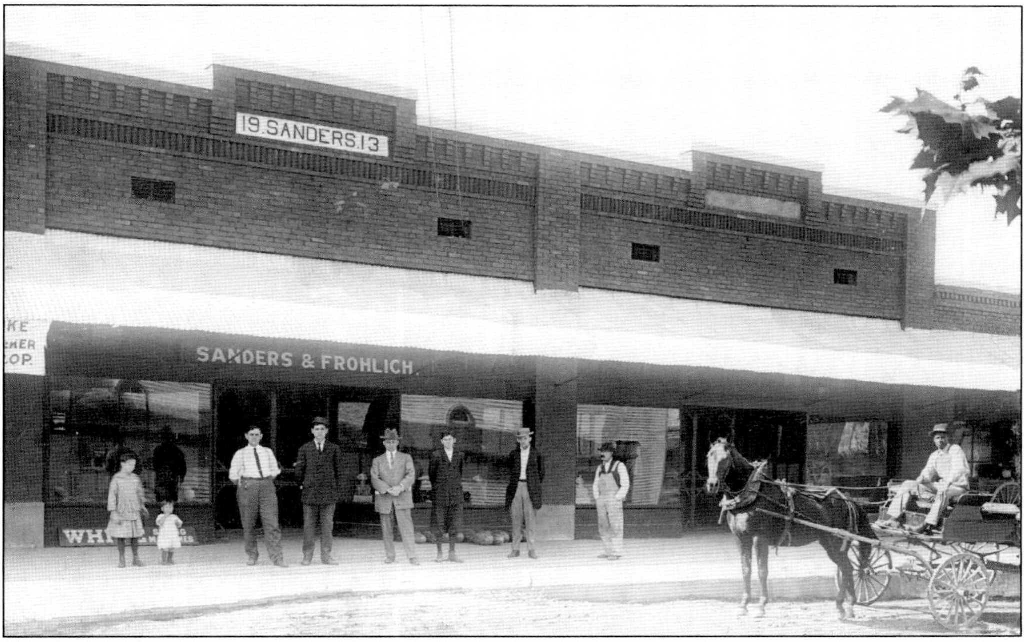

Reuben H. Sanders and Jacob Frohlich entered into a partnership in 1913 and created the largest general store in town. Mary and Robert Parker appear on the far left and Jacob Frohlich is fifth from the left. Others known to be in the photograph are Ben F. House, Claude Lumpkin, Thomas P. Atkins, and Archie ?. (Courtesy of James Rhodes.)

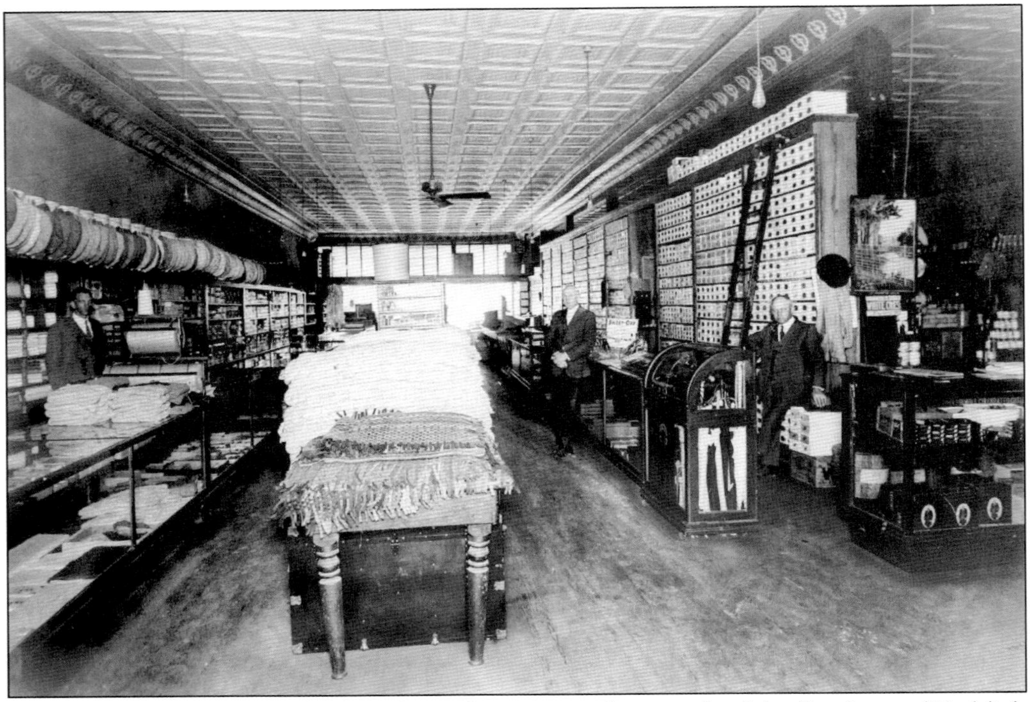

Jacob Frohlich appears on the far right in this interior photograph of the Sanders and Frohlich store. All others are unidentified. (Courtesy of James Rhodes.)

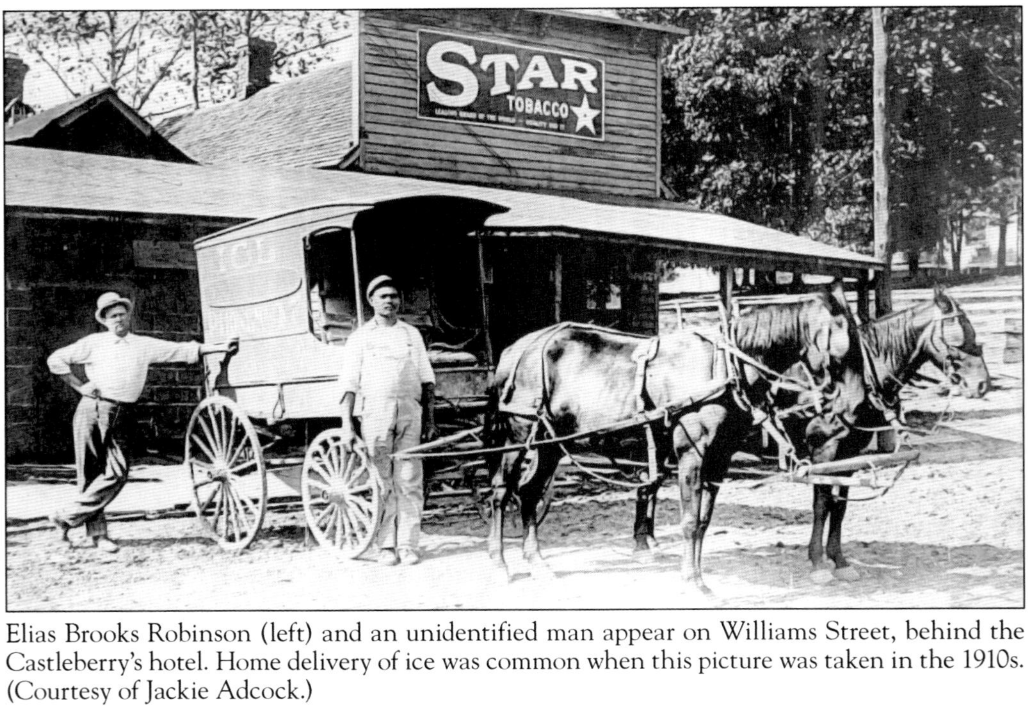

Elias Brooks Robinson (left) and an unidentified man appear on Williams Street, behind the Castleberry's hotel. Home delivery of ice was common when this picture was taken in the 1910s. (Courtesy of Jackie Adcock.)

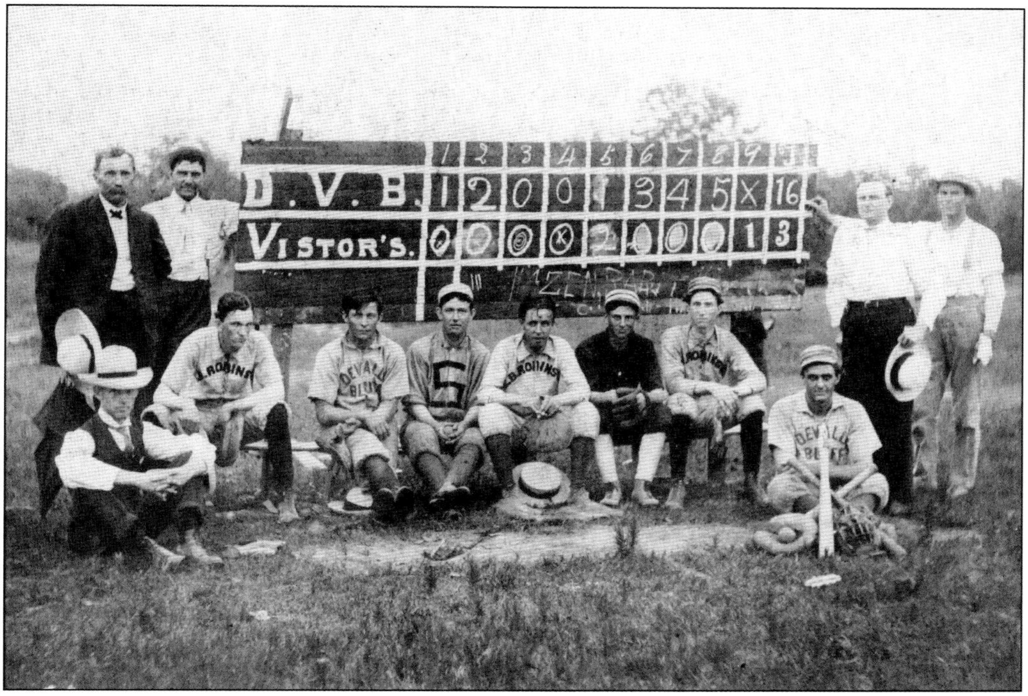

Local merchant Elias Brooks Robinson, who later married Hester Buck, apparently was the sponsor of the visiting team that played the DeValls Bluff schoolboys. (Courtesy of Troy Tacker.)

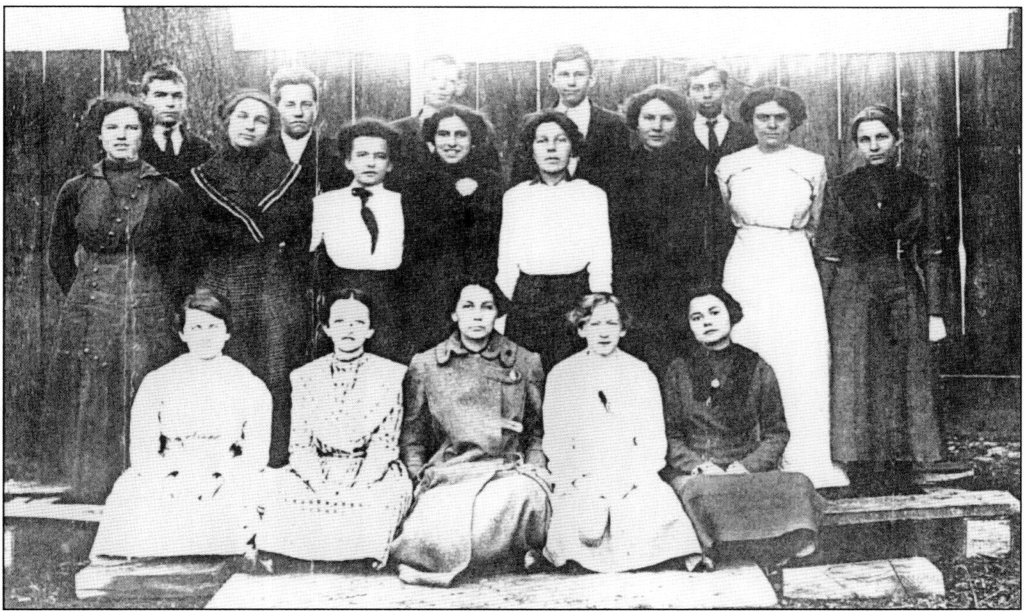

The graduating students of the class of 1915, appearing here among other young people, had attended school in the three-story frame building in use then. In the first row, Hester Buck and Mildred Morrow are third and fourth from the left; in the second row, Hortense Bizot is fourth from the left; and in the third row, John Dale Thweatt is second from the left. All others are unidentified. (Courtesy of Jackie Adcock.)

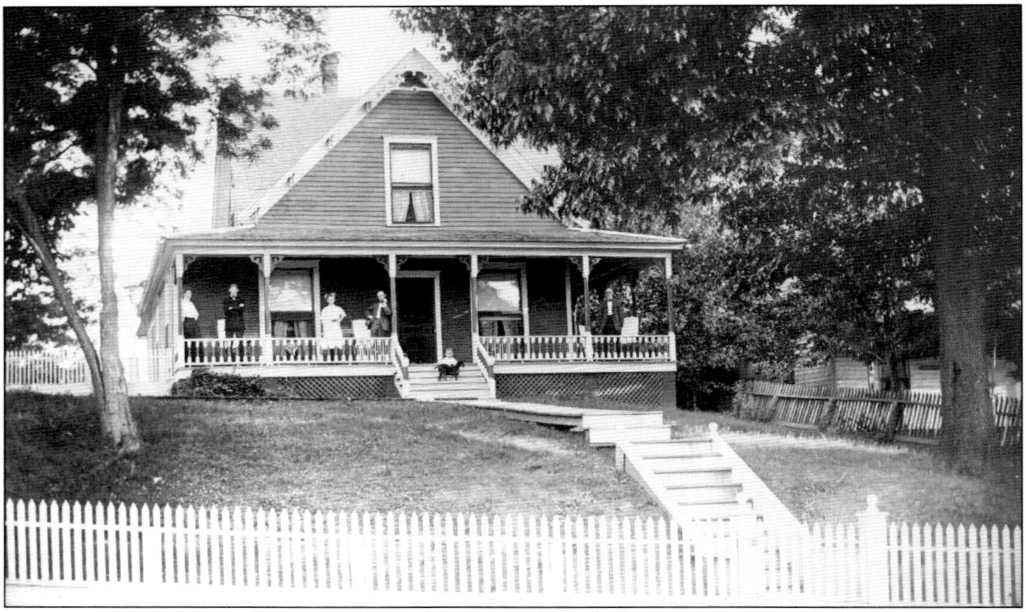

This house at the southwest corner of Main and Market Streets was built in 1872 and purchased in 1913 by Jacob Frohlich, a prominent merchant. His daughter Regina and her husband, James R. Rhodes, and family lived here for many years. Steven Ingle now owns the house. (Courtesy of James Rhodes.)

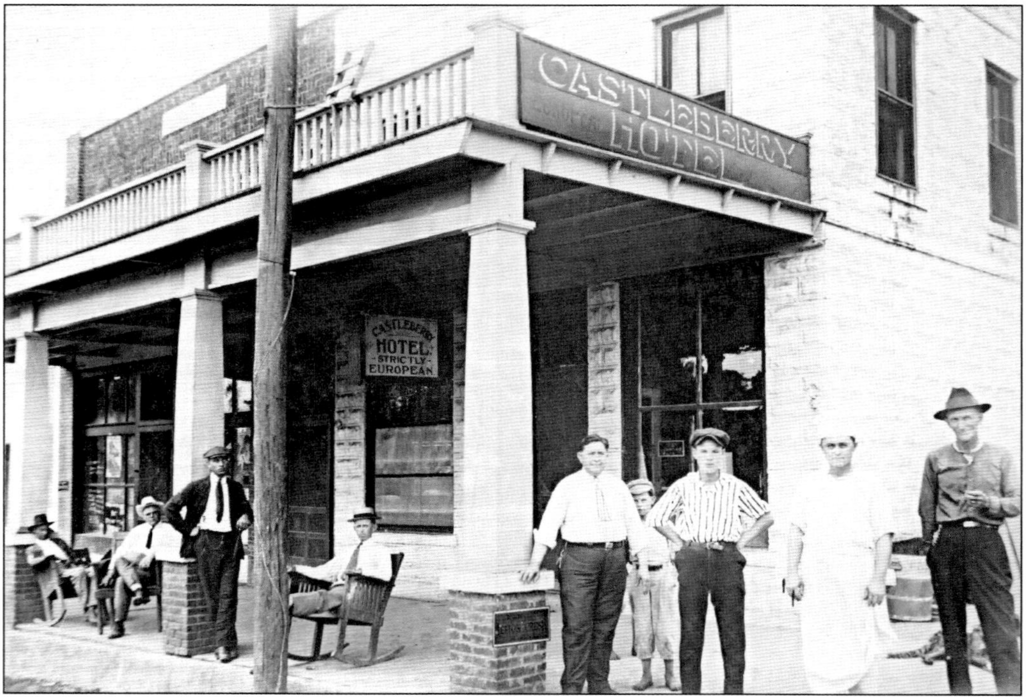

The sign at the front of the Castleberry Hotel in this undated photograph indicates that it operated under the European plan. The hotel burned in 1924, and Wesley and Doss Edward Castleberry rebuilt it in 1925–1926. (Courtesy of Harry Mason Jr.)

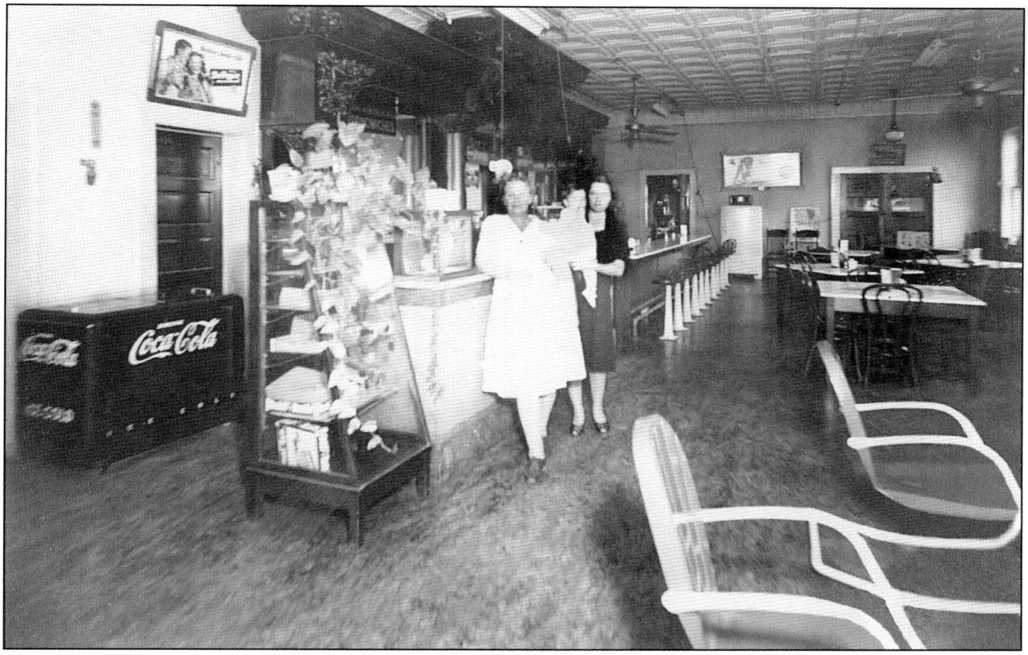

Pictured in the 1940s on the left is Myrtle Buck Rogers in the restaurant of her hotel in DeValls Bluff, formerly the Castleberry Hotel. The woman holding the child is unidentified. Myrtle was a sister of Hester Buck Robinson. (Courtesy of Linda Park Schwede.)

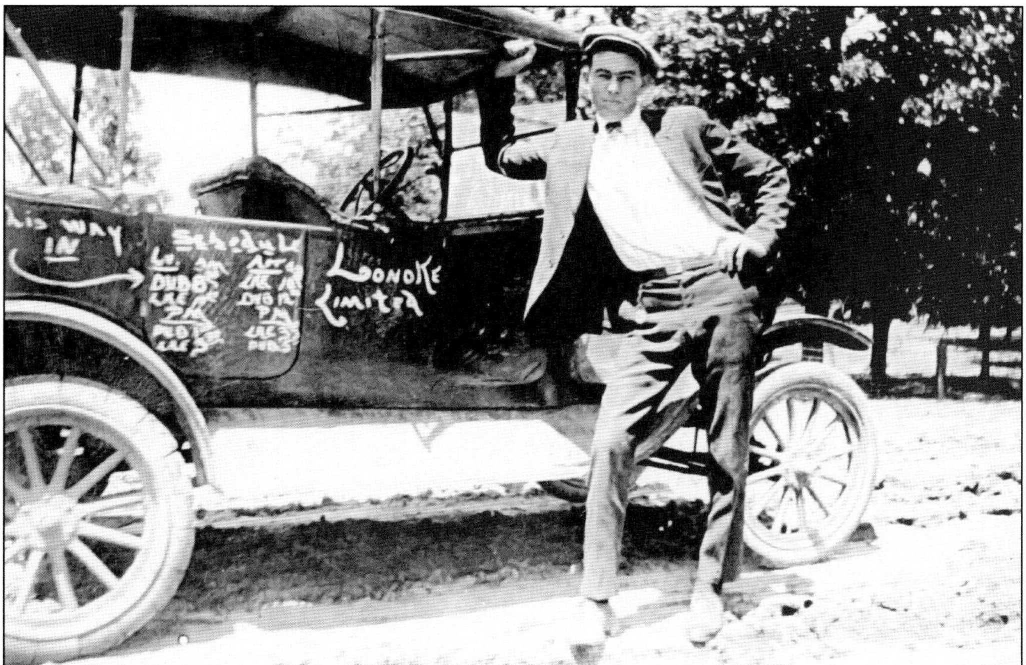

There was possibly no bus service between DeValls Bluff and Lonoke when this photograph was taken about 1920. The unidentified young man made one round trip daily between the towns, as posted on the car door, in his "Lonoke Limited" taxi. (Courtesy of Harry Mason Jr.)

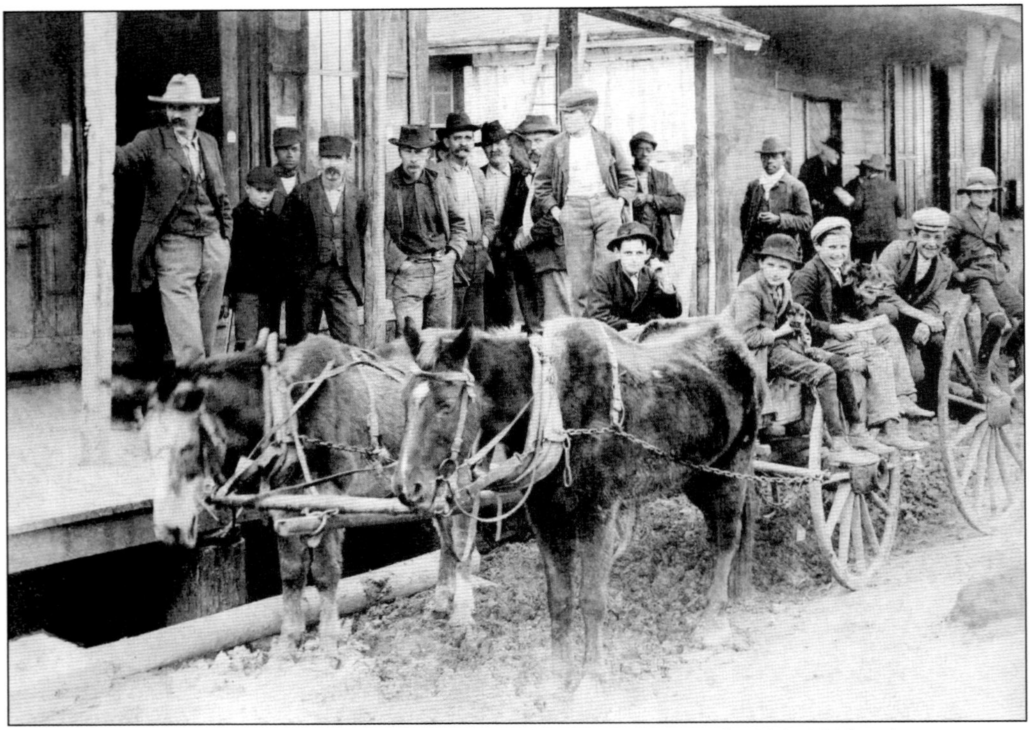

The reason for these gentlemen congregating downtown around 1900–1910 is lost in time. (Courtesy of Harry Mason Jr.)

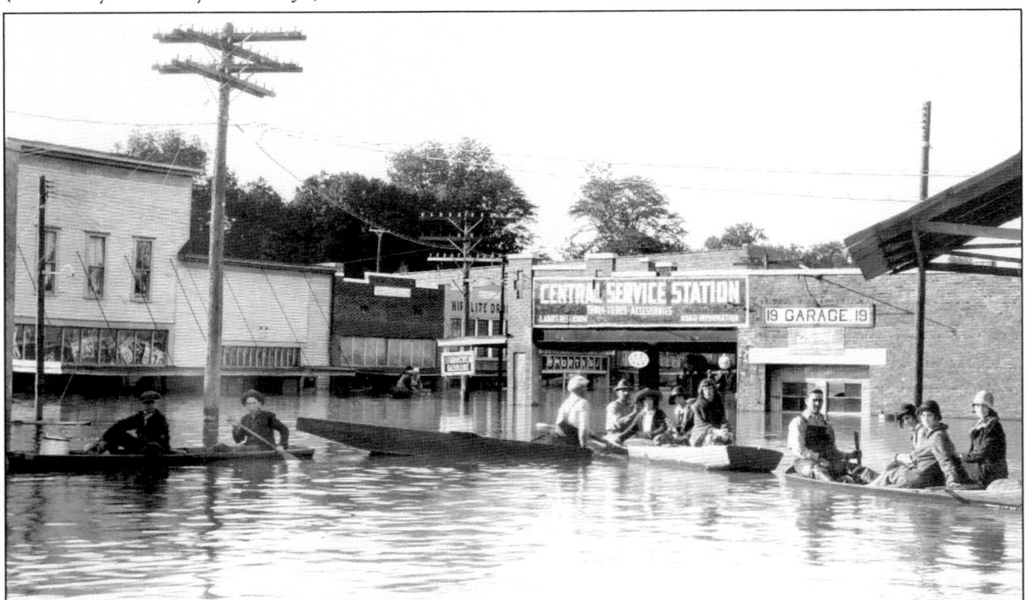

The Mississippi Valley flood in the spring of 1927 forced nearly 150,000 Arkansans into refugee camps and claimed 98 lives, besides doing untold damage to newly planted crops. The water was perhaps at its highest level when this photograph was taken at the intersection of Main and Market Streets. (Courtesy of James Rhodes.)

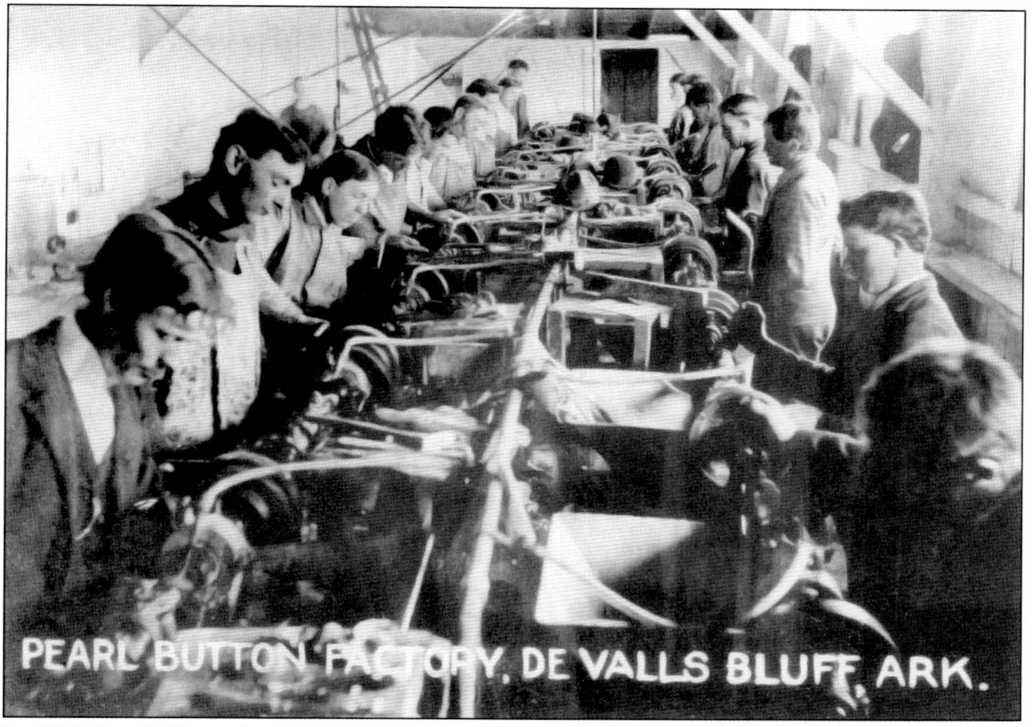

In 1896, Jim O'Hara of Memphis started a button factory using the mussel shells harvested primarily from the White and Cache Rivers. The 1910 DeValls Bluff area census listed 45 men working as button cutters, 3 as shell diggers, and 9 as shellers. Button factory operations ended about mid-century. Today, the shells are cut into pellets and placed in oysters to grow cultured pearls. (Courtesy of Ray Hanley.)

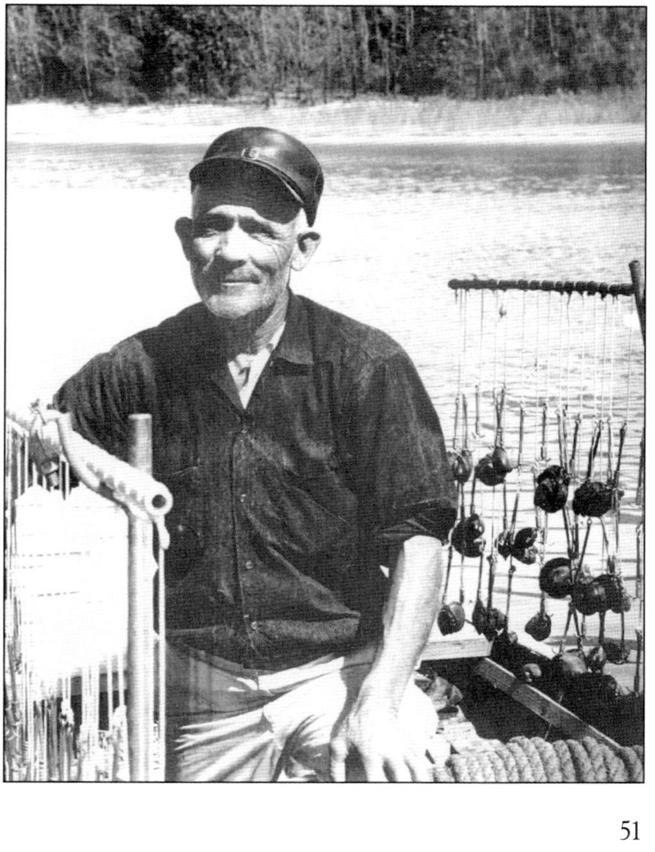

Marion Griffin (born 1911) of DeValls Bluff was a commercial fisherman and sheller on the White River. On the device to his left hang "crows' feet" with three hooks on each line. The apparatus was dragged over the river bottom where mussel shells lay. Some mussels would close and attach themselves to the passing barbs. (Courtesy of Dora Griffin Redmon.)

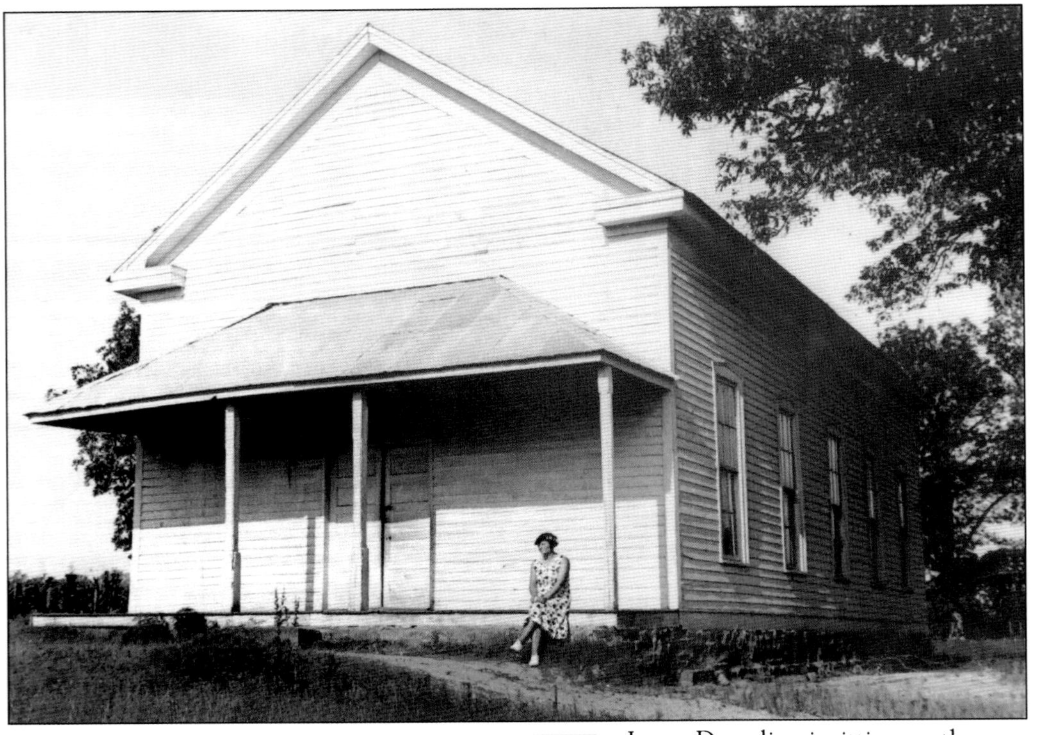

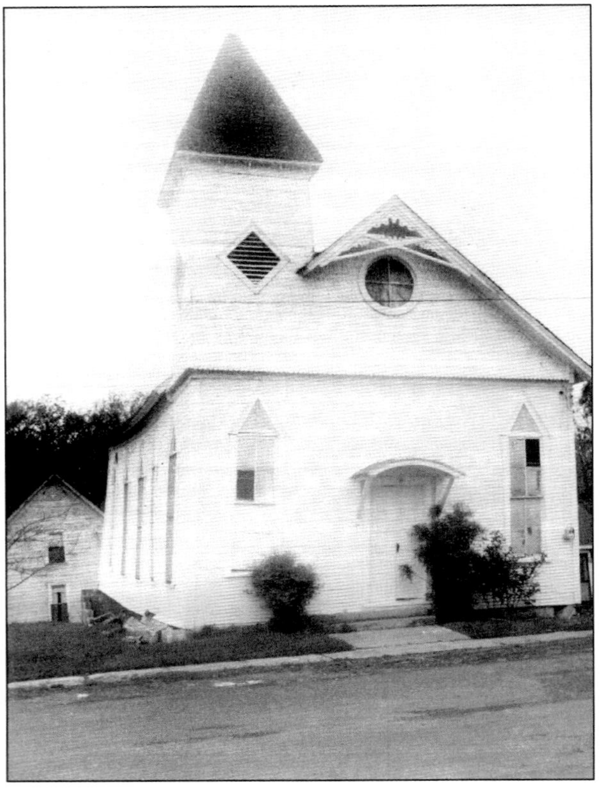

Laura Deuerling is sitting on the porch in this 1940 photograph of DeValls Bluff's St. Elizabeth Catholic Church, which was formerly called Sacred Heart of the Prairie. Fr. Robert Jeanne built a church on the site in 1904. In 1912, that building was wrecked by a storm and was torn down. It was rebuilt through the efforts of Fr. Henry Frommer, with the financial support of the townspeople, including Protestants. (Courtesy of Angela Wiesle Hinton.)

This church was built in the mid-1880s for the Methodists of DeValls Bluff on land donated by Logan Roots. The Assembly of God Church congregation later used it. (Courtesy of Linda Park Schwede.)

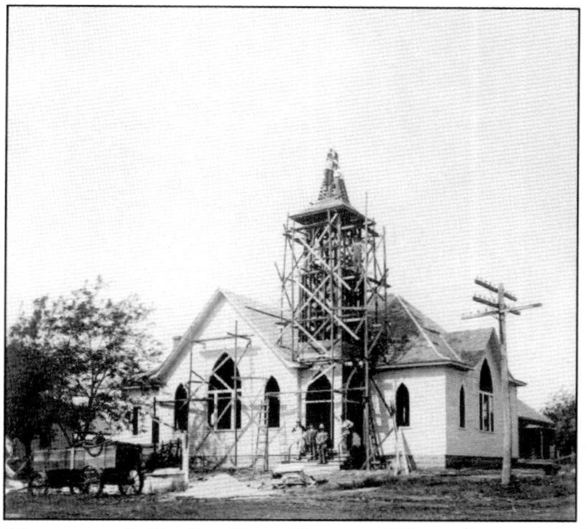

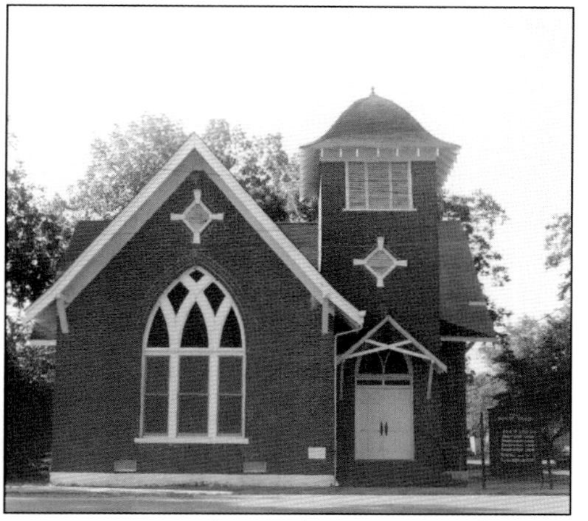

Shown at left, the First Baptist Church was under construction at the northeast corner of Prairie and Mason Streets in 1913. At right is the church as it appeared before it burned in the early 1990s. (Courtesy of Ray Hanley and Bill Sayger)

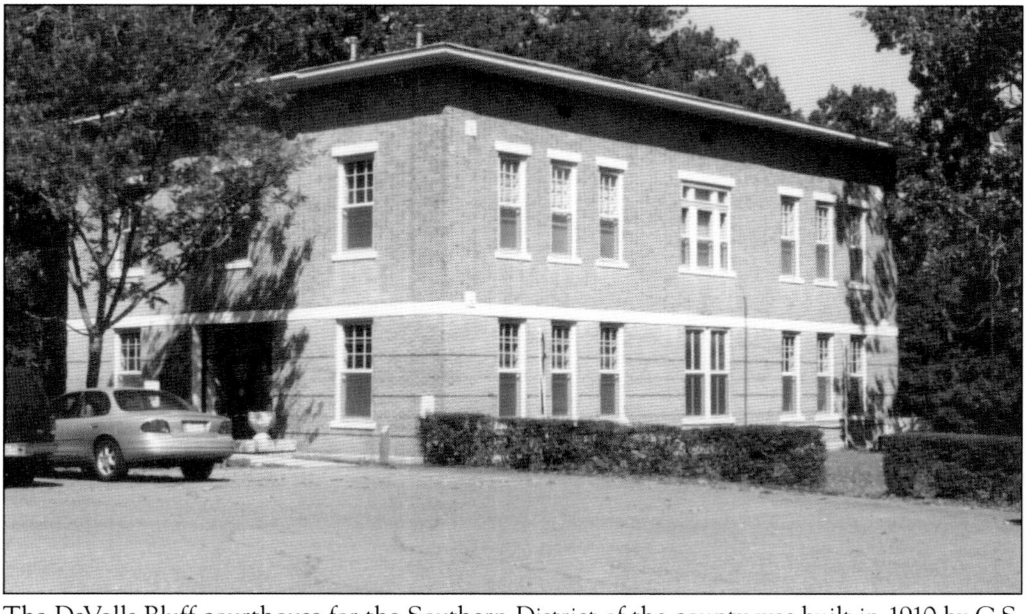

The DeValls Bluff courthouse for the Southern District of the county was built in 1910 by C.S. Proctor. The architect was H.J. Harker. Additional work was done on the building in the 1930s. (Courtesy of Bill Sayger.)

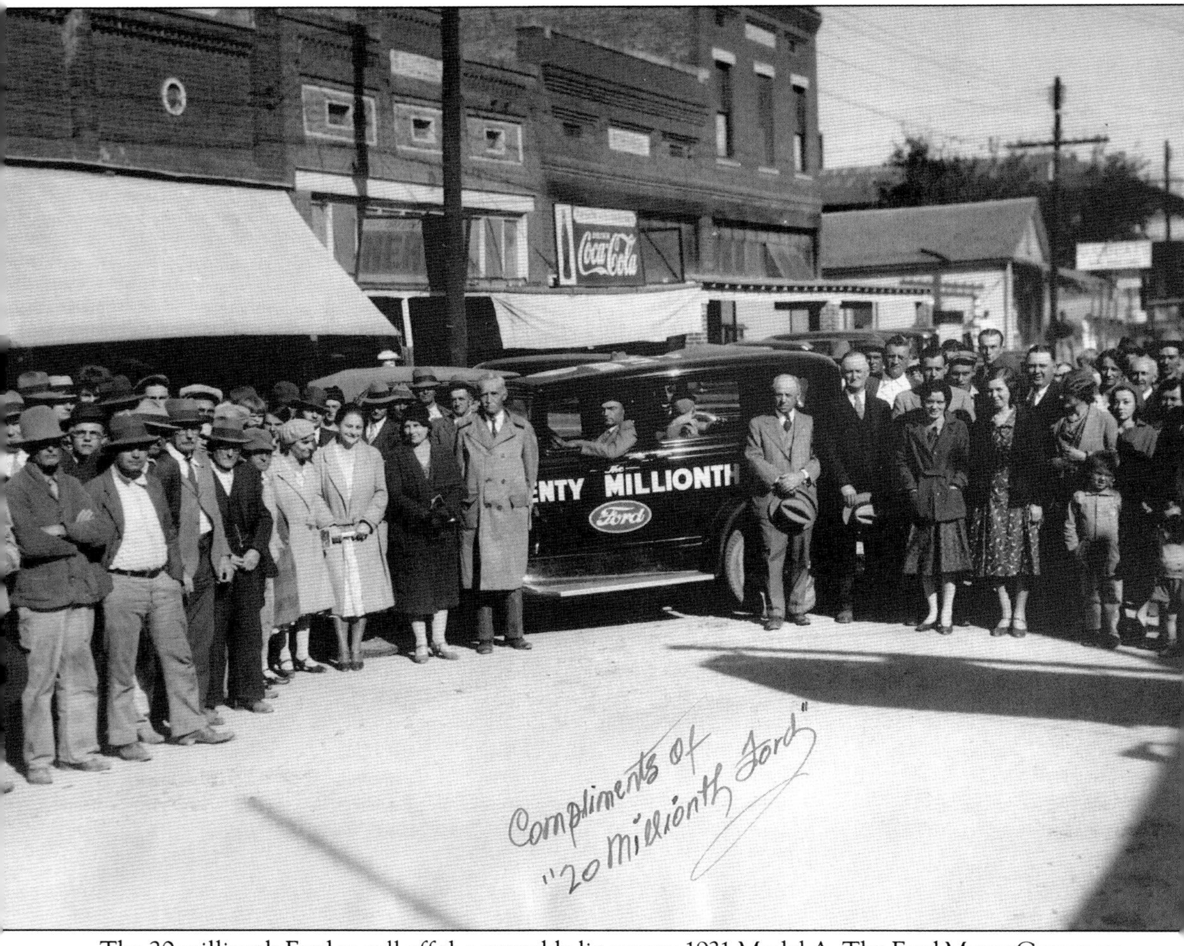

The 20 millionth Ford to roll off the assembly line was a 1931 Model A. The Ford Motor Company sent it on a publicity tour during the summer and winter of 1931 with "Twenty Millionth Ford" displayed on both sides of the automobile. When it arrived in DeValls Bluff, the automobile was accompanied by a caravan of Model As, radio cars, and filmmakers who shot the reception on Main Street (Highway 70). On the left side of the car are (first row) Mark Brooks, Frank Nelson Welty (man with glasses peeking over Brooks's shoulder), unidentified, L.K. Armstrong, Dr. James Parker, two unidentified, Lucy Whitcomb, Bessie Welty, J.A. Welty, and John Whitcomb in the driver's seat. Standing to the right of the driver are Jacob Frohlich and Michael Gillespie. (Courtesy of James Rhodes.)

James R. Rhodes purchased the service station at the corner of Main and Market Streets in 1945 from John Whitcomb's widow, Lucy. Porter Hurt, shown here in the late 1940s, operated the station for Rhodes. Hurt drove the school bus for the Biscoe and Brasfield area for many years. (Courtesy of James Rhodes.)

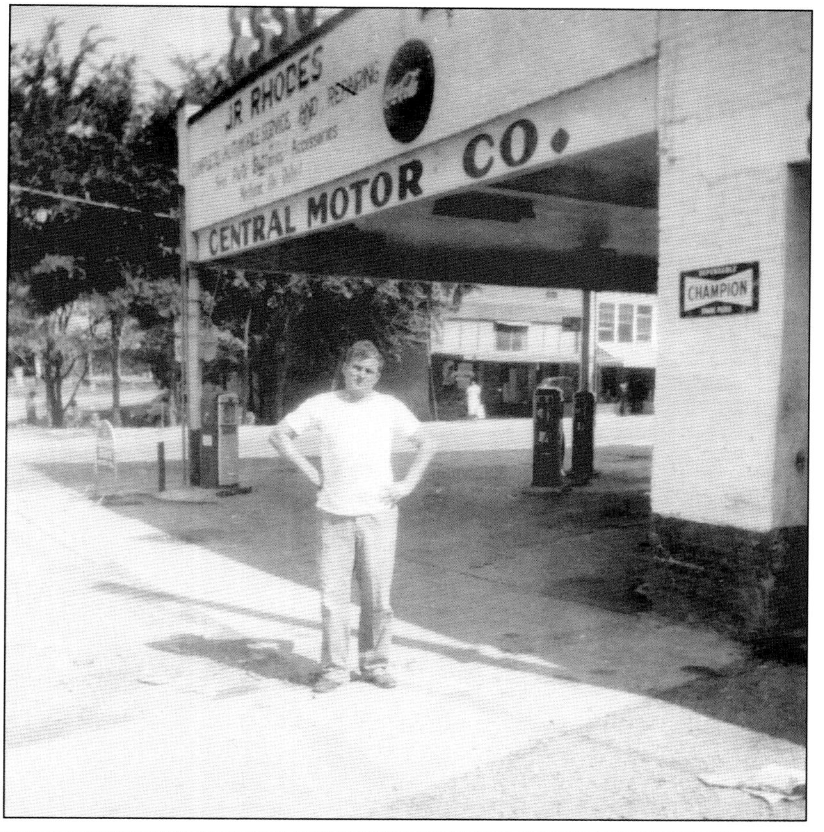

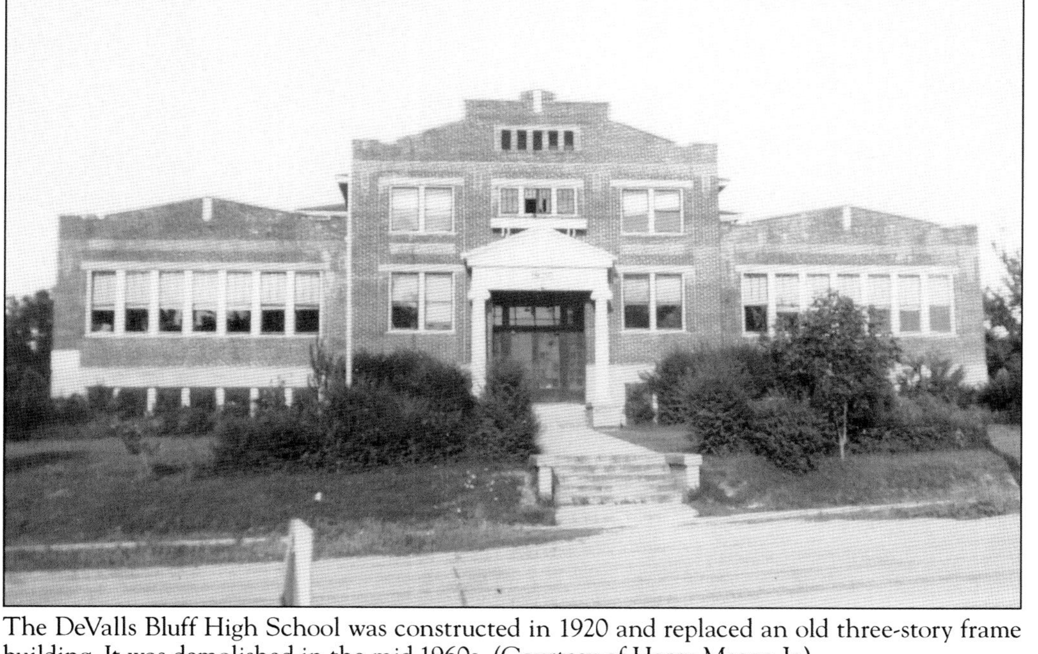

The DeValls Bluff High School was constructed in 1920 and replaced an old three-story frame building. It was demolished in the mid-1960s. (Courtesy of Harry Mason Jr.)

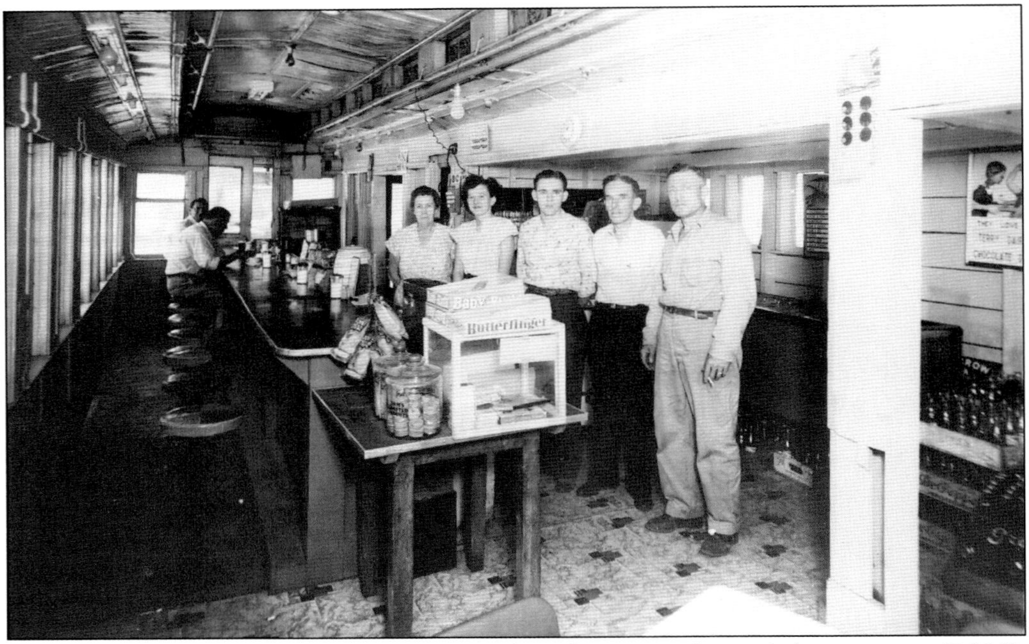

Mom and Lorraine's Lunch Car (or Mom's Lunch Car) was one of several places to eat in DeValls Bluff when this photograph was taken about 1960. One of the two men sitting at the lunch counter is Vernon Minton; standing, from left to right, are Eva Mason, two unidentified, Fitzhugh Motley, and Frank O'Rouke. (Courtesy of the Torreyson Library, University of Central Arkansas.)

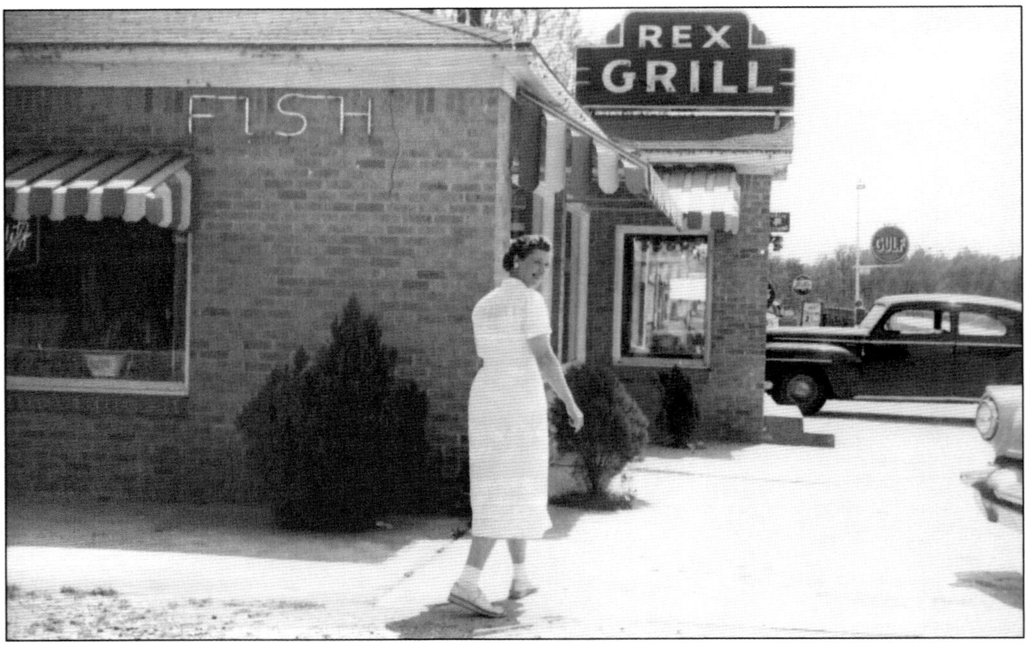

Rex's Grill was located at "the Grove" just across the White River from DeValls Bluff and was a popular place to dine on fried catfish, steaks, and beer. Next door was Rex's Dairy Bar, a gathering place for young people in the 1940s, 1950s, and 1960s. It featured an outdoor jukebox. Cordelia Hall is shown arriving for work in the 1950s. (Courtesy of Barbara and Rex Williams Jr.)

Rex Williams Sr. was working at his restaurant when this undated photograph was taken. (Courtesy of Barbara and Rex Williams Jr.)

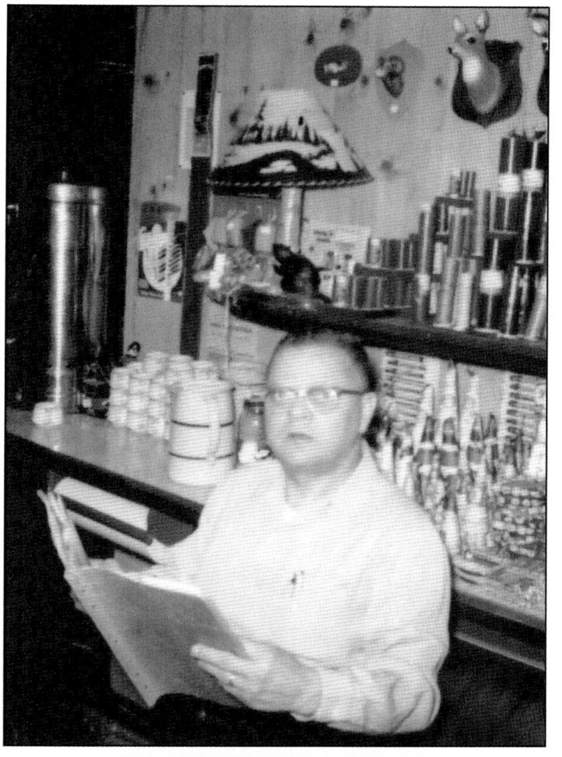

The Alley Cats was a local combo that played in area nightclubs and for other engagements. Shown in this 1952 photograph are, from left to right, James R. Rhodes Sr., saxophonist; Al Avery Moss, trumpeter; Mack ?, bass viola; Porter Hurt, drummer; and Charles Stuart, pianist. (Courtesy of James Rhodes.)

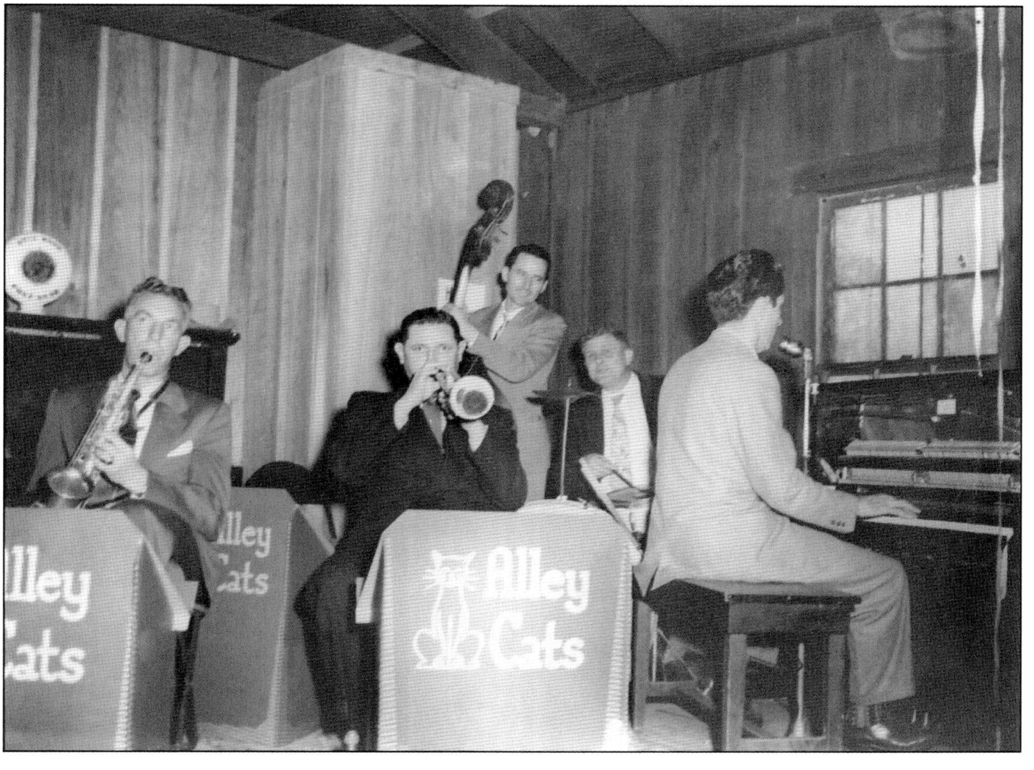

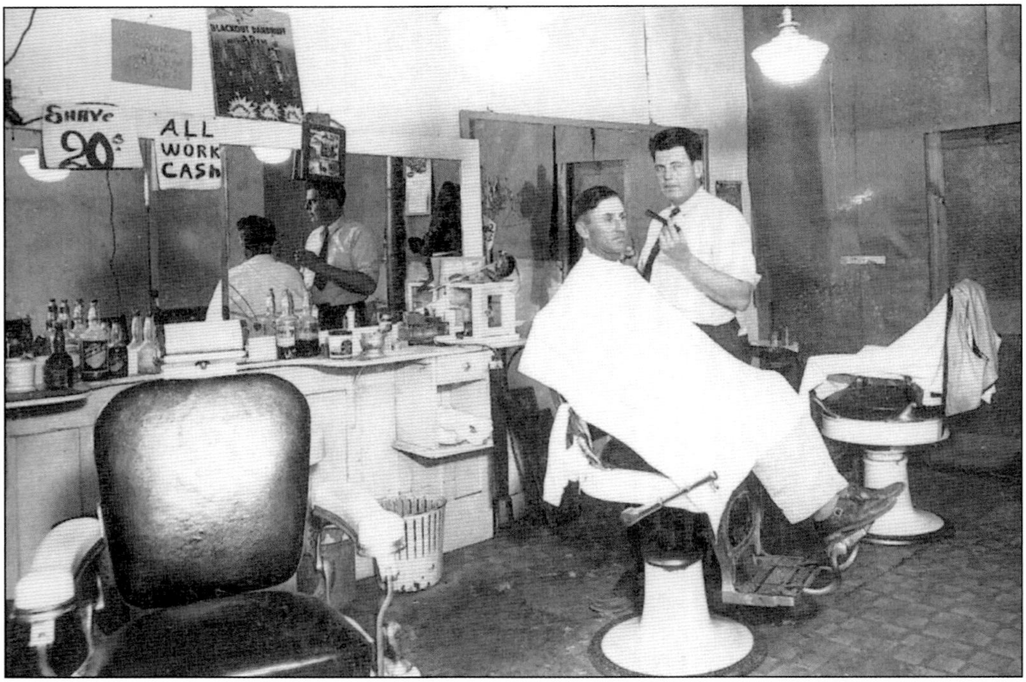

Charles N. Sparks is shown in his Main Street barbershop with an unidentified customer in 1943. High on the wall is an advertisement headlined "Blackout Dandruff" for a product possibly promising to cure (or conceal) the common malady. (Courtesy of James Littell Sparks.)

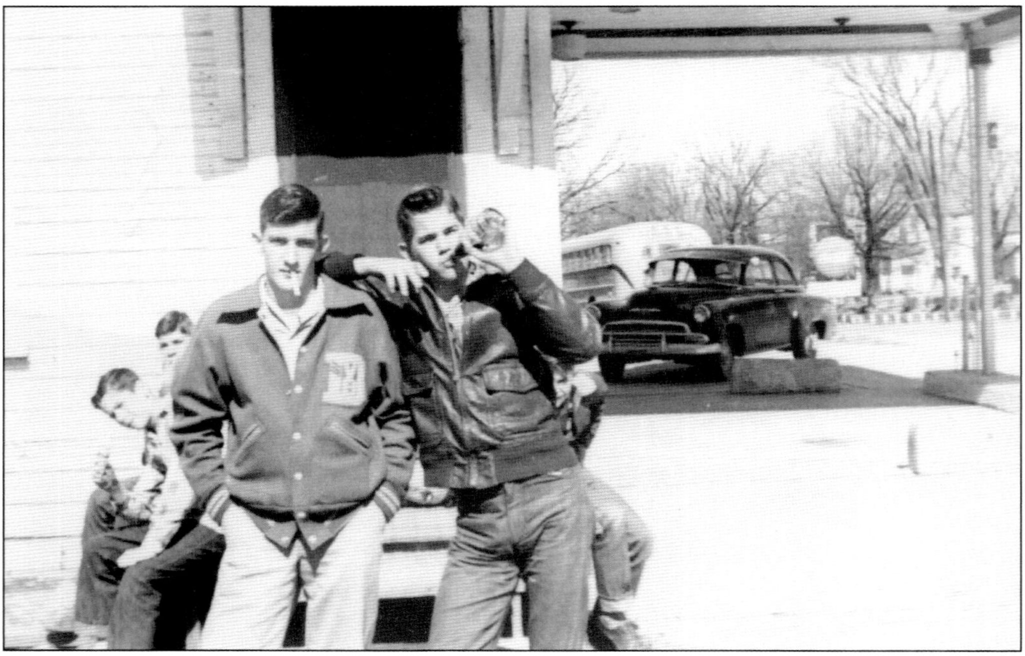

These cool dudes hanging out at Fitzhugh Motley's Service Station across from the DeValls Bluff High School are, from left to right, J.C. Humble, Lawrence Riba, Tommy Aycock, and George Earl Carter. (Courtesy of David Smith.)

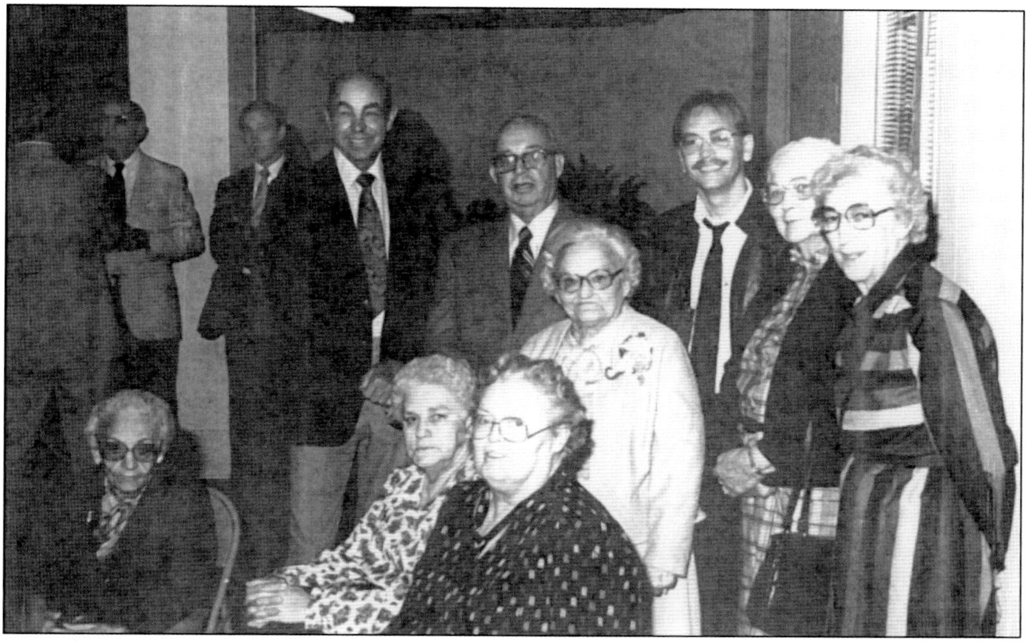

Several prominent citizens of DeValls Bluff appear in this December 6, 1984, photograph. They are, from left to right (first row) Pearl Higgins Hill, Mary Louise Hill, Margaret Buck George, Midget Higgins Mills, Mary Carrick O'Rourke, and Patricia Hill Craig; (second row) two unidentified, Clarence Craig, Conway George, and ? Craig (Patricia and Clarence's son). (Courtesy of Jackie Adcock.)

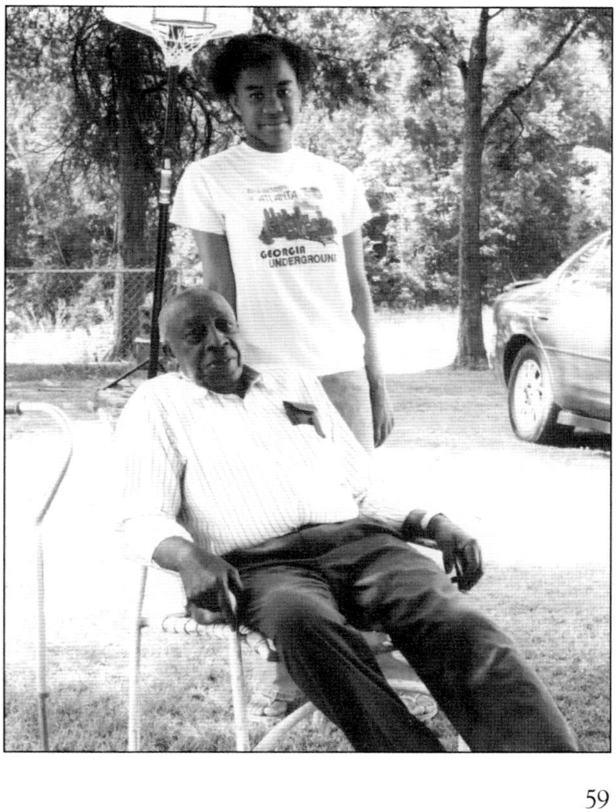

Lawrence Craig is shown with granddaughter Jesmire. He worked on the river's dredge and snag boats where he developed skills as a cook. In the 1930s, riverboats had no refrigeration, so live chickens were kept in cages and dressed as needed. Lawrence and his brother Wes opened Craig Brothers Café in 1947, which is still in operation today. They are most notably known for their pork barbecue slathered with a signature barbecue sauce. Craig's has been featured in several national magazines. (Courtesy of Bill Sayger.)

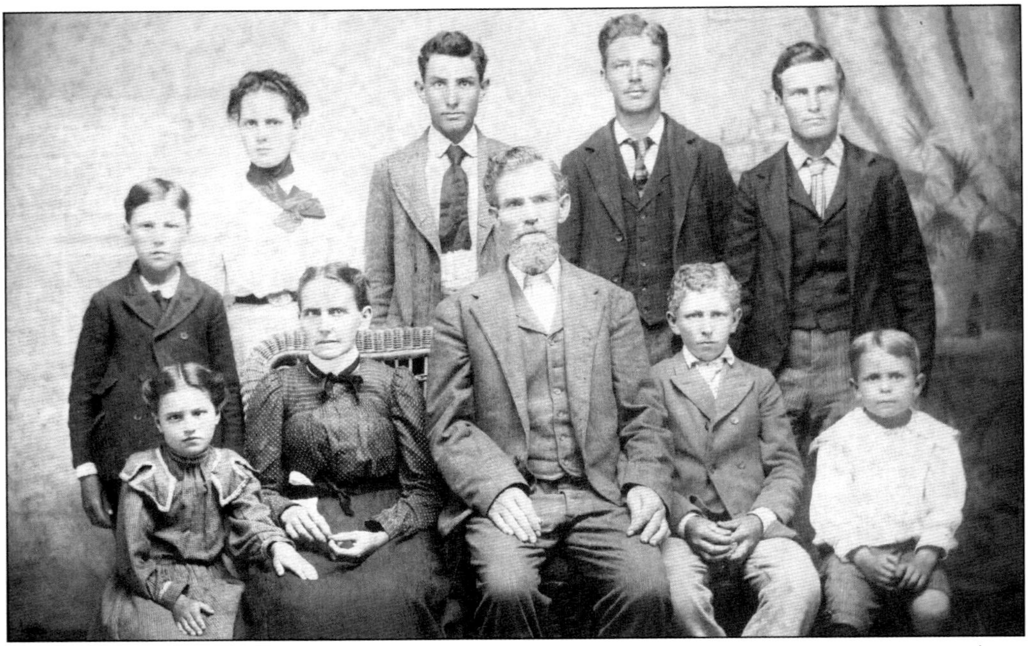

The Alexander family moved from Missouri about 1908 to the Peppers Lake community about three miles southeast of DeValls Bluff. Pictured around 1900 are, from left to right, (first row) Grace, Anna, Milton, Arthur, and Grover Alexander; (second row) Jo, Ethel, Paul Hubert, and Everett Alexander. (Courtesy of Margie Alexander Saul.)

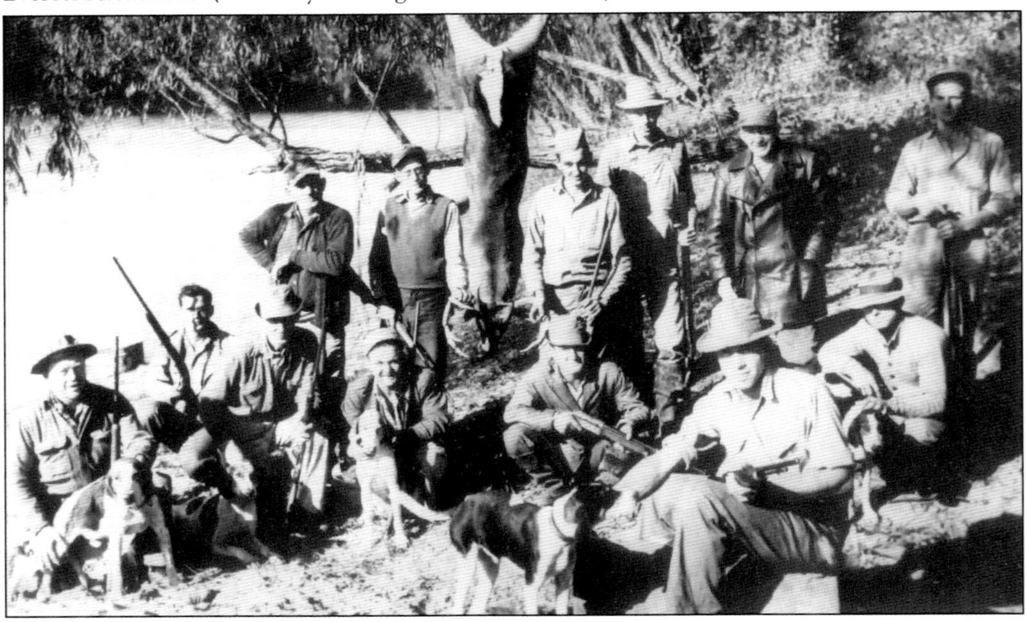

The deer population was very low in 1946 in Arkansas when these men went hunting at Seven Mile in the Cache River bottoms. Pictured are, from left to right, (first row) Buster Claussen, Marion ?, Henry Ulry, Columbus Treadway, Robert Treadway, K.W. Dodson, and Harry Higgins; (second row) Bill Booth, Harvey Hall, Harry Saul (who killed the deer), Frank Kirkemier, ? Kaman, and Carl Mathis. (Courtesy of Margie Alexander Saul and James Saul.)

Three

New Town Takes Pioneer's Name

Hazen

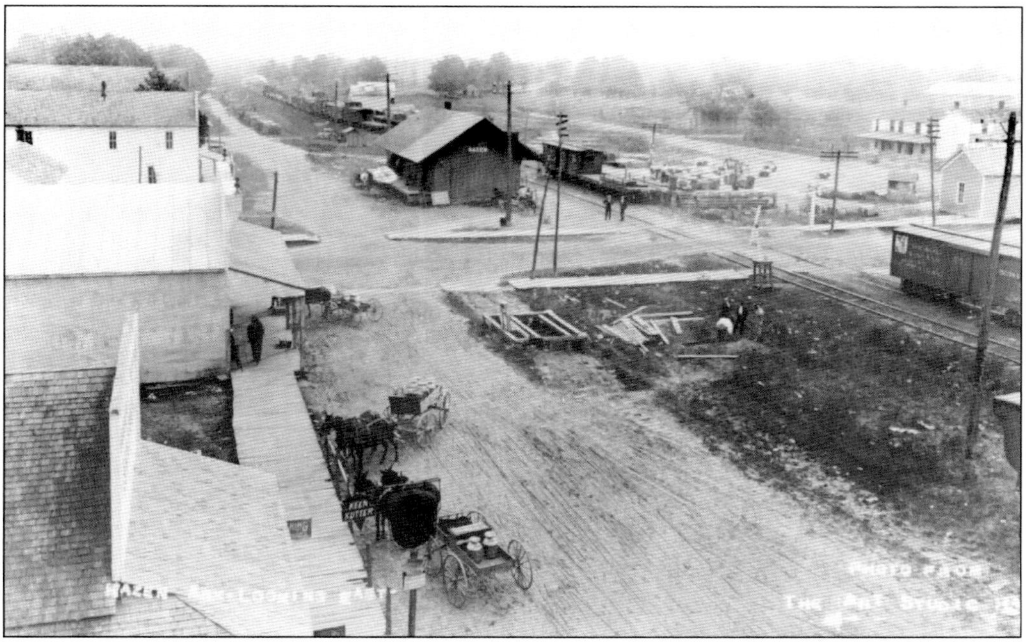

The Rock Island depot is the centerpiece of this photograph taken about 1905. In the foreground is the Kocourek and Benish Hardware Store, followed by the Brockway Building. In the early days, prairie grass was cut for hay and shipped out by rail. (Courtesy of Torreyson Library, University of Central Arkansas.)

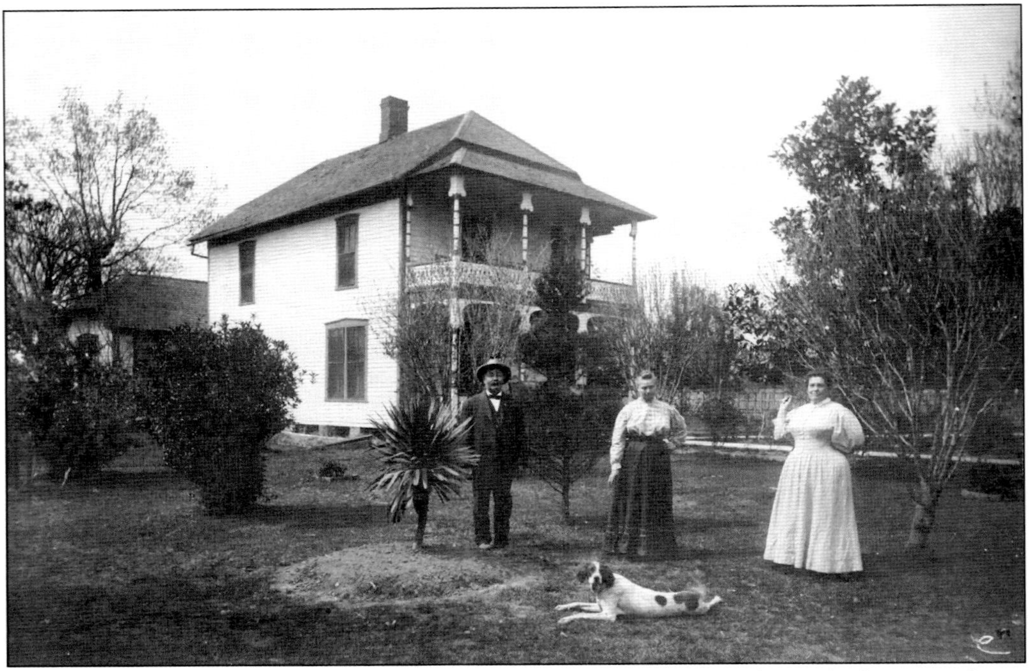

John Kocourek and his wife, Anna, came to Hazen in the 1880s where he worked as agent for an Iowa real estate company selling farmland on the Grand Prairie. He also established a hardware business in a small frame building on Front Street. From left to right are John and Anna Kocourek and an unidentified woman. (Courtesy of Judith Toll-Booher.)

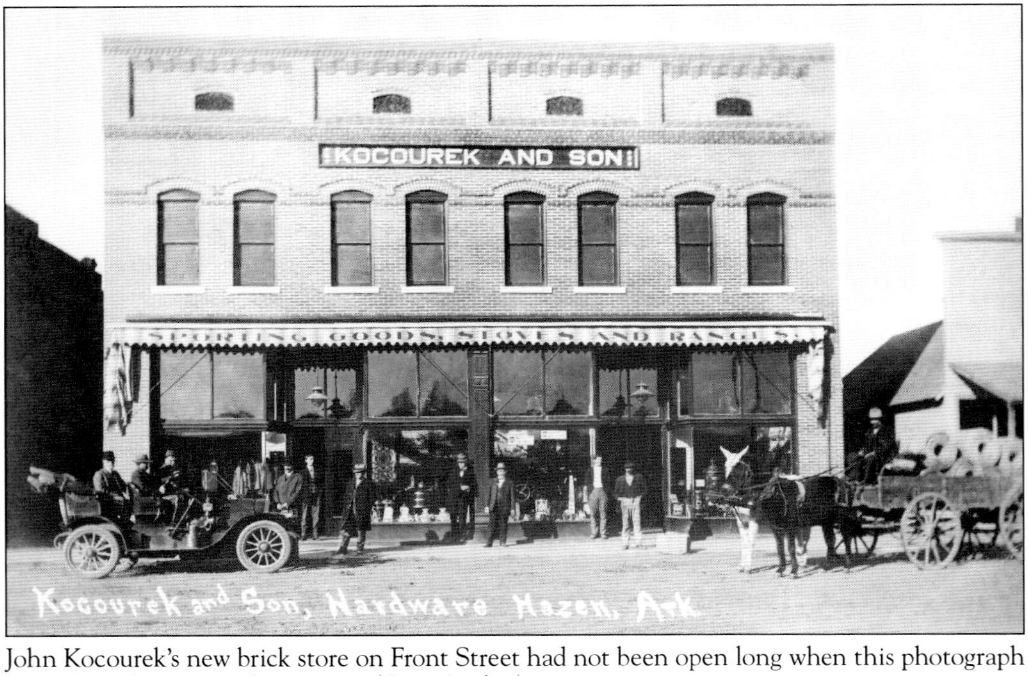

John Kocourek's new brick store on Front Street had not been open long when this photograph was taken about 1915. (Courtesy of Ray Hanley.)

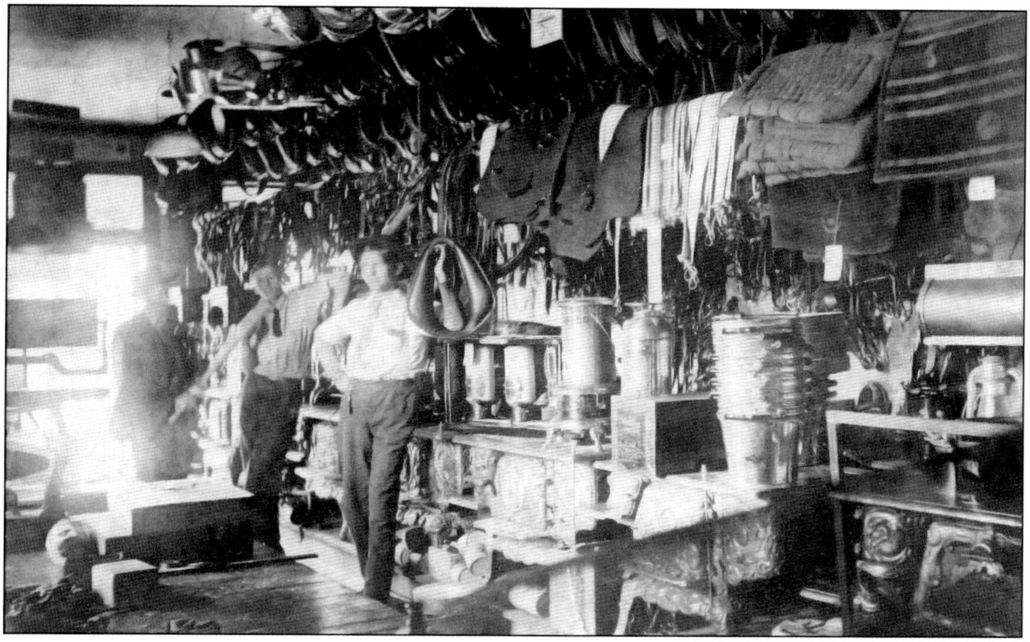

Note the display of horse collars hanging from the ceiling in this undated photograph of the Kocourek store. The building has the only elevator in Hazen, which is hand operated. Today, it is an antiques and collectibles shop. (Courtesy of Judith Toll-Booher.)

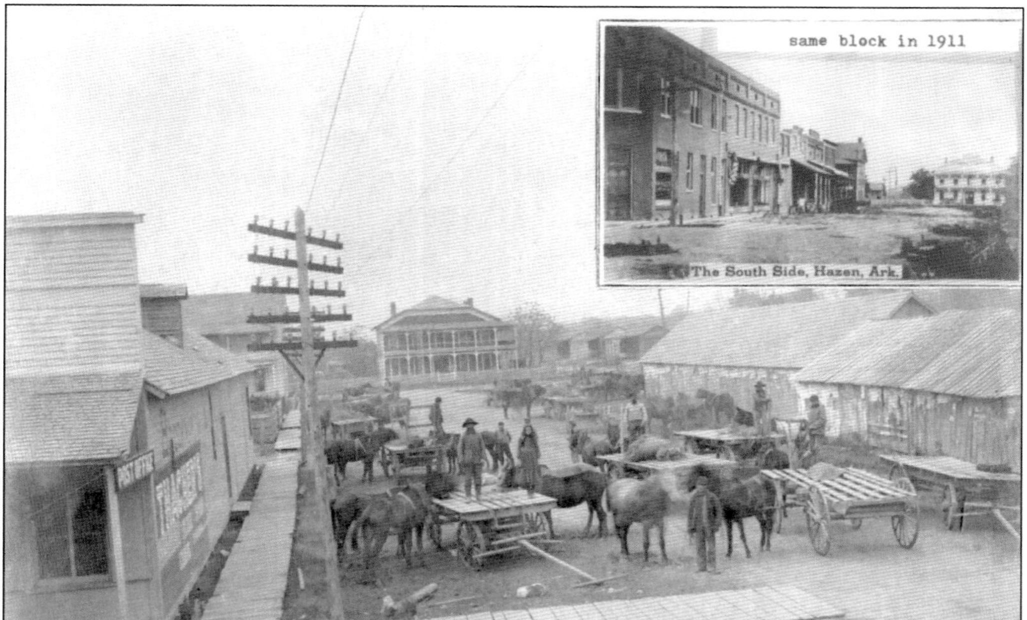

Pointing west, this photograph was taken at the intersection of what is now Highway 70 and Livermore Streets about 1905. The "Betzner House" hotel with its stacked porches was later owned and operated by R.H. McGeorge. The insert shows the same block a few years later. (Courtesy of Torreyson Library, University of Central Arkansas.)

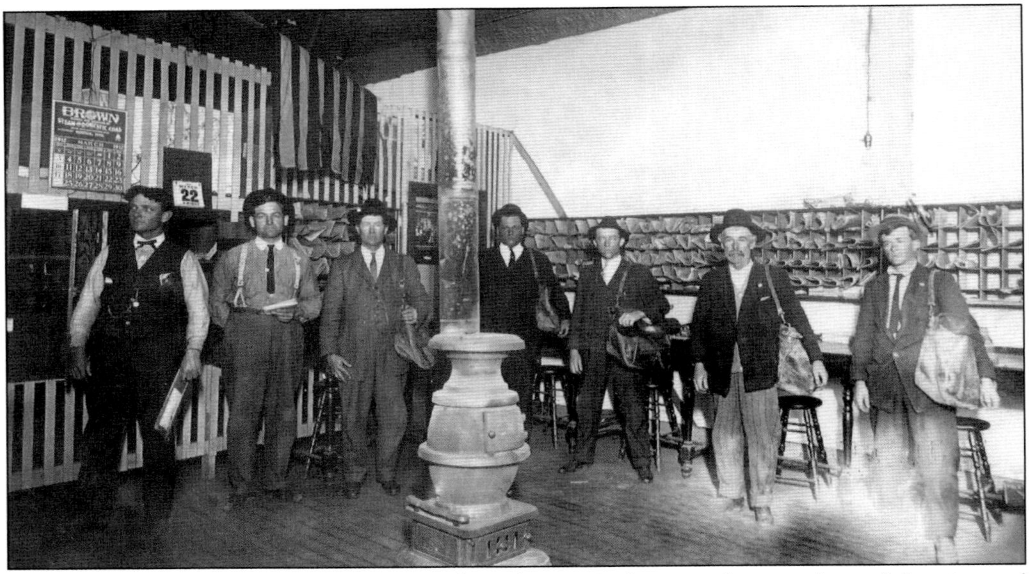

Hazen had a population of around 700 when this 1912 photograph was taken of the city and rural mail carriers. From left to right are postmaster Charles H. Tisdale, clerk Robert Hazen, Leroy Hendricks, Walter Percy Bowman, Clifton Eiland, James A. Crowley, and Joe H. Crowley. (Courtesy of Lew and Pat Sorrells.)

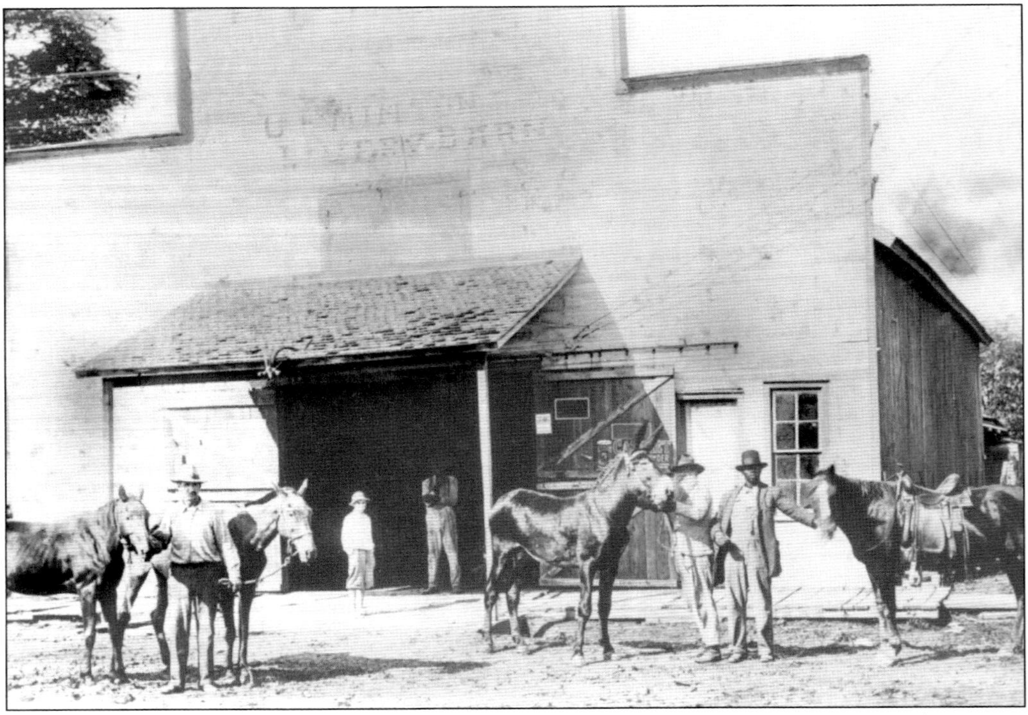

Shown in this undated photograph of Overman's Livery Stable are, from left to right, John Eaton, Bowman Hammond, George Braddix, ? Overman, and Cal Gordon. A Cyrus V. Overman appears on the 1920 census and is listed as a breeding stock buyer. (Courtesy of Torresyson Library, University of Central Arkansas.)

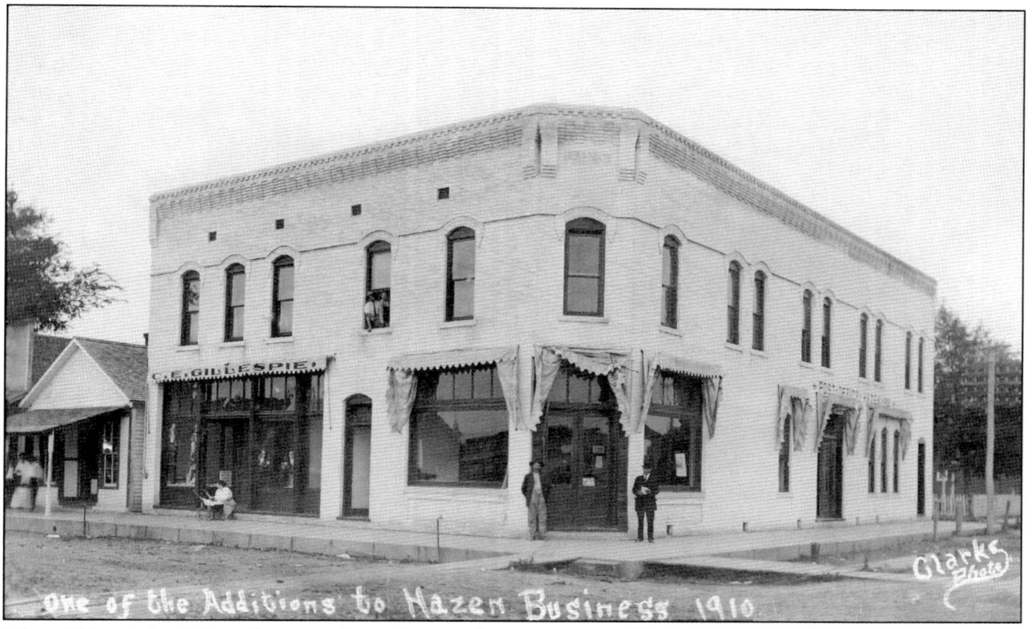

The old bank building that stands at the northeast corner of Livermore and Front Streets in 1920 also housed the town's post office and Dr. Charles E. Gillespies's drugstore. During the 1950s, Dr. Travis Matthews and dentists Drs. Neel and Yeager had offices on the second floor. The street-level floor became known as Reid's Furniture and Appliances. (Courtesy of Judith Toll-Booher.)

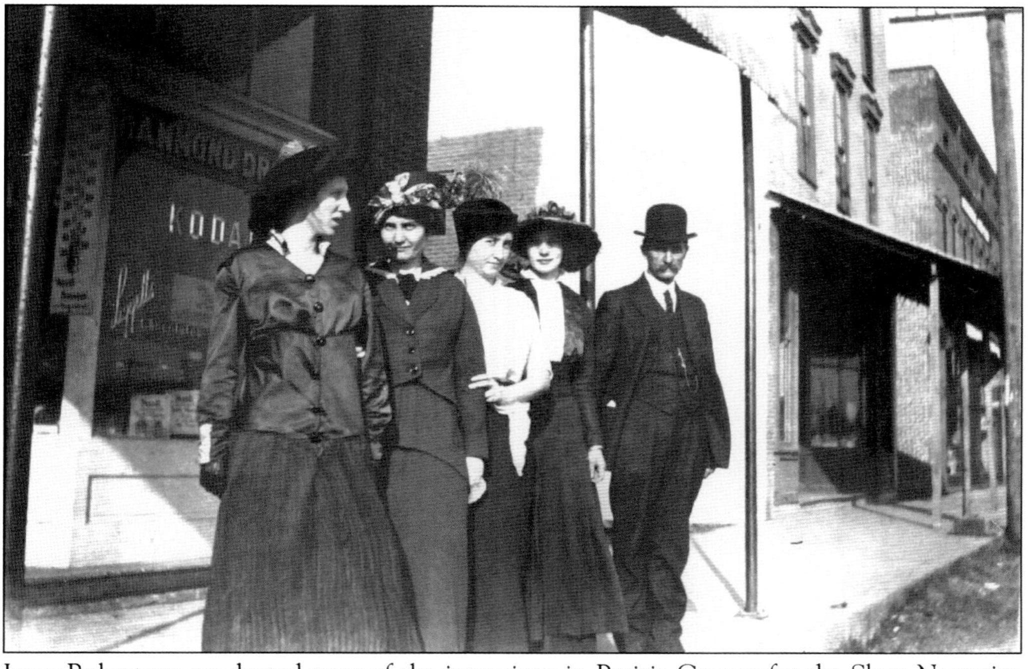

Irene Robertson conducted most of the interviews in Prairie County for the Slave Narrative Collection of the Federal Writers' Project in the 1930s. Standing in front of the Hammond Drugstore in 1914 are, from left to right, Robertson, Ruth Carlley, Lola Bowman, May Page, and Hugh B. Wheatley. (Courtesy of Torreyson Library, University of Central Arkansas.)

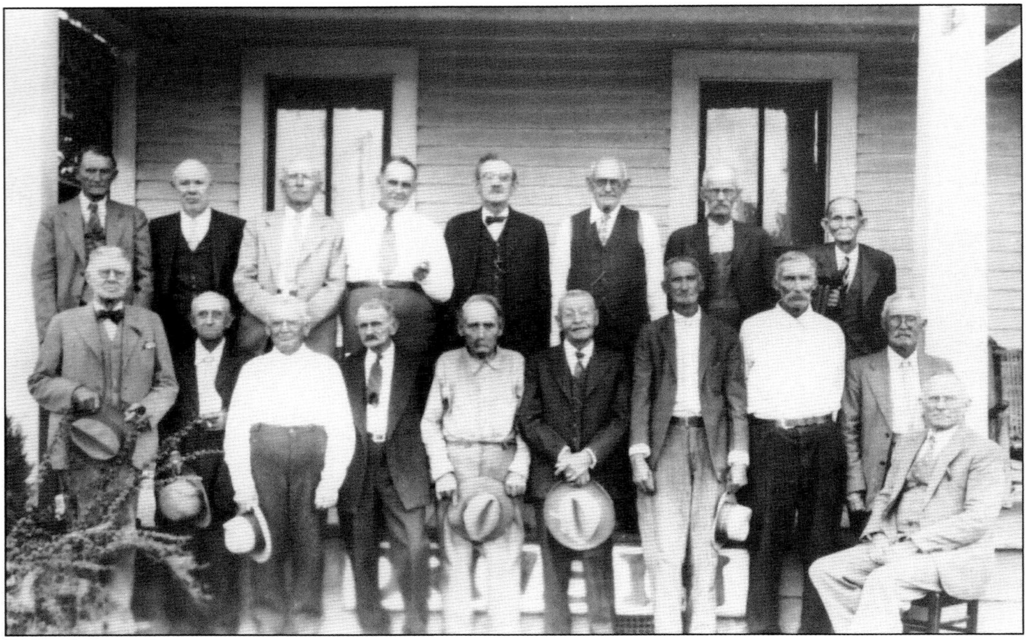

At his hotel, R.H. McGeorge hosted a dinner party for many pioneer residents of the Hazen area. Pictured are, from left to right, (first row) A.J. Barnett, George M. Kreger, A. Woodall, J.D. Cash, W.E. Worley, John Kocourek, W.H. Jessup, G.G. Rasor, J.A. Crowly, and R.H. McGeorge (seated); (second row) Hugh B. Wheatley, Dr. J.R. Lynn, J.C. Melton, R.W. Larkin, W. Radican, J.H. Rounsavall, Z.M. Turley, and A.B. Hudson. (Courtesy of Lew and Pat Crowley Sorrells.)

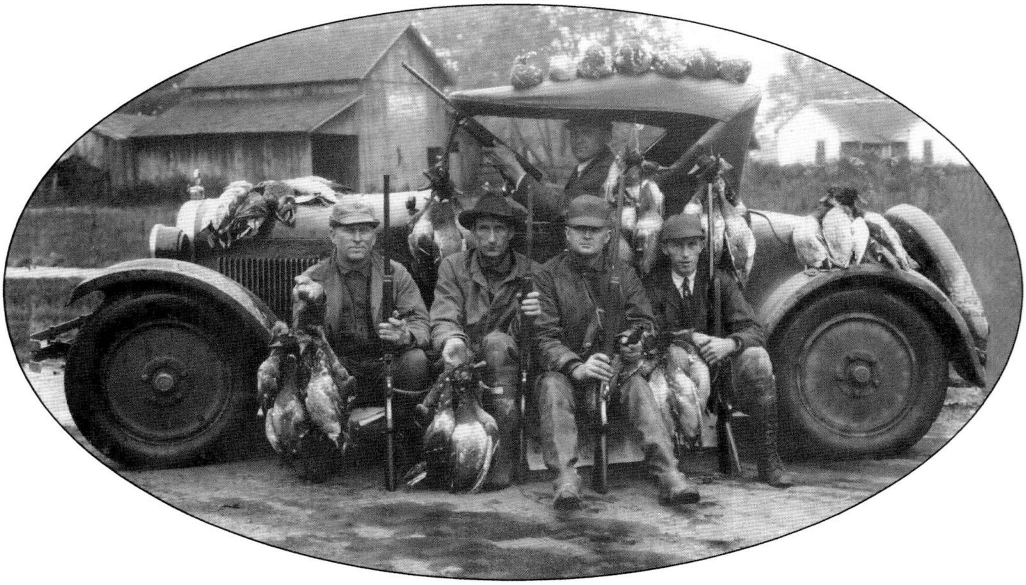

An unidentified driver is pictured with, from left to right, J.A. Hale, Graham Carlley, John Sims, and unidentified. The party of five successful hunters is proudly displaying ducks taken during the hunt. All have automatic shotguns and are dressed in drab-colored hunting clothes (no camo). The 1920s Dodge Roadster provides a very sporty backdrop for the picture. (Courtesy of Judith Toll-Booher.)

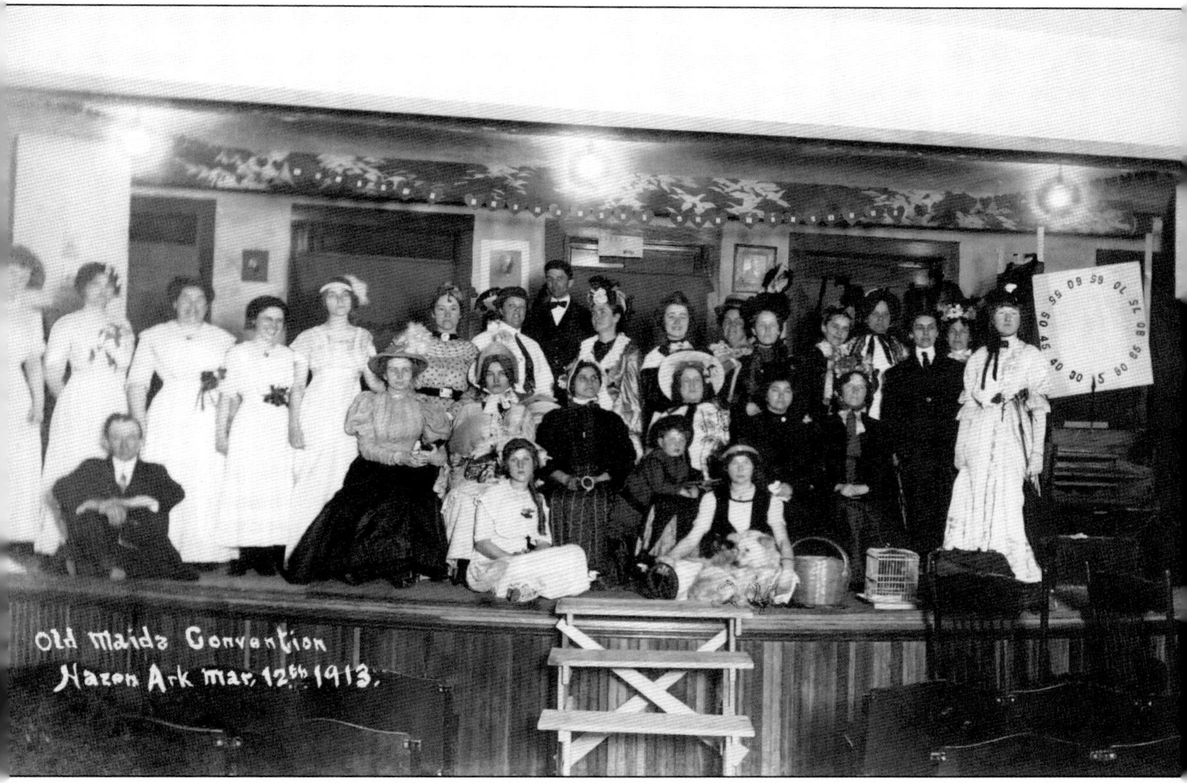

Old Maids Convention was a play performed in the spring of 1913 on the stage at Hazen High School (HHS). The 1912–1913 graduating class was the first to be offered a 12-year course of study. This was likely a community fundraising performance, as most in the cast were not students. The banner of valentines at the top of the stage reads, "Welcome bachelors and widowers." From left to right are (sitting on floor) J.A. Wright, Georgia Wimberly, unidentified boy, and Darrence Ealy; (sitting in chairs) Elmo Bowman, Ruth C. Carlley, Mrs. A.H. Wimberly, Mrs. R.L. Felts, and two unidentified; (standing) Alouise Miller, Iona McCain (HHS faculty), Lillian Woodworth (HHS music teacher), Goldine Grove, Lola Brewer, Mrs. Dr. Porter, Mrs. W.W. (Ruth) Fox, Prof. A.C. Reagan (HHS principal), Dora Radican, Ellie Clyde Crowly, Etta Lynn (HHS faculty), Mrs. R.H. (Mary) Hazen, Mrs. C.S. Proctor, Mrs. A.B. Hudson, Elma Yopp, Mary English, and Grace Carraway. Ruth Carlley Austin made these identifications in her later years. (Courtesy of Ray Hanley)

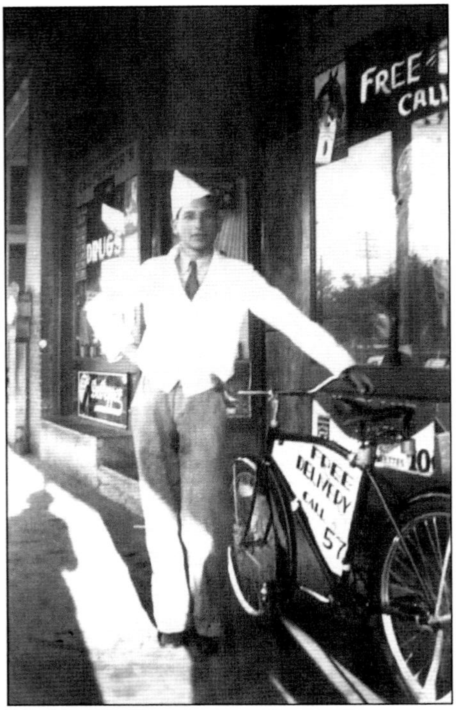

A young Carlley, a delivery boy, poses in front of the Culpepper Drugstore in this undated photograph. Customers received prompt service by dialing 57. (Courtesy of Judith Toll-Booher.)

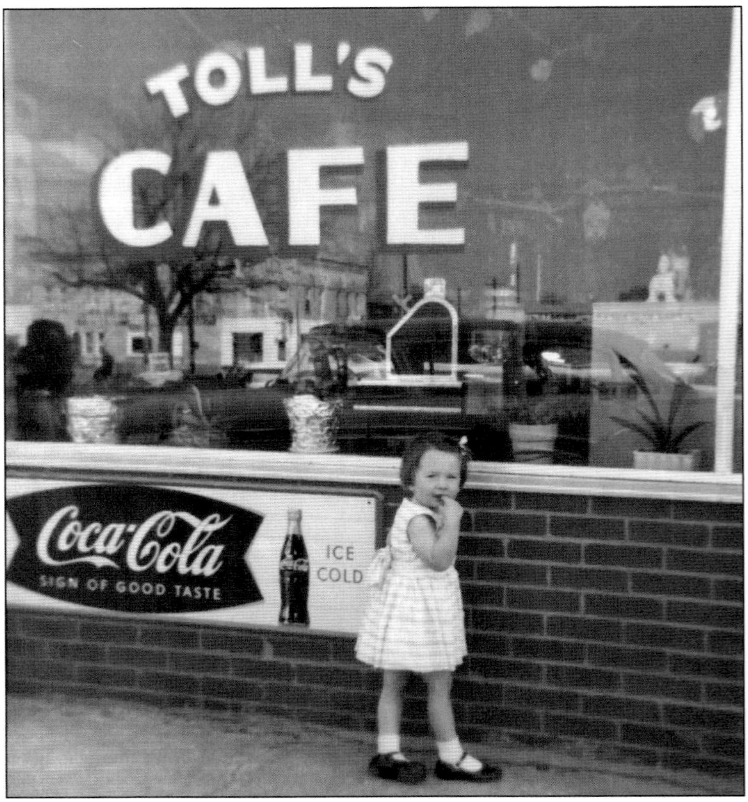

Karen Black is adorning the front of her grandmother Nellie Newkirk Toll Thacker's café on Main Street about 1956. The old bank building on Front Street is reflected in the glass. During the 1950s and 1960s, Toll's Café not only served delicious home-cooked food (her pies were memory-makers) but it was also the meeting place for everyone from "wee-hour" breakfasts for hunters to hamburger and fries for school children after ball games. During these times, it was not uncommon to see waiting lines. (Courtesy of Judith Toll-Booher.)

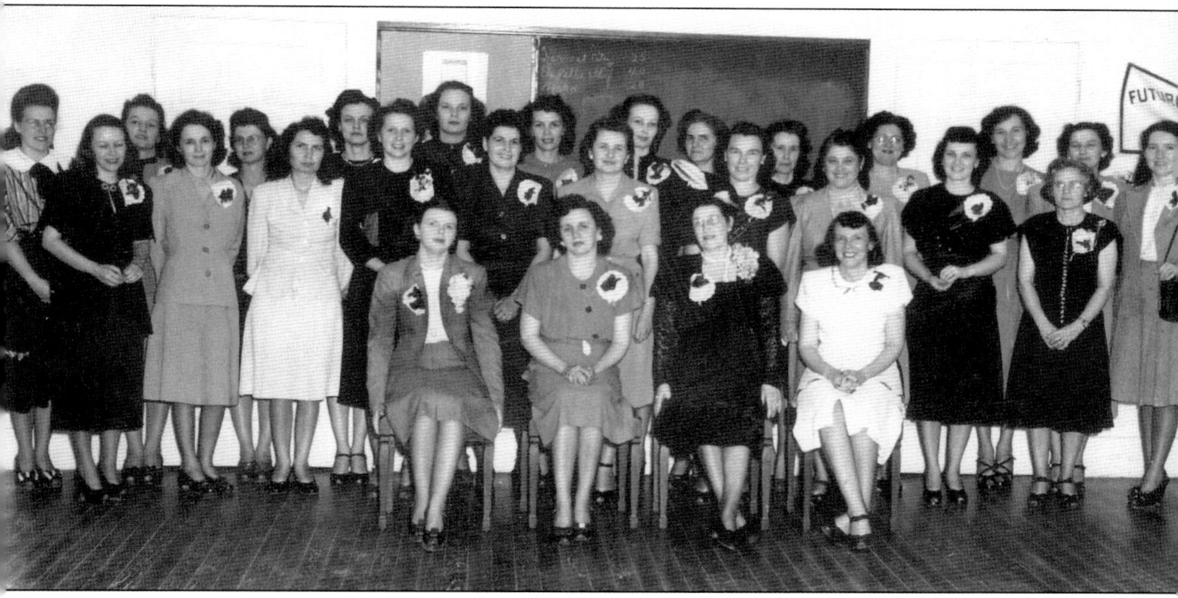

This 1950s photograph includes Hazen and Tollville chapter members at a General Federation of Women's Clubs gathering. From left to right are (seated) Jane Sims Jackson Louck, Hazel Page Oliver, Edna Toll Clayton, and Ruby Luebke Toll; (standing) Pat Trunkfield Gaddy, Olivia Jensen Maxon, Elizabeth Sims Hutson, Dora Grace Toll Huffer, Rosetta Auersperg Van Houten, Emaline Strohl Newsome, Martha Pirtle Huffer, Evelyn Turner Larkan, Christine Smith, Geraldine Pitts Crowly, Dorothy Sanders DeVorak, Leona Sullivan Crowly, Margaret Rounsavall Rieke, Evelyn Hampton, Katherine Toll Stipp, Sallie Mae Crowly Coyle, Willene Sparks Clayton, Cecile Holmes Chudy, Geraldine Aycock Rhodes, Cecile Melkovitz Dunar, Neva Tallent Miller, Etta Lynn Fischer Toll, and Eloise Burnside. (Courtesy of Judith Toll-Booher.)

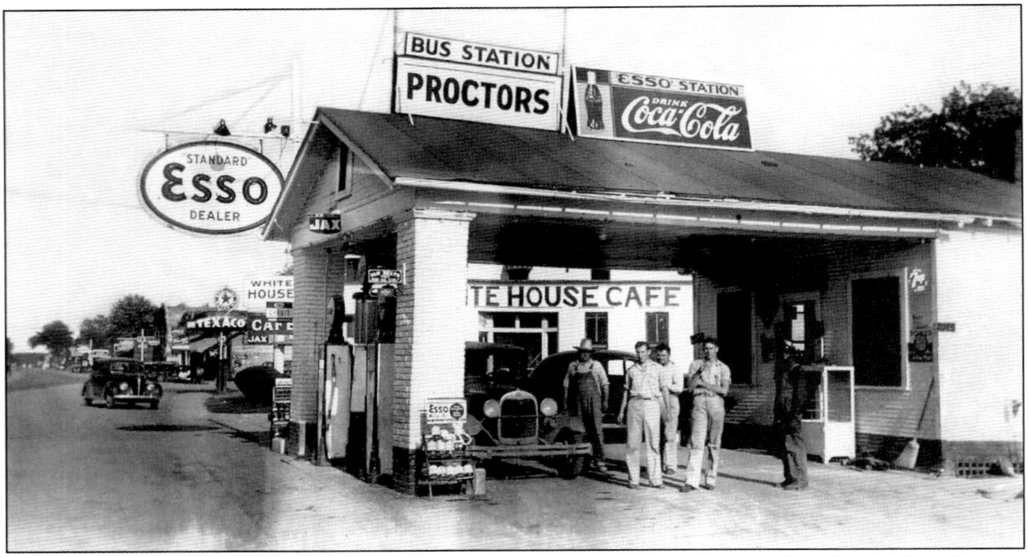

C.S. Proctor's Service Station, shown here about 1936, was on the south side of Main Street, about one block east of Livermore Street. Today, the Main and Livermore Streets intersection has the only stop light in Prairie County. (Courtesy of Judith Toll-Booher.)

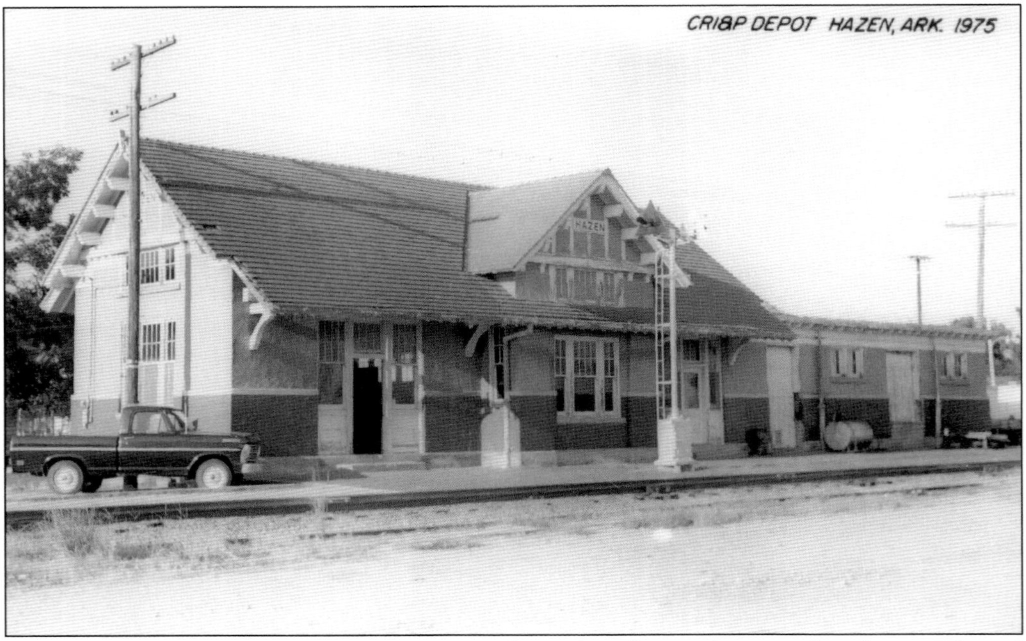

All the Rock Island train stations between Little Rock and Memphis varied in design. The rail line went bankrupt in the 1970s, and in the 1980s, most of the track between Brinkley and North Little Rock was removed. The branch line from Mesa to Searcy had already been abandoned. (Courtesy of Judith Toll-Booher.)

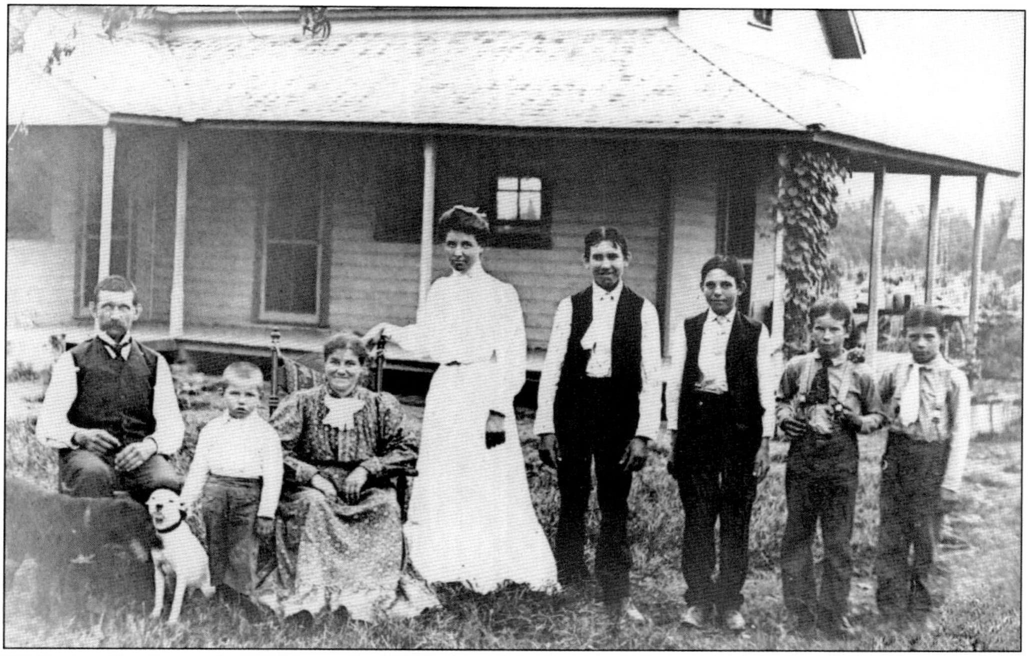

Wilhelm Ferdinand and his wife, Wilhelmina "Hermine" Gnadt Hardke, immigrated from Germany in 1892 and, in time, settled on a farm about four miles southwest of Hazen. Pictured at their home are, from left to right, Wilhelm Ferdinand, Otto Ferdinand, Hermine, Emma Mari Therese, Karl "Charles" August, Herman Albert, Emil August, and Wilhelm Otto Hardke. (Courtesy of David Hardke.)

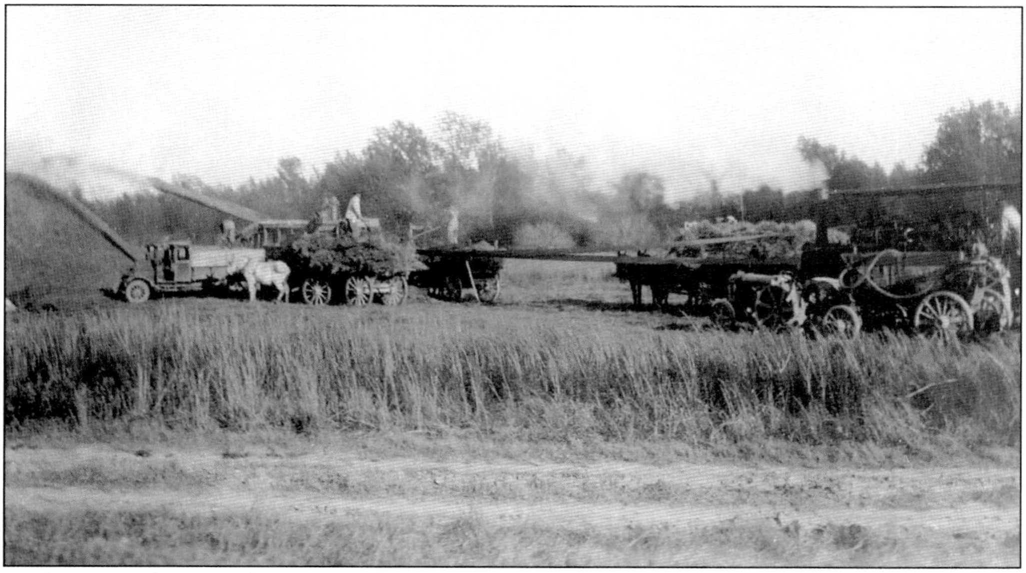

In this 1926 photograph, men are threshing oats and wheat on the Wilhelm Hardke farm using a John Deere tractor and two-cylinder Decal threshing machine. The Hardkes installed the first electric-powered irrigation well in Prairie County. Charles Hardke operated a general mercantile store and was also a wholesale hay dealer at Screeton Switch, four miles west of Hazen. (Courtesy of David Hardke.)

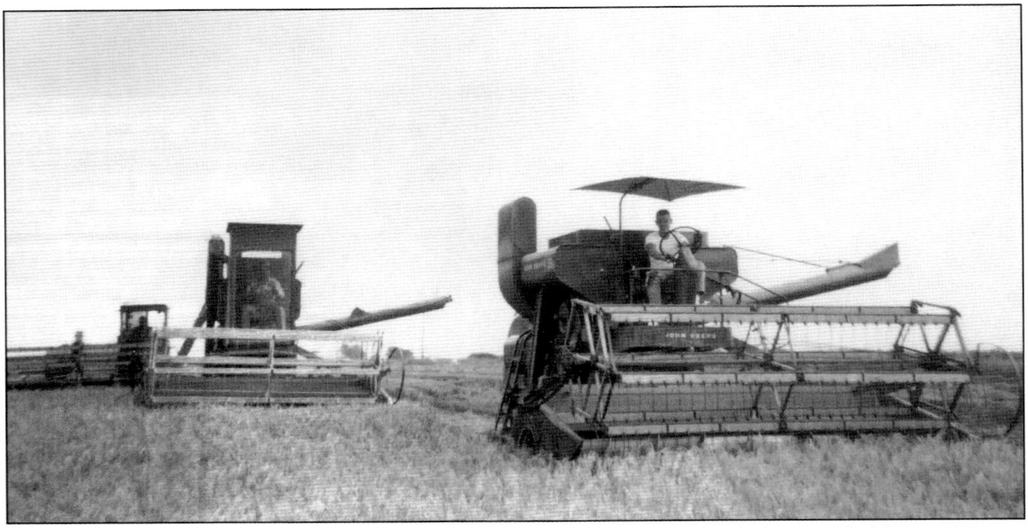

Thirteen-year-old Limon Clayton is on the lead combine on Wachal's rice field near Hazen on September 28, 1963. The header was 12 feet wide, and 60 years later, one combine with a 25-to-30-foot header would nearly replace all three in cutting power. The average yield then was 120 bushels per acre, and today's average yield in Prairie County approaches 200 bushels per acre. (Courtesy of Judith Toll-Booher.)

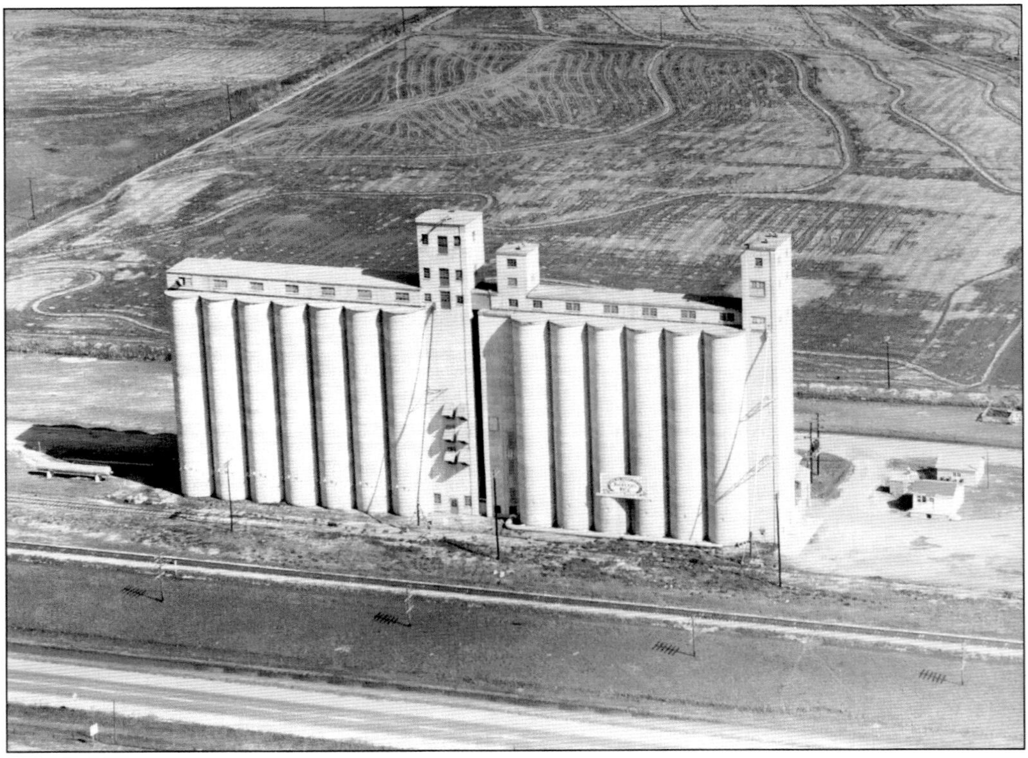

The first grain drying and storage unit in Hazen was built in 1948 for local farmers, and the organization was named the Hazen Grain Drying Cooperative. It became part of Riceland Foods in 1980. (Courtesy of Riceland Foods-Hazen Division.)

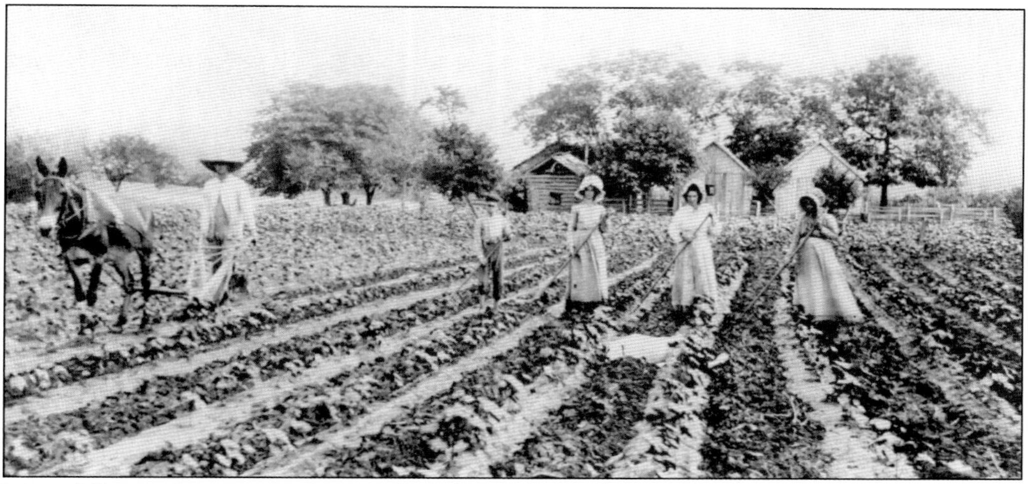

These folks are chopping cotton on a farm four miles northwest of Hazen. The cotton crop, as late as the mid-20th century, was planted in a continuous row, which had to be "blocked" or thinned with the hoe. Before herbicides came into common use, labor-intensive hoeing was also done to cut down the weeds and grass. (Courtesy of Torreyson Library, University of Central Arkansas.)

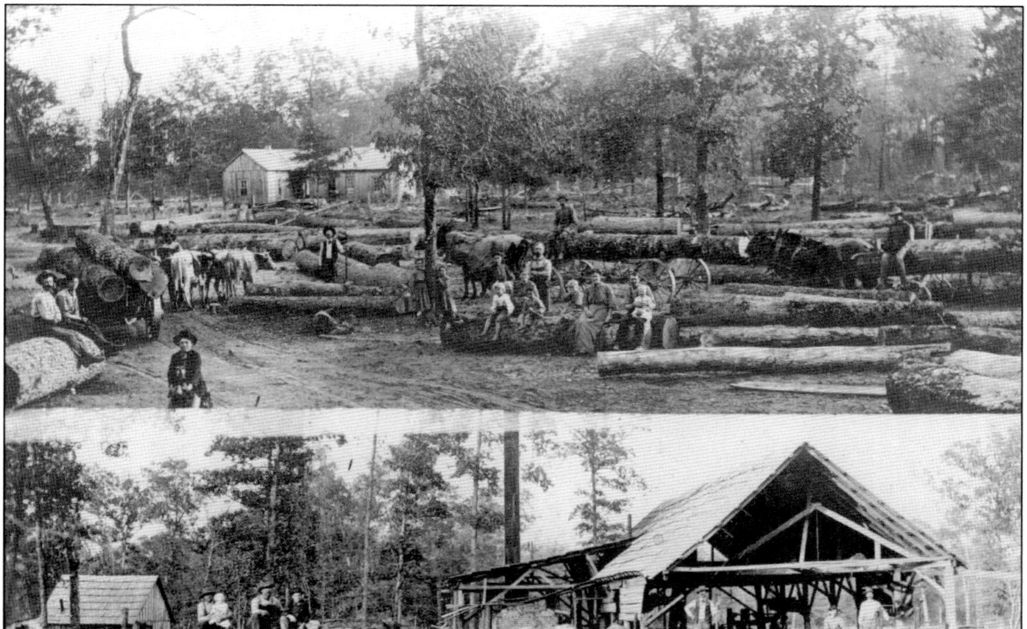

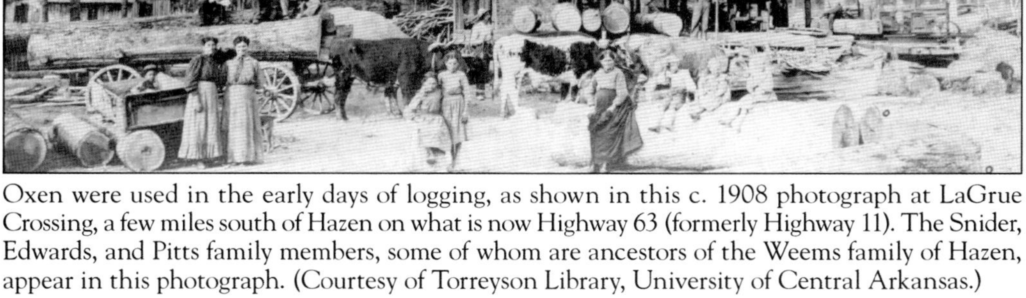

Oxen were used in the early days of logging, as shown in this c. 1908 photograph at LaGrue Crossing, a few miles south of Hazen on what is now Highway 63 (formerly Highway 11). The Snider, Edwards, and Pitts family members, some of whom are ancestors of the Weems family of Hazen, appear in this photograph. (Courtesy of Torreyson Library, University of Central Arkansas.)

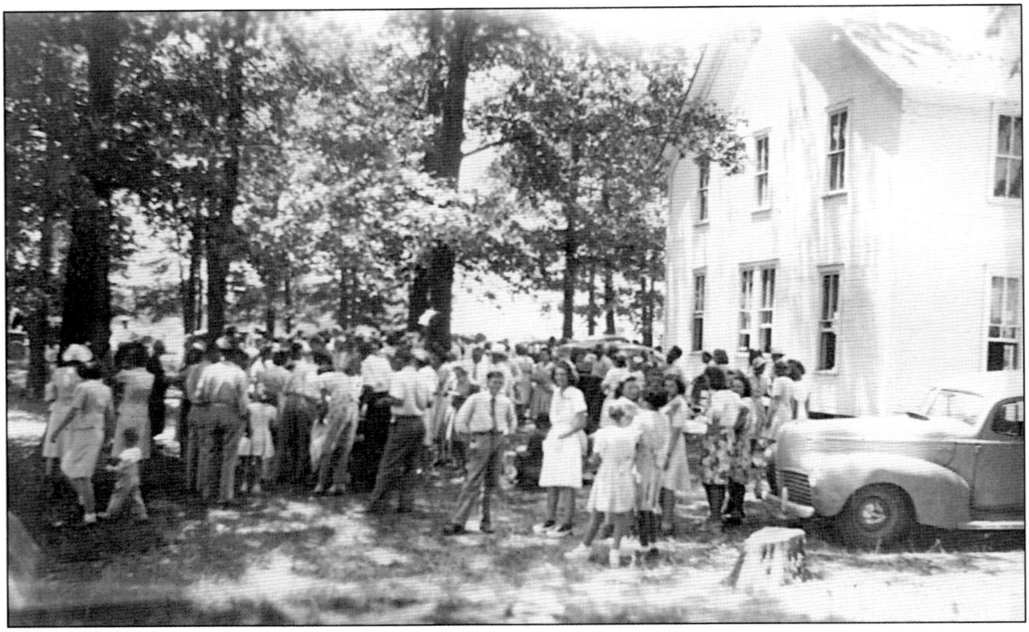

In 1874, Baptist minister Sylvanus Minton played a leading role in organizing the Center Point Baptist Church, five miles northwest of Hazen. The congregation first met in a log cabin, which was also used as a schoolhouse. The third building used by the members, shown here, was destroyed by a 1952 tornado, and the present church was constructed on the site. (Courtesy of Tim Harper.)

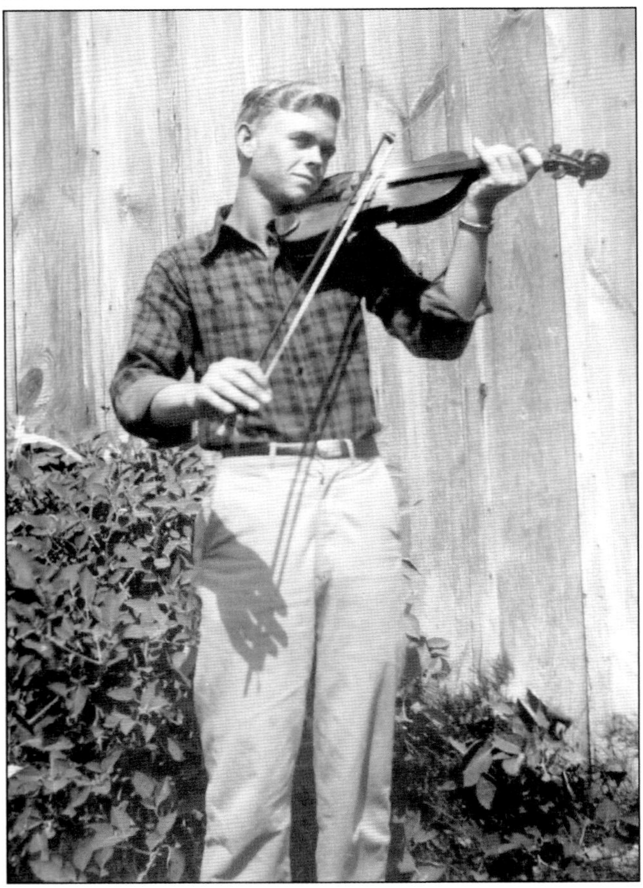

Lee King, who played the fiddle, mandolin, and banjo, would gather with other musicians and vocalists in and around the Center Point community north of Hazen to relax and entertain friends. The sessions began in the 1960s in private homes, but by about 1990, they were performing in Lamar Raper's shop. They later performed in a room provided by Virgil Mills, which adjoined his Center Point store. (Courtesy of Wanda King Sayger.)

Four

The British Are Coming

Tollville

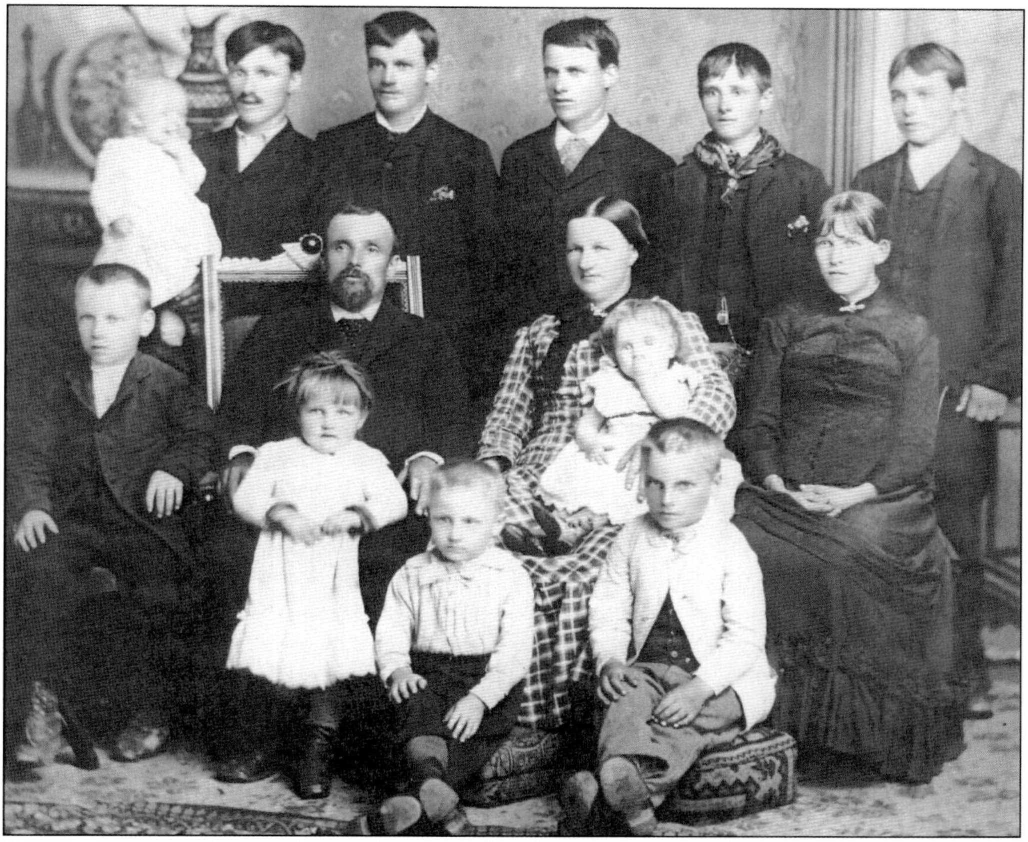

Prior to moving to Prairie County from LaSalle, Illinois, Burgess Toll had a family portrait made around Christmas 1884. The family members are, from left to right, (first row) Mary Louise "Polly," William Andrew "Will," and Samuel Robert "Sam;" (second row) Frederick Thomas "Fred," Burgess, his wife Jane Oliver Hill holding Sarah Elizabeth "Sadie," and daughter-in-law Adaline Catherine "Addie" Reynolds; (third row) John Burgess holding son William Godfrey, Richard Henry "Dick," George Oliver, Edward William "Ned," and Charles Frederick "Charlie." A few years later, Burgess Toll migrated to Prairie County, Arkansas, with his extended family, including his father, two sisters, and brother and sister-in-law. The area where they settled was soon called Tollville. On November 13, 1910, Dick and Fred Toll hired surveyor George C. Lewis to lay out 100 acres in Tollville. The enterprise sold residence lots for $50 and business lots for $100. The town itself did not become a reality; however, the community of English-descent families grew and prospered. (Courtesy of Judith Toll-Booher.)

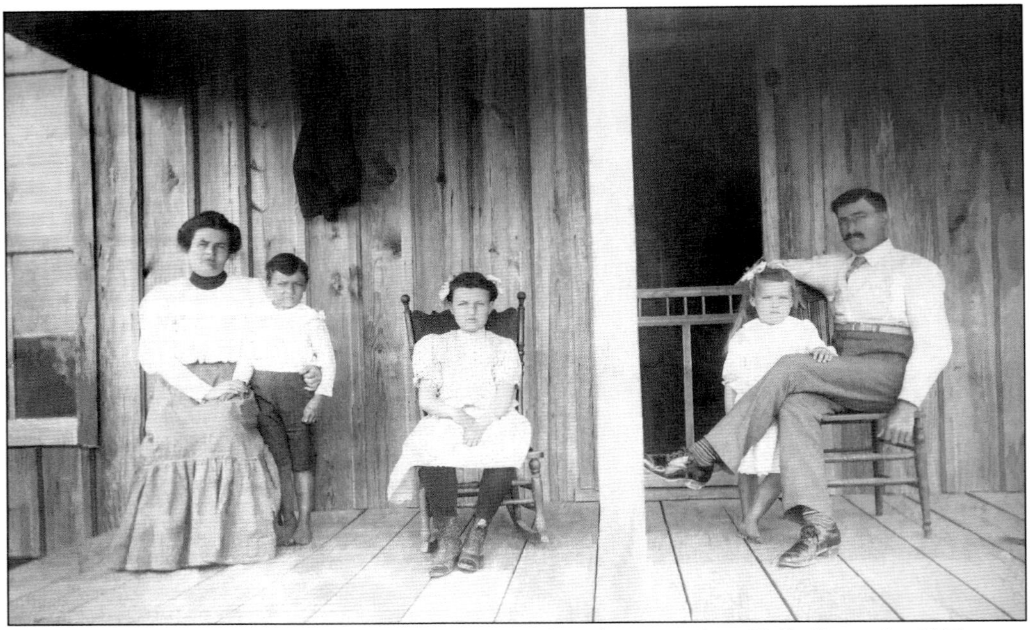

The James Roger Foot family members, shown on their front porch in Tollville in the 1890s, are, from left to right, Mary Janie Newman, Elizabeth "Lib," Phyllis "Philly," Bess, and James Roger. Roger and Mary Janie emigrated from England to America on their honeymoon. The couple had two other children, Evelyn and Roland, not pictured. Mary Janie became a widow in 1900 and later married Ned Toll. They had twins, Edward and Edna Toll. The Foot, Newman, and Toll families were friends when living in their native England. (Courtesy of Judith Toll-Booher.)

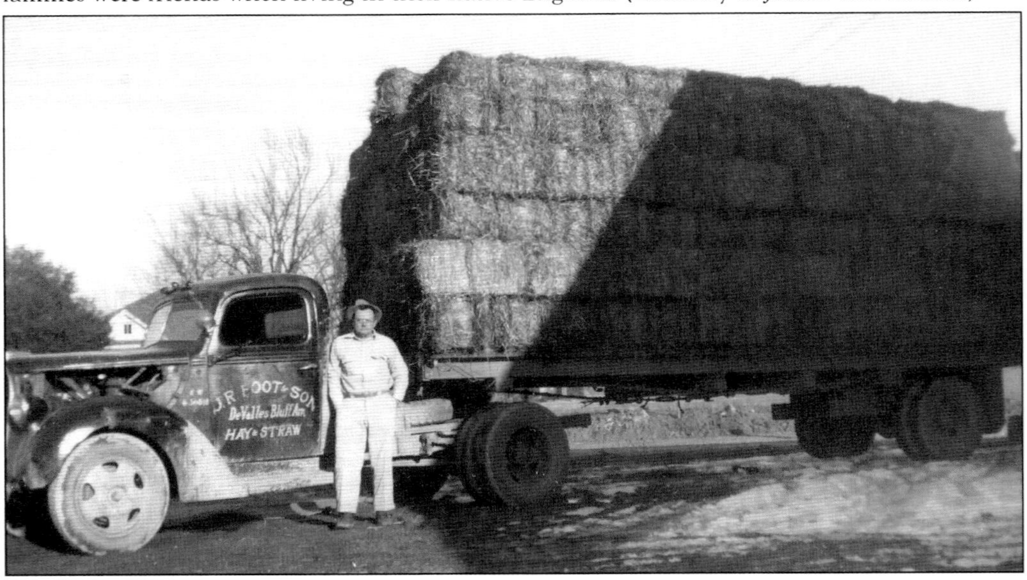

Prairie hay and straw from rice and oats were cash crops as part of the J.R. Foot & Son farm operation in Tollville. Roland sold hay and straw to brick companies around the state. Year-round, hay and straw were delivered to feed stores and stables as far away as Memphis, Tennessee. Pictured is Roland Foot standing near his loaded flatbed trailer truck in the early 1940s. (Courtesy of Judith Toll-Booher.)

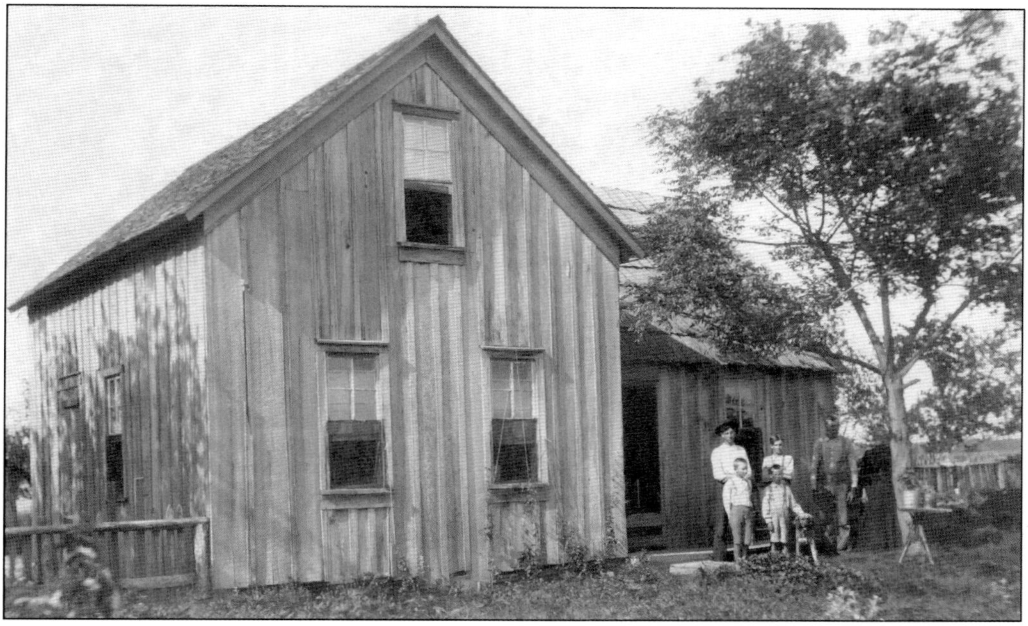

Pictured is the home of John and Alice Wade Clayton. The board-and-batten siding was typical of the early prairie homes. The Claytons, who also have English heritage, came to Arkansas from Kansas in 1906. Standing are, from right to left, Alice, John, their daughter Daisy, and her husband and two sons. (Courtesy of Judith Toll-Booher.)

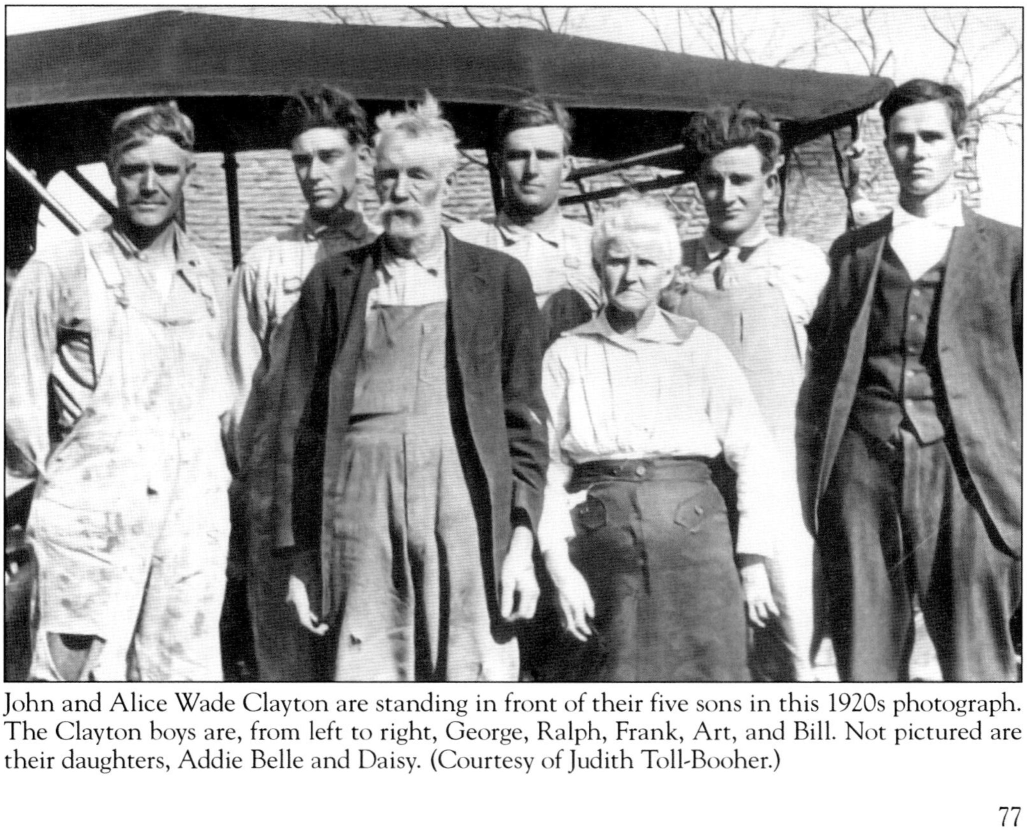

John and Alice Wade Clayton are standing in front of their five sons in this 1920s photograph. The Clayton boys are, from left to right, George, Ralph, Frank, Art, and Bill. Not pictured are their daughters, Addie Belle and Daisy. (Courtesy of Judith Toll-Booher.)

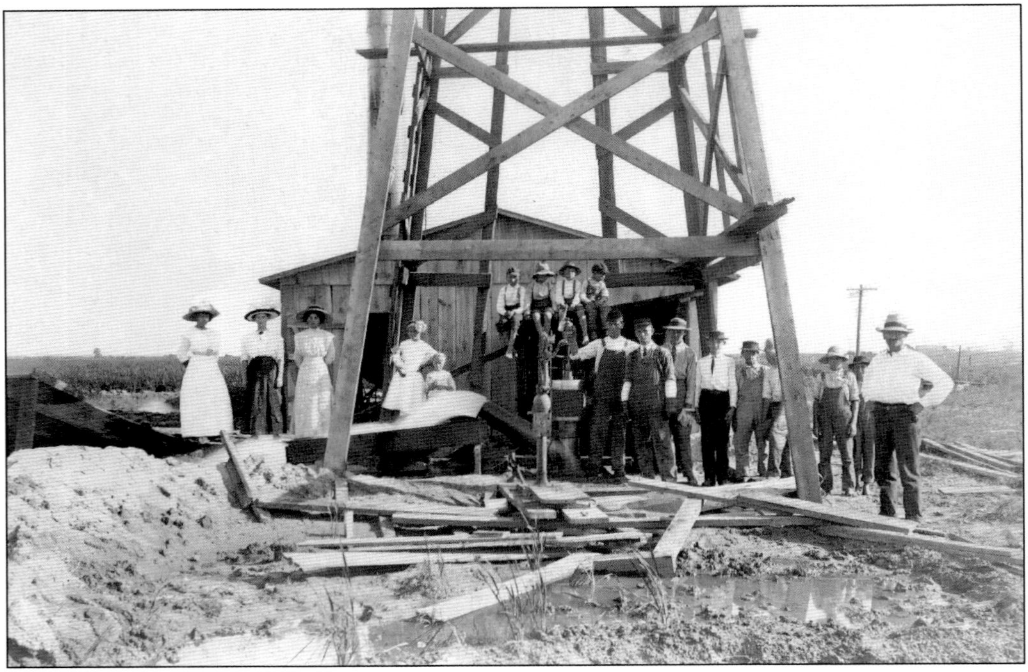

Essential to the production of rice is a good well to provide fresh water for irrigation. A new well was reason for a family celebration, complete with "Sunday best" attire and a photographer. (Courtesy of Judith Toll-Booher.)

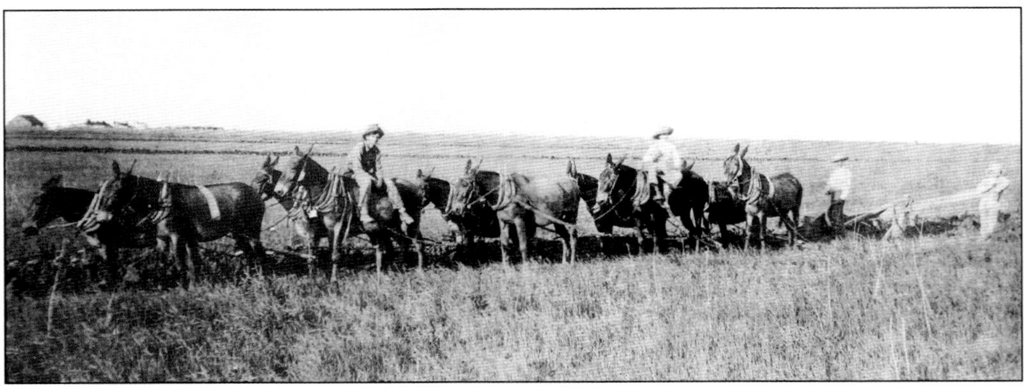

On virgin prairie land in Tollville, it took as many as 10 mules to push levees necessary for rice irrigation. The first method used was to plow three or four furrows and lap them over to the middle as much as possible and then use a horse or mule team (pictured here) to pull the pusher along the furrow to create the levee. Usually, it was necessary to make at least two passes over each side of the levee. Early attempts to irrigate rice often ended in failure because levees washed out and water was lost. Equipment to build levees had to be developed through trial and error. (Courtesy of Judith Toll-Booher.)

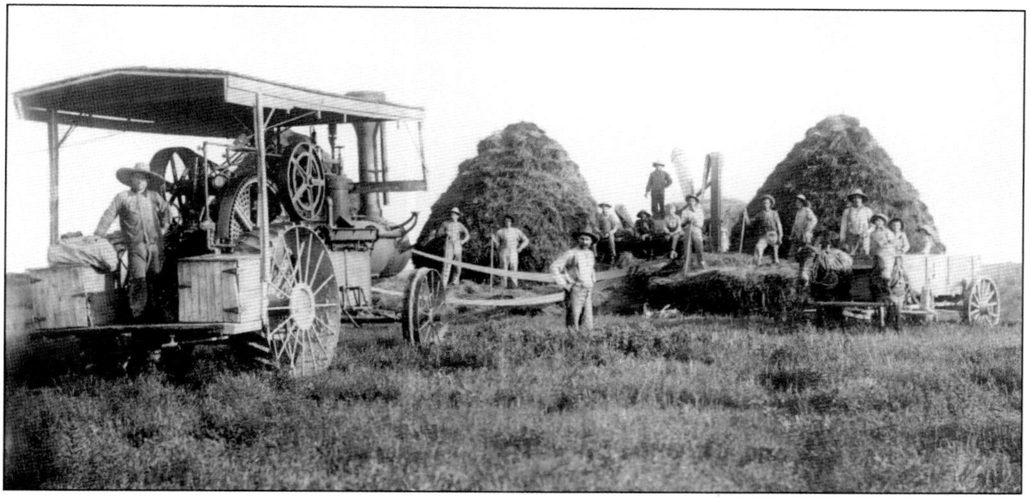

This rice threshing operation is the Will and Sam Toll Brothers Partnership, around 1913. Their steam-powered rice thresher and straw baling machinery was used on family lands and neighboring farms in Tollville. The whole neighborhood would feel the ground shaking when the gigantic steam tractor was moved from field to field. It was described as like a circus train with the huge machinery, the bundle wagons, wagons hauling water and wood, bagging materials, and the threshing crew. (Courtesy of Judith Toll-Booher.)

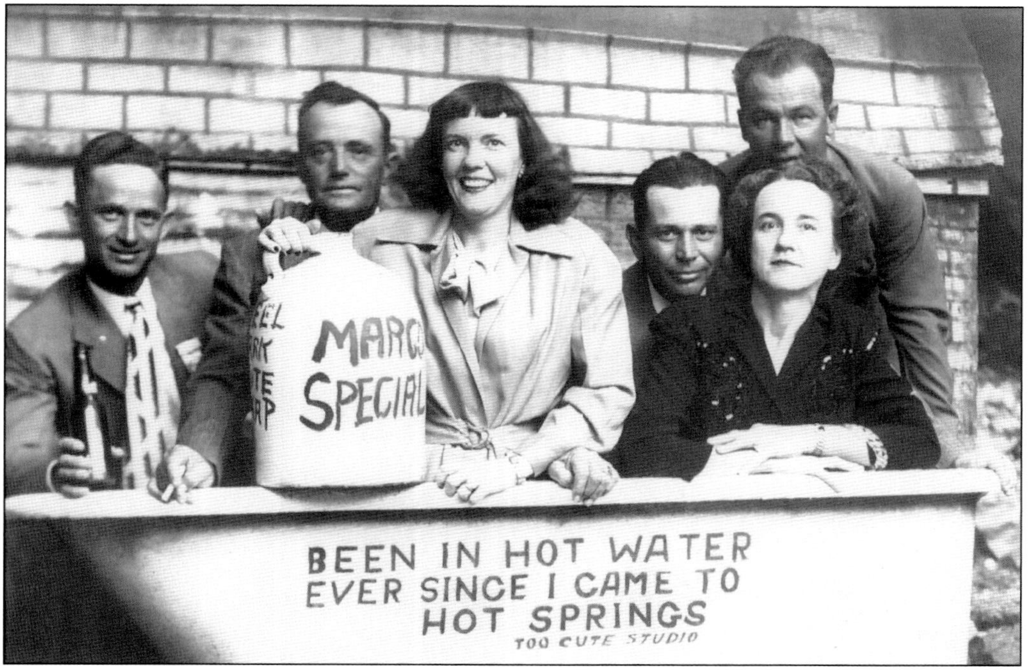

This 1940s "smile-maker" photograph was taken in Hot Springs. For decades, annual pilgrimages were made to Hot Springs by those in the Tollville community to celebrate the end of harvest season. They enjoyed the famous healing baths on bathhouse row, auction houses, ostrich races, the alligator farm, and so much more. Pictured are, from left to right, Warren Clayton, Roland Foot, Ruby Toll, Odie Fowlkes, Charlene Fowlkes, and Teddy Toll behind her. (Courtesy of Judith Toll-Booher.)

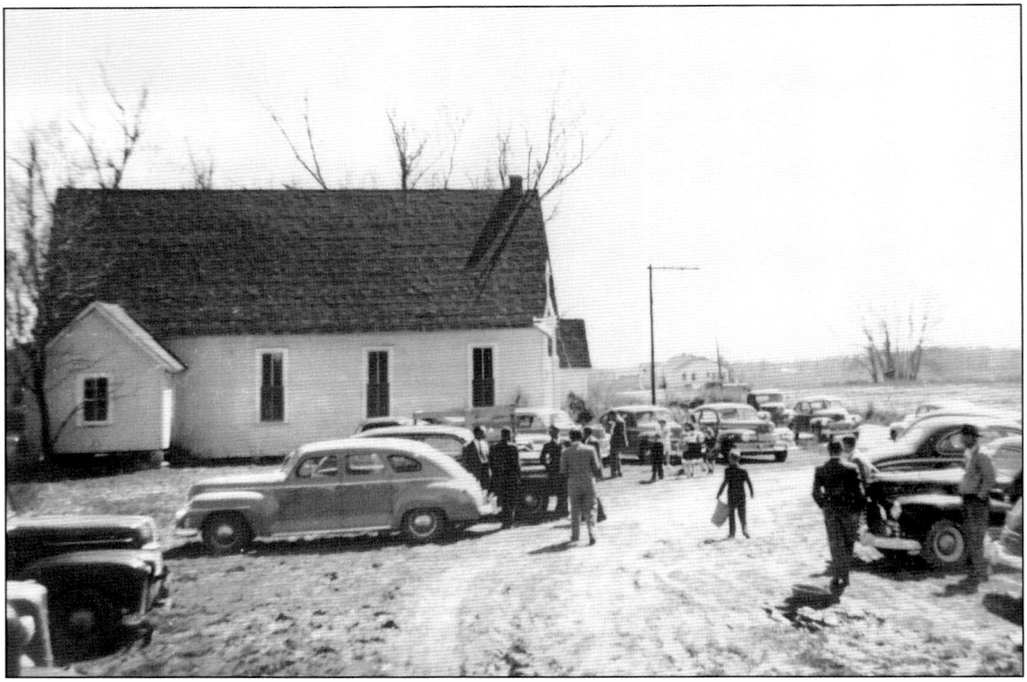

Tollville's family traditions are woven through the history of St. Peter's on the Prairie Episcopal Church, the heart of the community. The 1940s picture above shows the original church, which was built in 1905. The photograph below, taken around 1970, shows the new brick church that was constructed in 1953 and called the "70-day wonder church" for having been erected in that period of time; the congregation was able to build it without going in debt. Also below in the background to the left is the Parish Hall, which was built in 1940 and served as the location for church school and family and civic activities. (Courtesy of Judith Toll-Booher.)

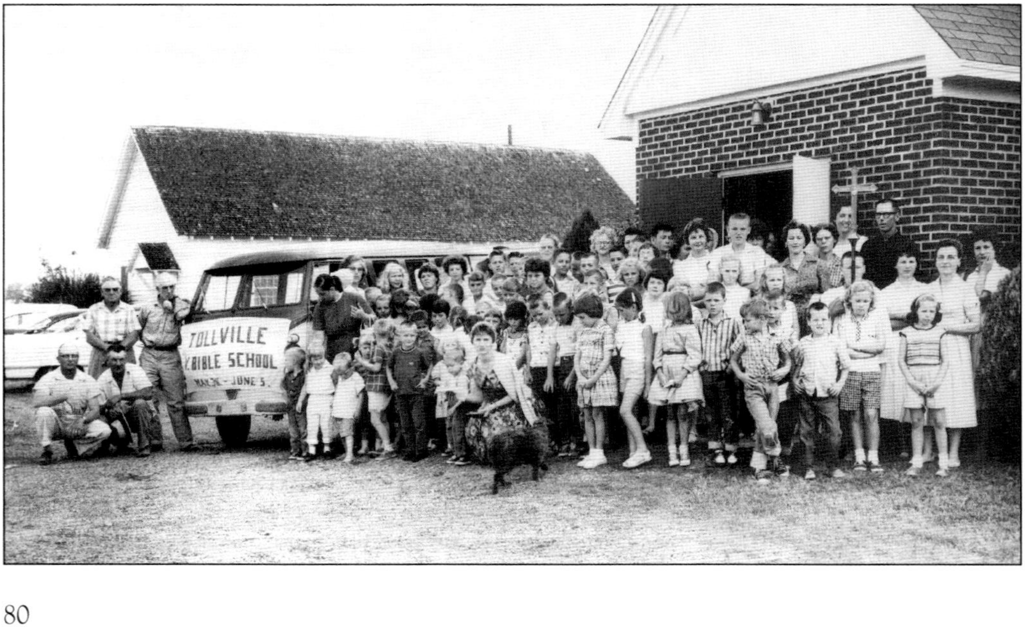

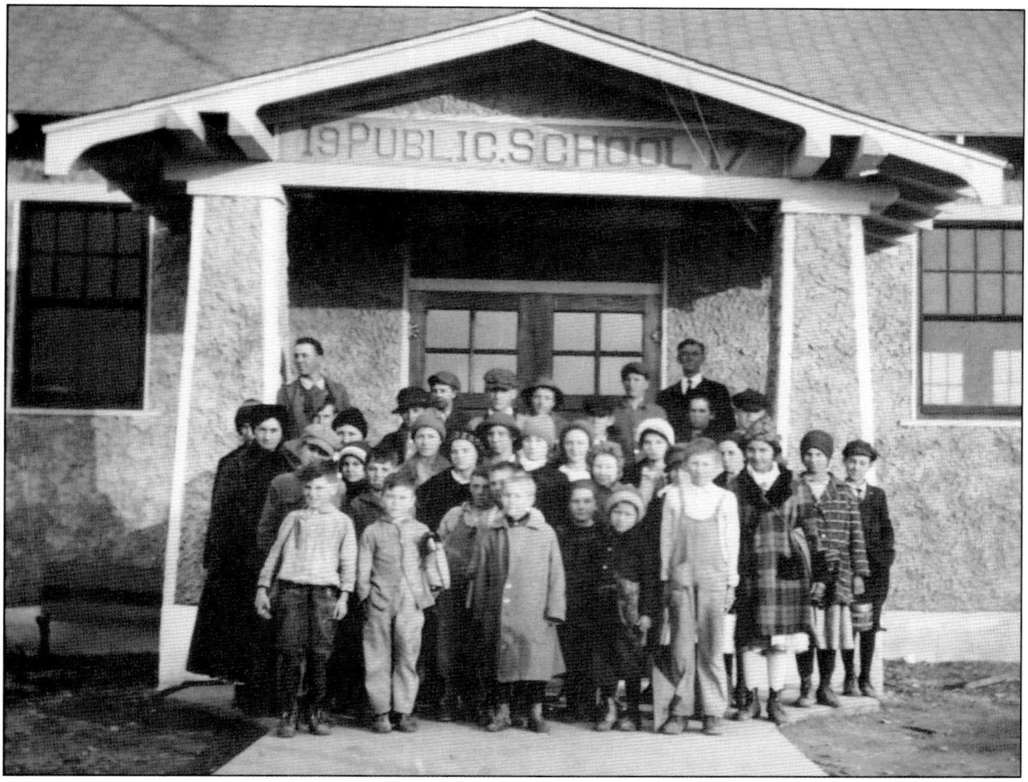

The Tollville children attended the one-room Fischer School and two other one-room schools in the early days. In 1917, a two-room stucco schoolhouse, shown above around 1924, was built to consolidate the classes. At the time, children brought their lunches in little pails, as can be seen in the picture. Once when Elias Toll opened his pail for lunch, there was nothing in it. His disappointment was so great that his former classmates called him "Empty" for the rest of his long life. Shown to the right are, from left to right, Evelyn Sickel, Pete Sickel, and Helen Clayton riding Helen's pet pony Toby. Children frequently used their horses to get to and from school. Katherine Toll had a cart and carried the younger children along the way. (Courtesy of Judith Toll-Booher.)

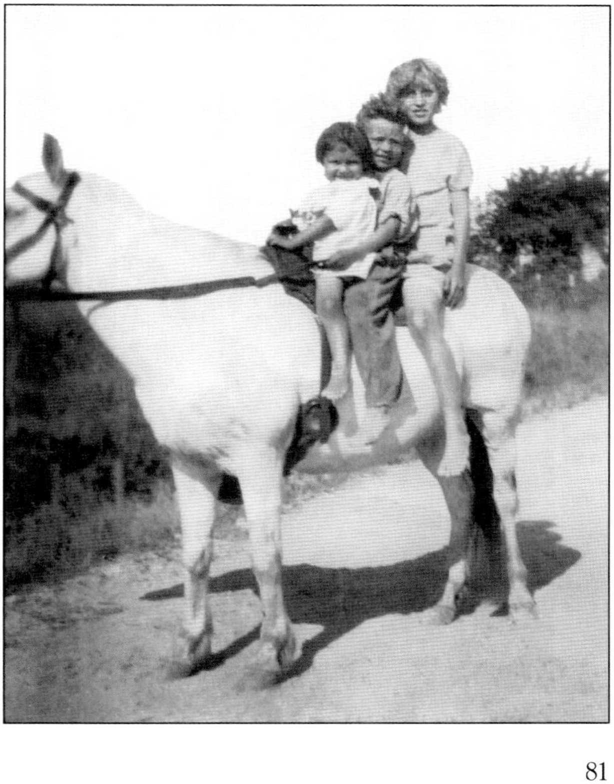

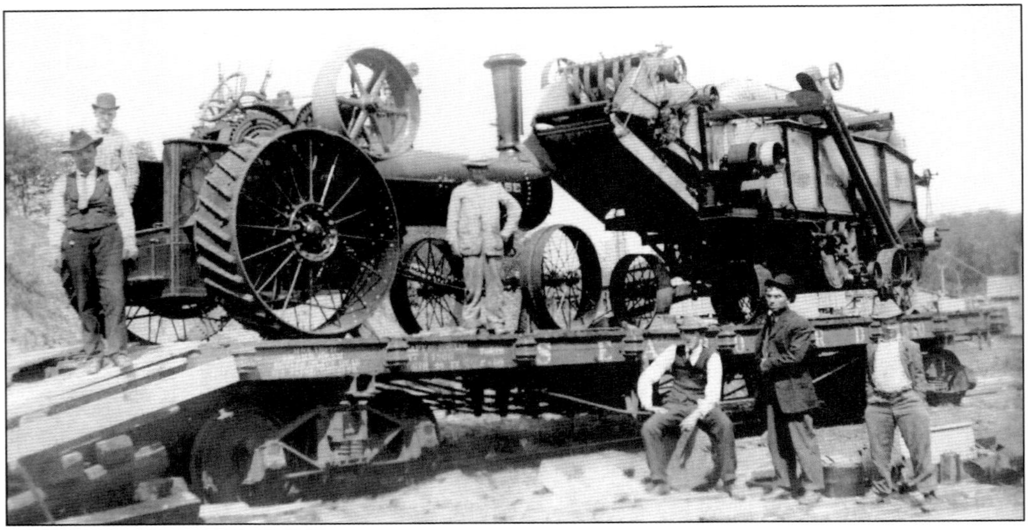

Richard Toll, on the far left, and Sam Toll, in the middle standing beside the tractor, are welcoming the rail delivery of a major investment in a steam tractor/power plant and threshing machine. (Courtesy of Judith Toll-Booher.)

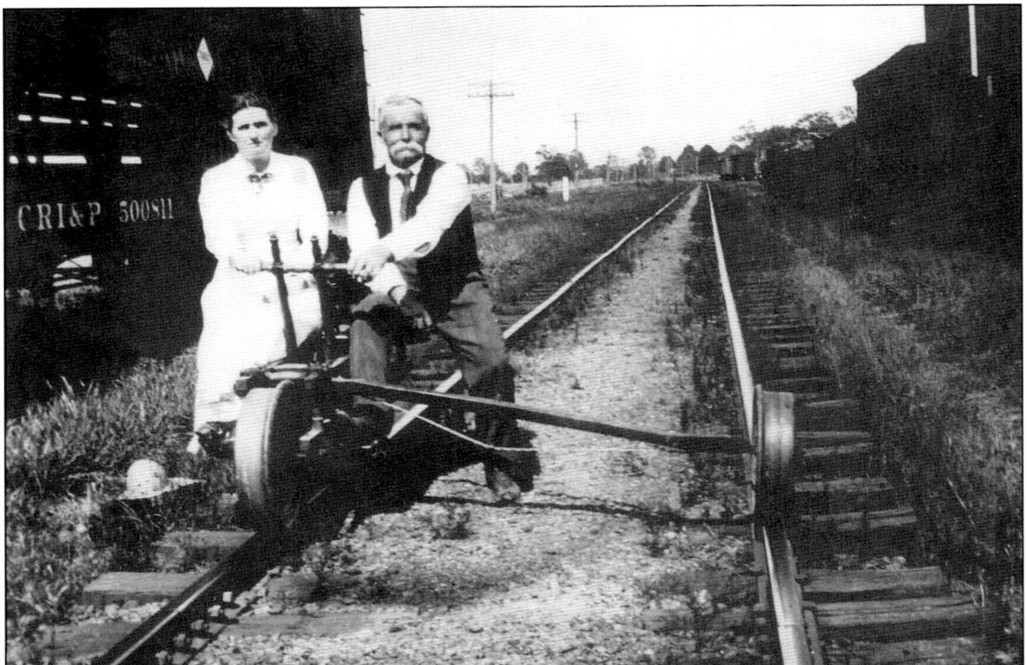

Burgess and Jennie Toll are shown on a handcart near Mesa where Burgess worked for the railroad in his later years. Before the railroad, the only public means of transportation was by stagecoach, which ran across the corner of Burgess Toll's farm in the route between Clarendon and Carlisle. There was a way station on the bank of Little Lagrue operated by a man named Mr. Overman. An open platform was built at this station, and dances were held there on Saturday nights. There was also an inn and stables, as this was a layover point. As late as the 1930s, the old Stagecoach Road was visible. (Courtesy of Judith Toll-Booher.)

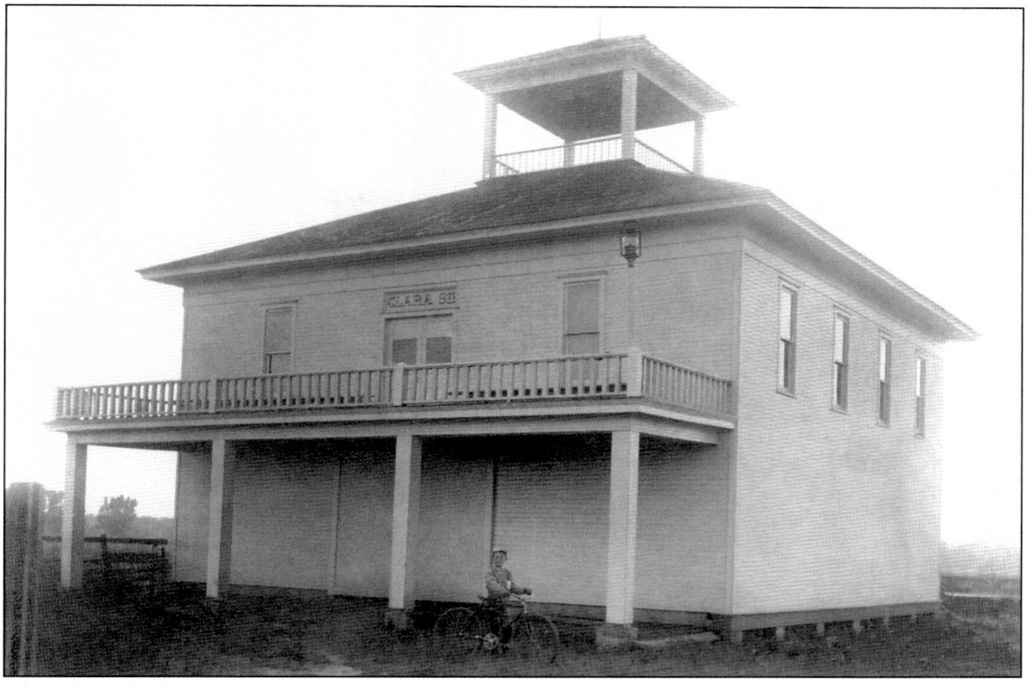

The Clara, built in Tollville in 1911, was designed after the home place built by the Tolls in the early 1870s in Illinois. There was a cupola to provide a natural updraft in the center of the building, bringing in cooler air through open doors or windows. A dance hall was on the top floor where prairie folks gathered, often along with visitors brought in by the nearby Rock Island Railroad. The second-generation Richard Toll is pictured on his bicycle around 1914. Burgess Toll & Sons sold buggies, wagons, and other farm equipment on the ground floor, as shown in the flyer pictured to the right. (Courtesy of Judith Toll-Booher.)

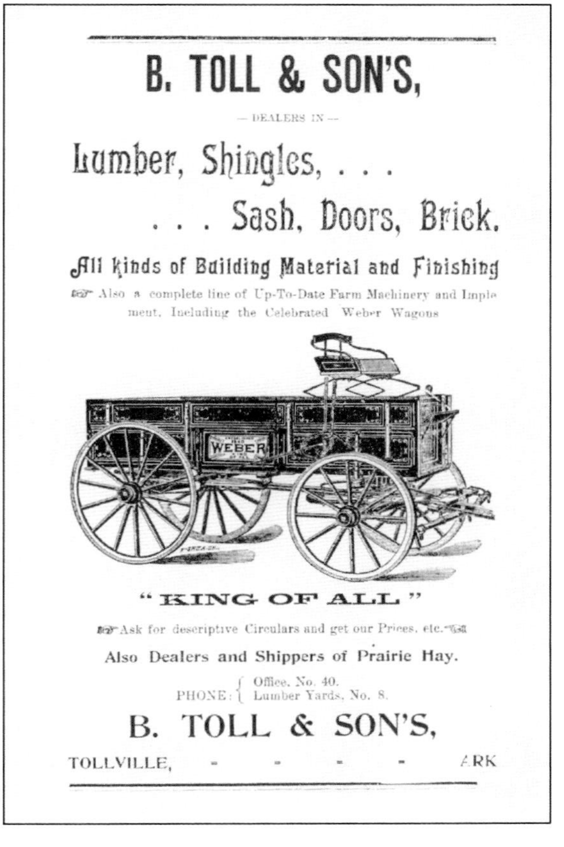

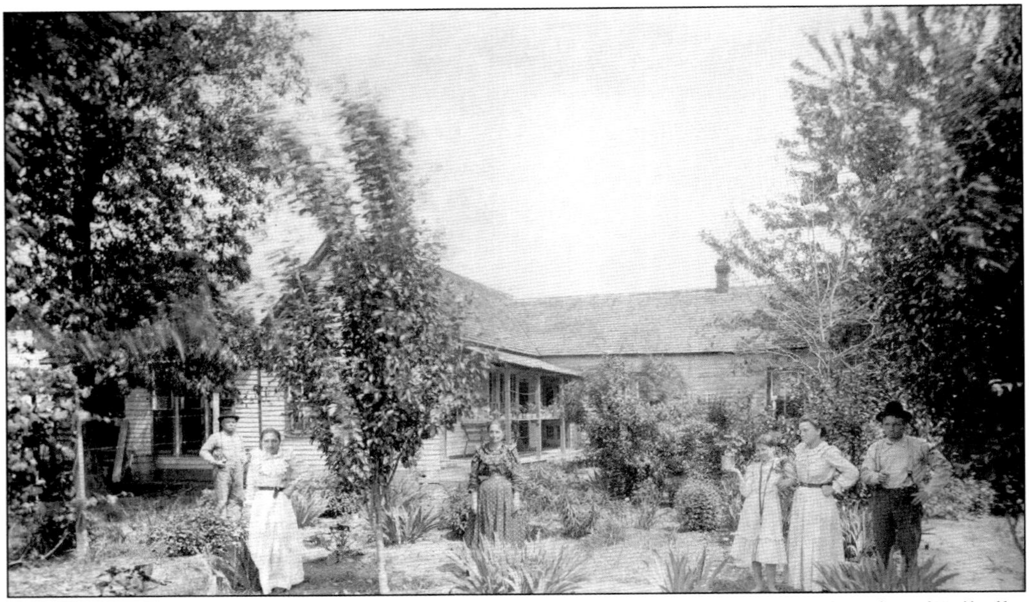

This 1907 photograph shows the expanded, original home place of Burgess Toll, founder of Tollville. It features a wing on the right, built to accommodate a long, custom-made table to seat 26 people for his large, close-knit family. Standing are, from left to right, Burgess Toll, daughter Sadie Toll, wife Jennie Welty Toll, granddaughter Selma Toll, daughter Polly Toll, and the youngest of eight sons, Fred Toll. (Courtesy of Judith Toll-Booher.)

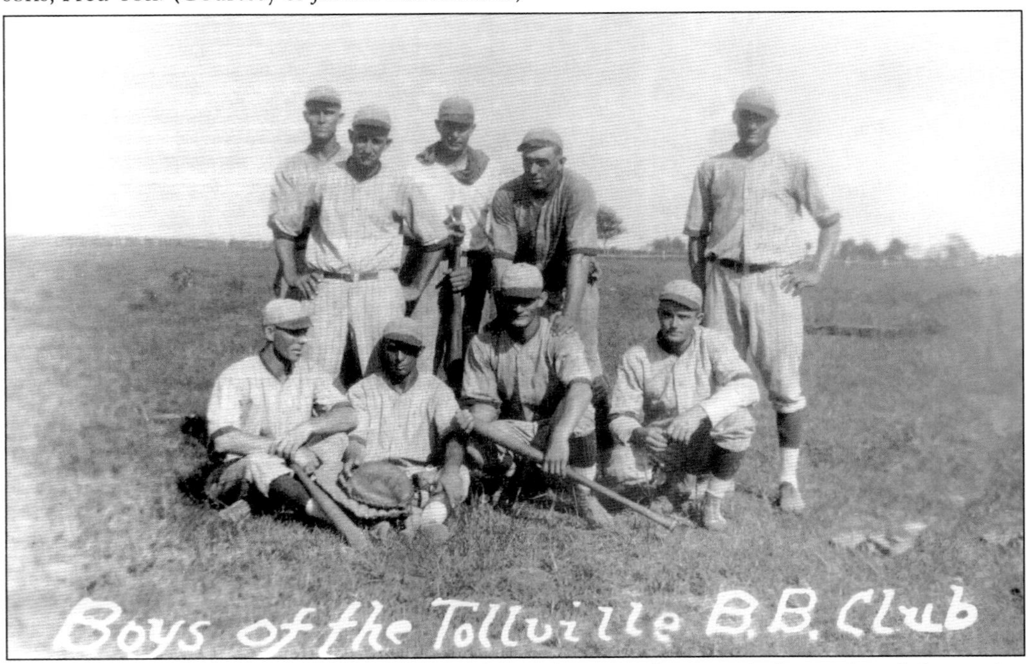

Baseball was a favorite pastime in Tollville. This early 1920s photograph shows, from left to right, (sitting) Lonnie VanHouten, Claude Prine, Orville Larkan, and Roland Foot; (standing) Bill Clayton, Art Clayton, Ernest Camm, Everett Adams, and Emil Hula. This team played together for many years. (Courtesy of Judith Toll-Booher.)

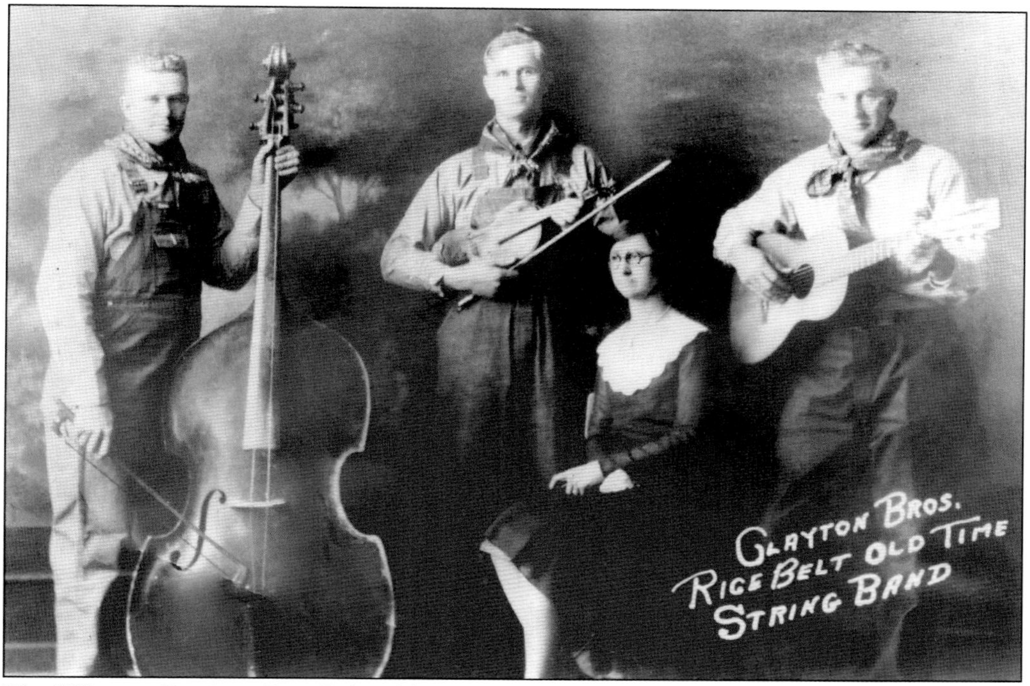

The "Clayton Brothers Rice Belt Old Time String Band," pictured above, gave renditions of popular music for more than half a century in Tollville and surrounding areas. They entertained at weddings, dances, and all kinds of gatherings. Frank Clayton, with his large build and strength, often picked up his stringed bass and held it like a guitar while playing. Bill Clayton was known far and wide for his fiddle playing and, in the 1940s and 1950s, for calling at square dances. Mae Camm, pianist, was a niece of the Clayton brothers. Art Clayton was guitarist. In later years, Bill's daughter Helen accompanied the group on piano. Below, the Tollville brass band members are gathered on the front stairs of Richard Toll's home. The group includes Roland Foot, Richard Toll Jr., Ernest Camm, Bill Clayton, Robert Toll, and Art Clayton. (Courtesy of Judith Toll-Booher.)

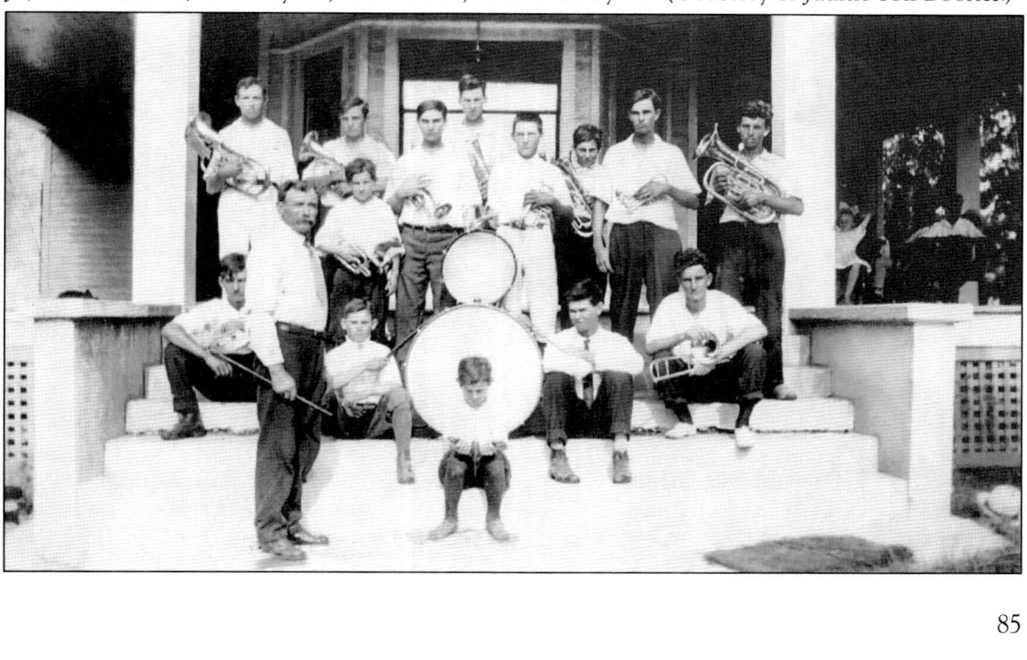

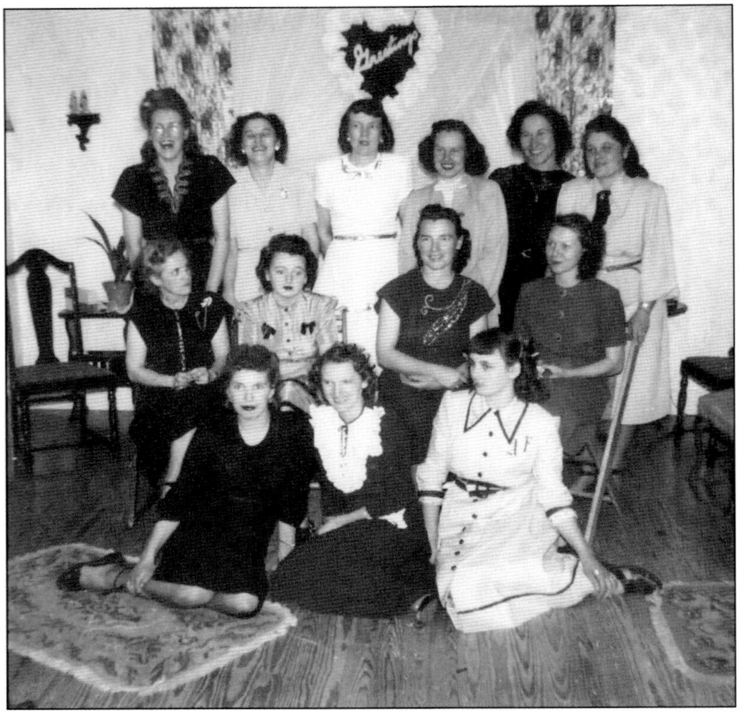

Tollville Progressive Club members are celebrating Valentine's Day at the home of Katherine Stipp in the 1950s. From left to right are (first row) Peggy Kocourek, Dora Faye Gutherie Roushall, and Alice Rosel Foot; (second row) Neva Tallent Miller, Sissy Kocourek, Katherine Toll Stipp, and Betty Williams; (third row) Pat Gaddy, Etta Lynne Fischer Toll, Ruby Luebke Toll, Ethalene Foot Golleher Bowen, Cele Melkovitz Dunar, and Willene Sparks Clayton. (Courtesy of Judith Toll-Booher.)

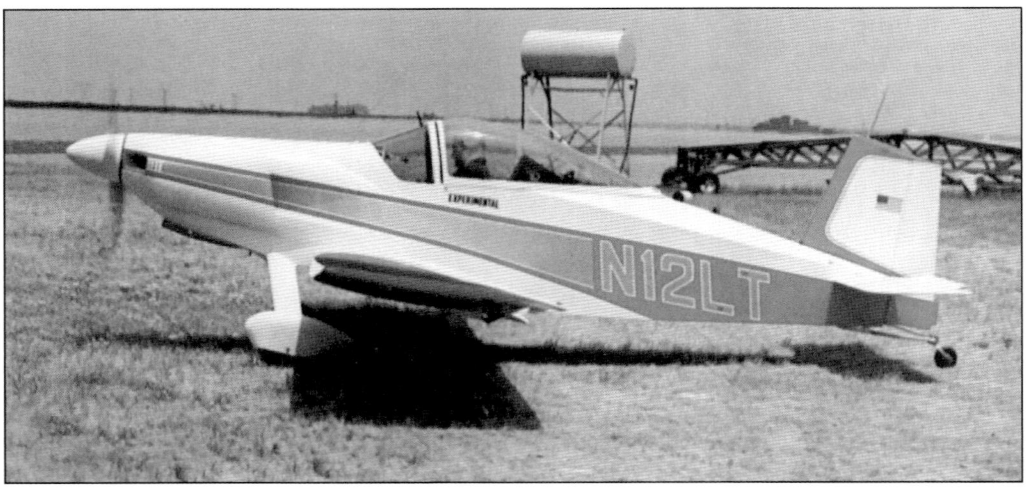

Lloyd Toll is shown ready for takeoff at the landing strip on his Tollville farm in 1972. He is in an all-metal experimental aircraft (T-18) that he built in his farm shop/hangar. This high-performance aircraft won international awards for best homebuilt and was featured in *Popular Mechanics* and *Sport Aviation* magazines. Lloyd was a farmer, welder, and master mechanic, even designing and building the land leveler shown in the background. (Courtesy of Judith Toll-Booher.)

Five

Eastern Europeans Seek Better Life

Slovak and Fairmount

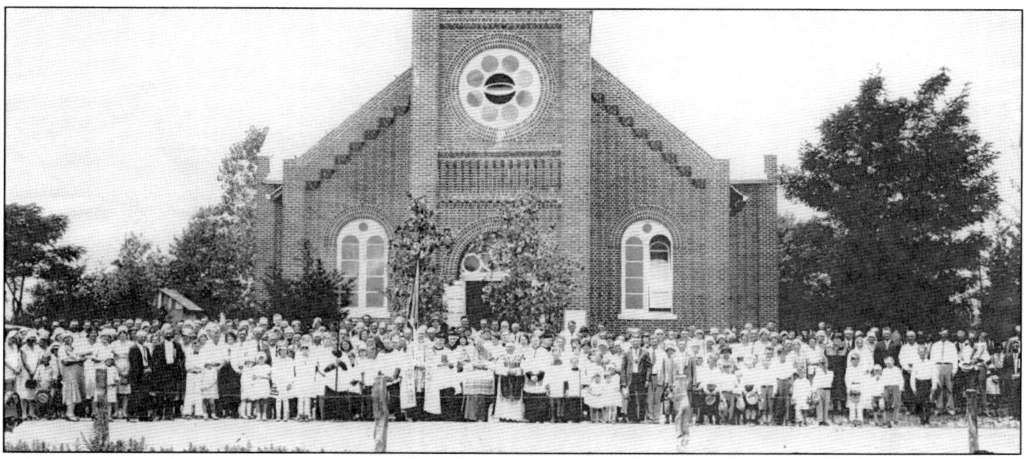

This photograph is believed to have been taken in May 1924 on the occasion of the dedication of a new parish hall located near the Ss. Cyril and Methodius Catholic Church of Slovak, shown here. Arkansas governor Thomas McRae and many dignitaries spoke before a crowd of 1,500 people. The brick church was completed in 1919, replacing the first frame church, which burned in 1914. Today's brick church was dedicated in 1961. (Courtesy of Linda Uhiren.)

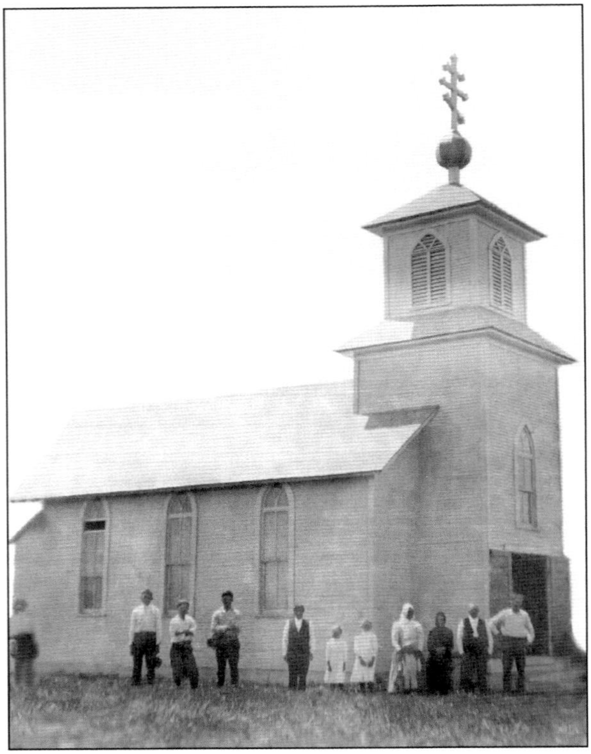

Pictured are members beside the first St. Mary's Russian Orthodox Church, built in 1918. It was struck by lightning and burned about 1940; the second church was completed in 1942. Ten years later, the congregation had dwindled, and the church building was moved to the grounds of St. Albans Episcopal Church in Stuttgart where it is used today as Sunday school rooms. Some members of St. Mary's joined the Episcopal church, and others united with Ss. Cyril and Methodius Catholic Church. (Courtesy of Linda Uhiren.)

The interior of Slovak's second Russian Orthodox church is shown at its dedication in 1942. Those identified are John Brasko, Joe Prislovsky Sr., Mike Prislovsky, Rev. John Tertichny (priest from St. Louis), George Brasko, Henry Brasko, Doris Seaser, and George Pich. (Courtesy of Robert Brasko.)

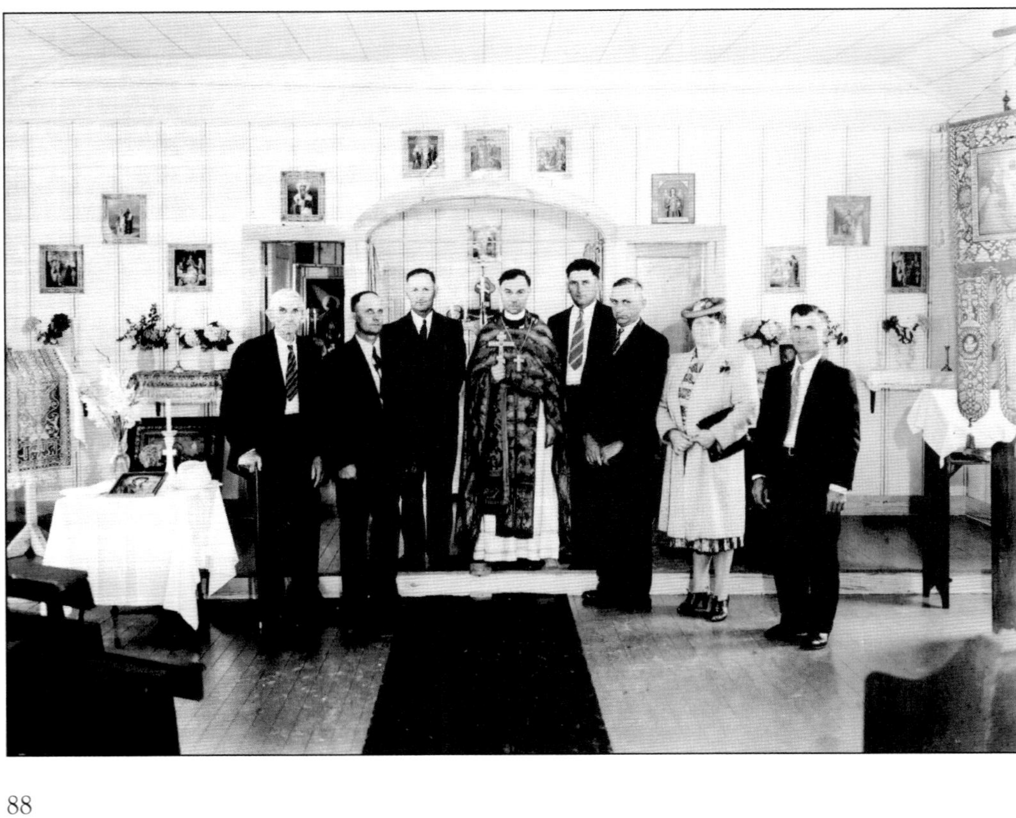

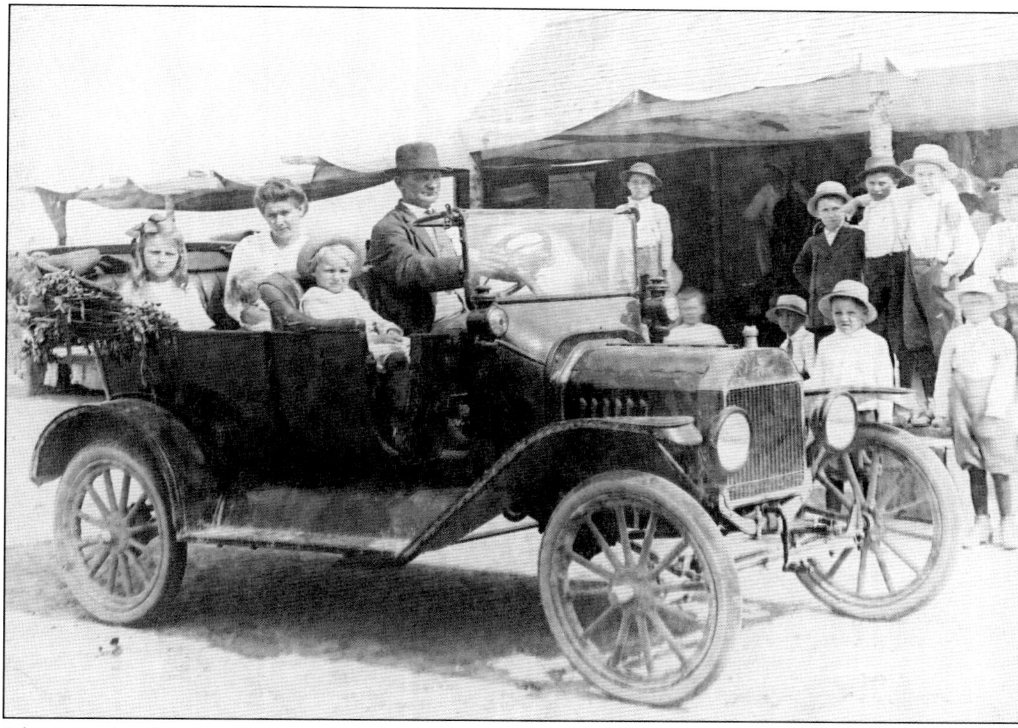

The Janesko family of Slovak is out for a drive around 1920. From left to right are Sophie (or Sophia), Suzie holding Alice, Louis, and John Janesko. Three of the Janesko sons became priests, and the daughter became a nun. (Courtesy of Linda Uhiren.)

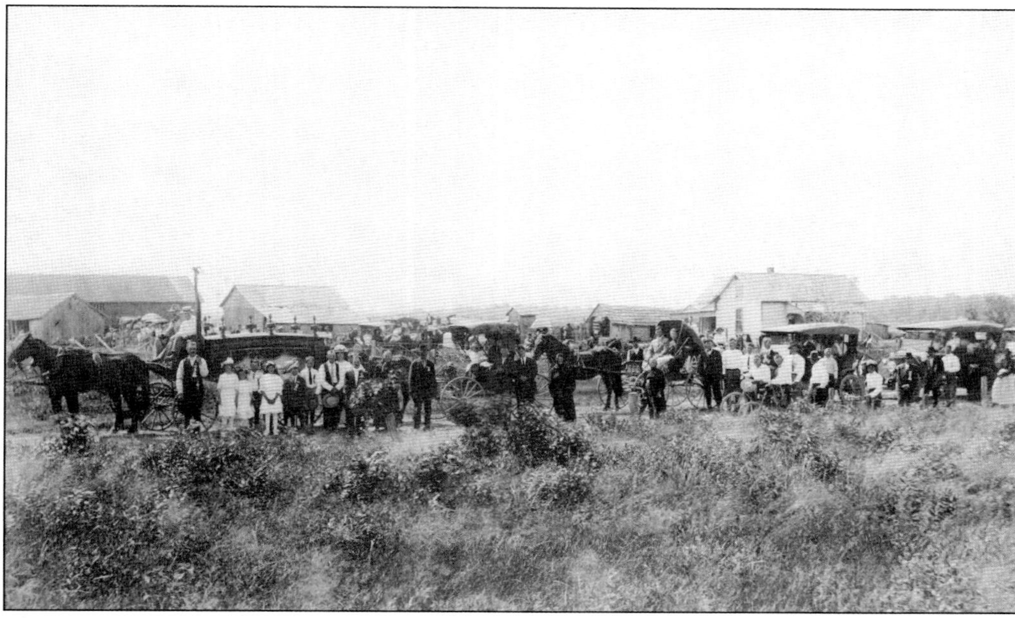

This undated photograph of the John and Suzie Janesko family shows a horse-drawn hearse and funeral procession. It is believed to have been taken in the Slovak area. (Courtesy of Linda Uhiren.)

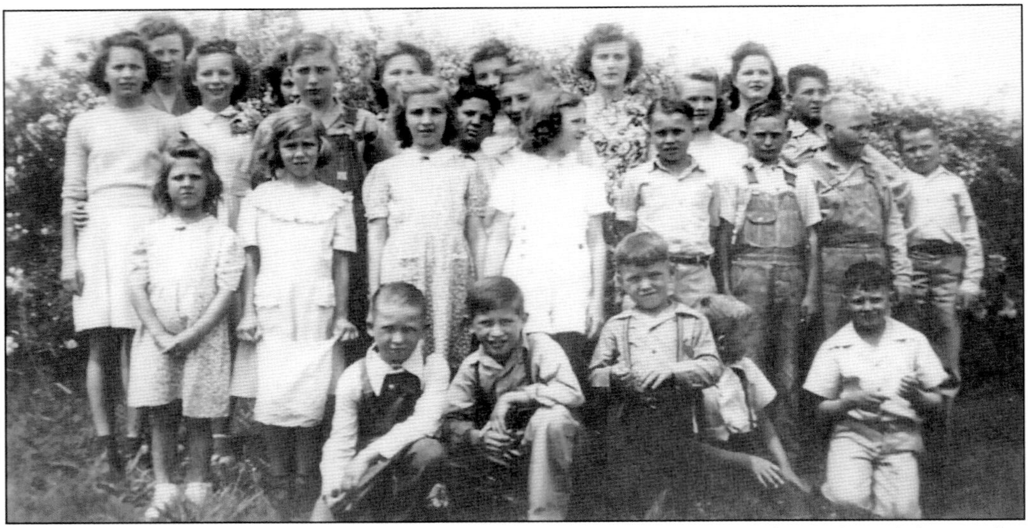

The Wylie school was located near Slovak in the early 1940s. Pictured are, from left to right, (first row) Tommy Uhiren, Paul Marek, Johnny Uhiren, and Martin Shimek; (second row) Betty Uhiren, Annie Marie Lisko, Angie Chlapecka, Harry Uhiren, Paul Chlapecka, Maymie Duch, Tommy Pitonyak, Veronica Bednar, Bobby Norman, Don Vaught, and Johnnie Lisko; (third row) Irene Marek, Francis Shimek, Steve Chlapecka, and Agnes Bednar; (fourth row) Geraldine Duch, Betty Marek, Theresa Uhiren, Dorothy Chlapecka, Lorraine Hooks, and Mike Uhiren Jr. (Courtesy of Linda Uhiren.)

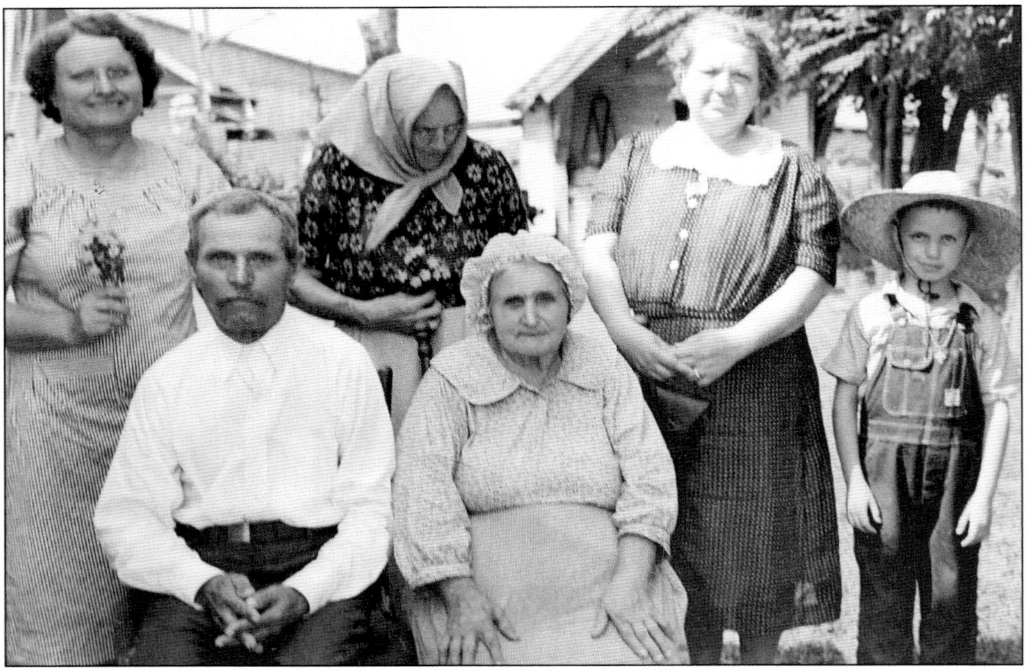

John M. Hooks Sr. and wife, Susie, shown seated, immigrated to America from the Slovakian region of Eastern Europe in 1882 and 1884, respectively, and settled north of Slovak in the mid-1890s. Standing are, from left to right, their daughter Rosie Hooks Lisko, two unidentified women, and Mike Pich. (Courtesy of Mrs. Edward D. Hooks.)

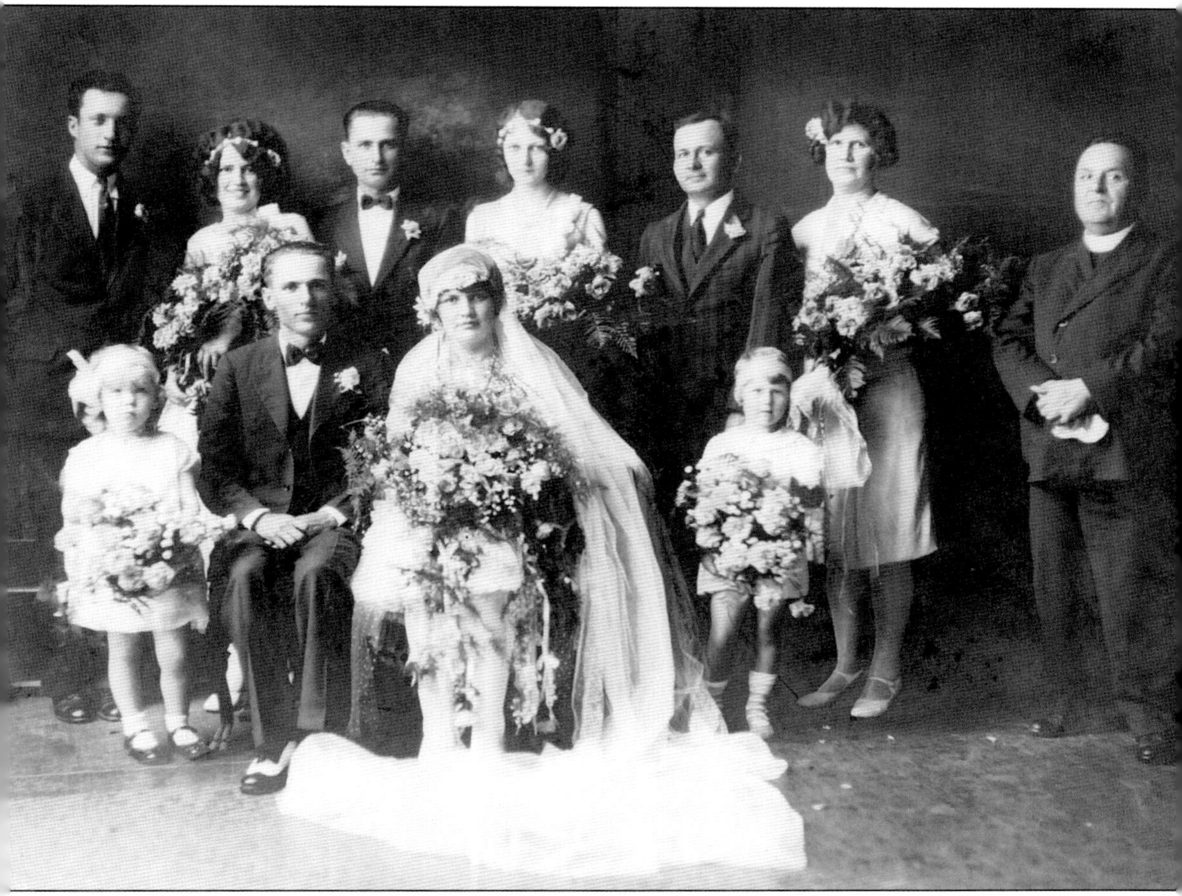

This is the lovely c. 1925 wedding party of Joseph, son of John and Susie Hooks, and his wife, Julie Makovec Hooks. The happy couple is seated between unidentified flower girls. In the second row are, from left to right, Johnny Prislovsky, Vernon and Mike Makovec, Viola Schroeder, Pete Nahay, Elizabeth Hooks Makovec, and Fr. Michael Judt. (Courtesy of Mrs. Edward D. Hooks.)

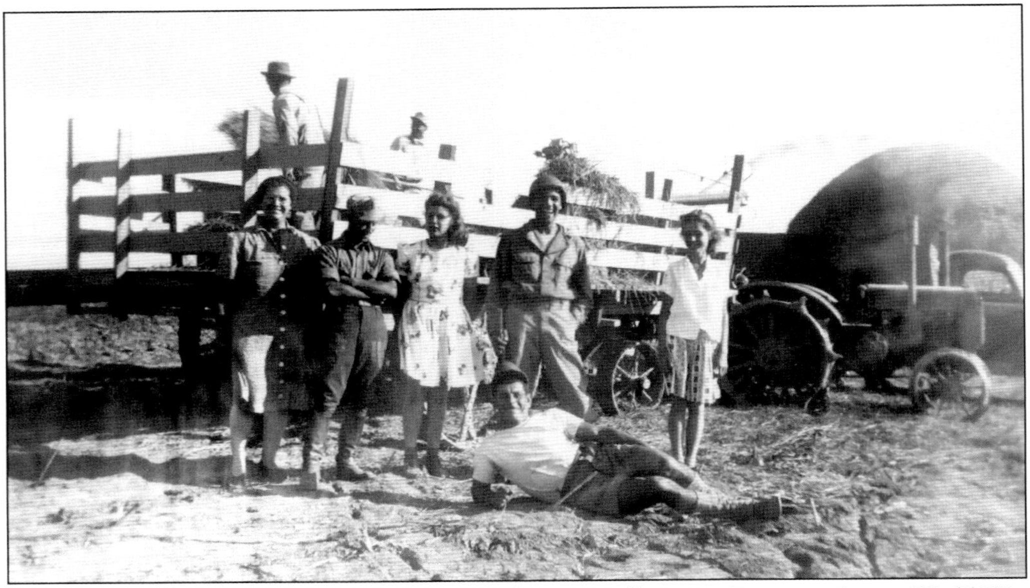

German and Italian prisoners were kept at a military installation at Stuttgart during World War II, and some of these men were hired to work area farms for less than a dollar a day. The Italian interpreter in the photograph relaxes in the foreground on John Hooks's farm. Standing, from left to right, are Elizabeth Hooks, a German prisoner of war, Lorraine Hooks, a US guard soldier, and Mary J. Hooks. (Courtesy of Mrs. Edward D. Hooks.)

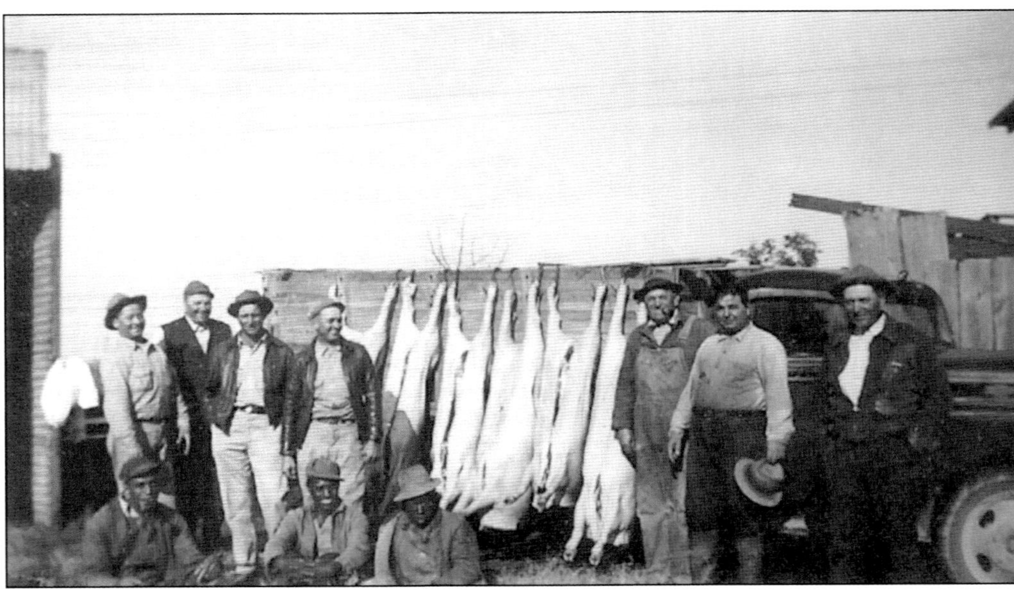

Cold weather brought these men together for a hog killing on the Lorince farm east of Slovak. Three unidentified men sit in the first row; in the second row, from left to right, are Charlie Papan, Mike Lorince, Orin Shirkey, Pete Matoske, John Lorince, Stanley Saranie, and Vince Sokora. (Courtesy of Brad Lorince.)

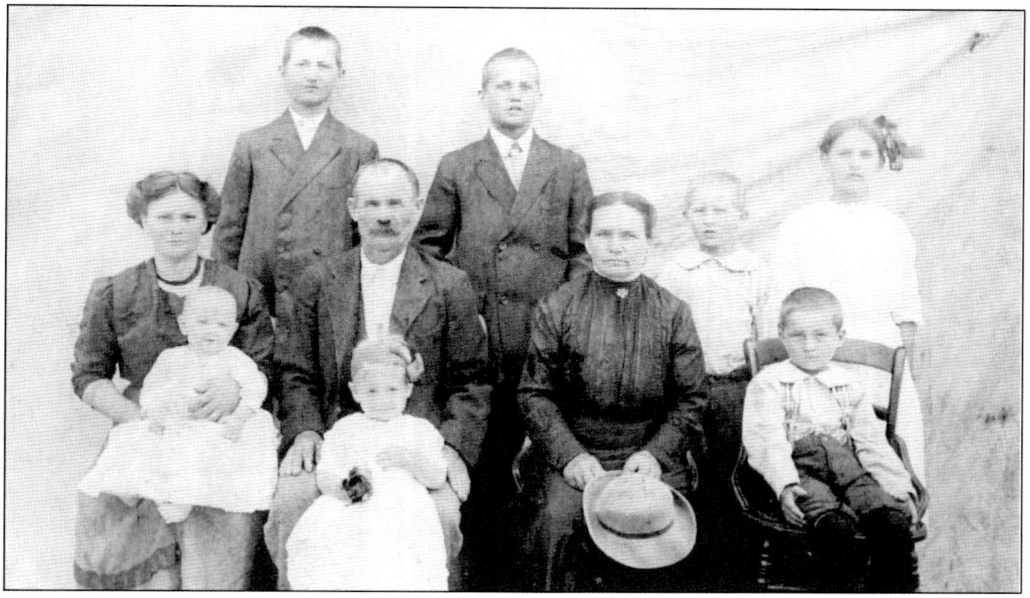

Shown above, the John Prislovsky family poses at its Slovak home in 1913. Members are, from left to right, (first row) Mary holding Rosa, John holding Julie, Barbara Lega, and Johnny; (second row) Mike, Joe, Andrew, and Anna. The family immigrated to America from Eastern Europe around 1886 and went west to find work. While mining in Montana, they learned of land for sale in Prairie County. John sent Barbara (who did not speak English) along with the children to Hazen by rail in 1900, where she got a wagon and went to Slovak (then called Slovac town) and bought a farm. They camped out until John could join after the mine closed. Slovak is a close-knit community with a very strong sense of family and fellowship. The Prislovskys are pictured below at their parents' home. They are, from left to right, (standing and drinking tankards of beer) Johnny, Andrew, Joe, and Mike; (sitting on the bench) Mary, John, Martha, Louie, and Julie. This was a typical Sunday after church in the mid-1920s. (Courtesy of Betty Lou Prislovsky Morris.)

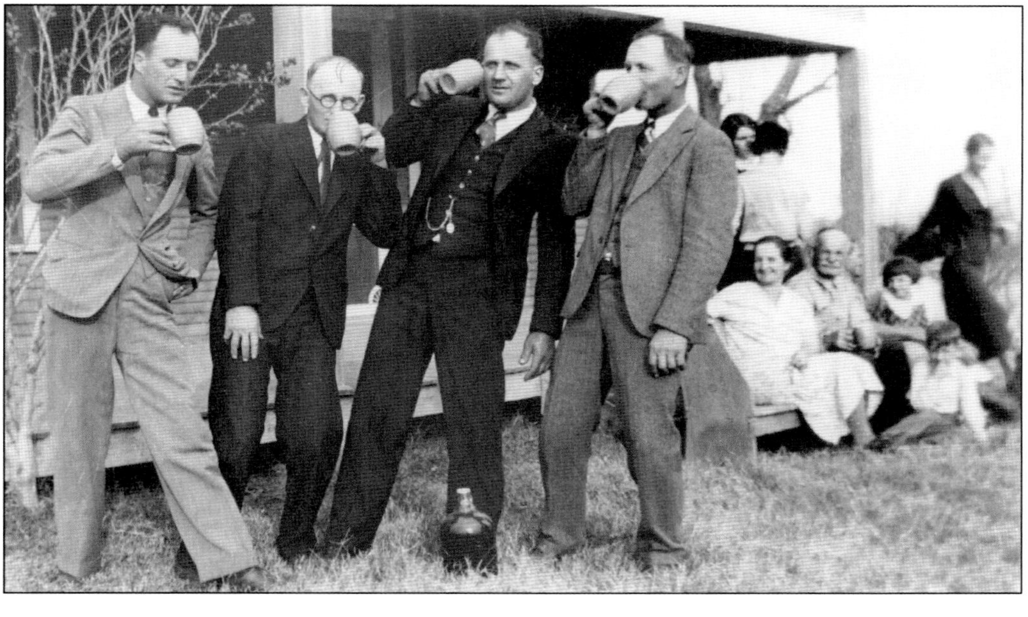

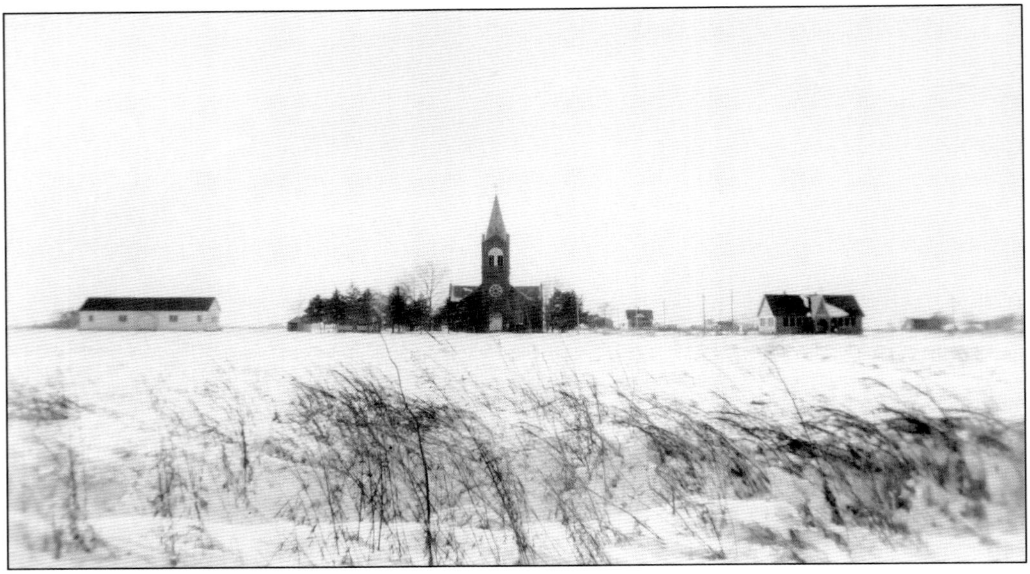

A heavy snow lay on the ground when these photographs were taken in the early 1950s. Shown above, on the far left, is the Catholic Hall where all community activities took place such as wedding and funeral receptions, Slovak dances with live music, oyster suppers, and reunions. The priest's house in front of the trees is adjacent to Ss. Cyril and Methodius Catholic Church. The larger building to the right is the Catholic School for grades one through six. This small community had three churches, three cemeteries, several schools, and a hotel. The scene below shows the intersection at the Andrew Konecny Jr. store. (Courtesy of Mrs. Edward D. Hooks.)

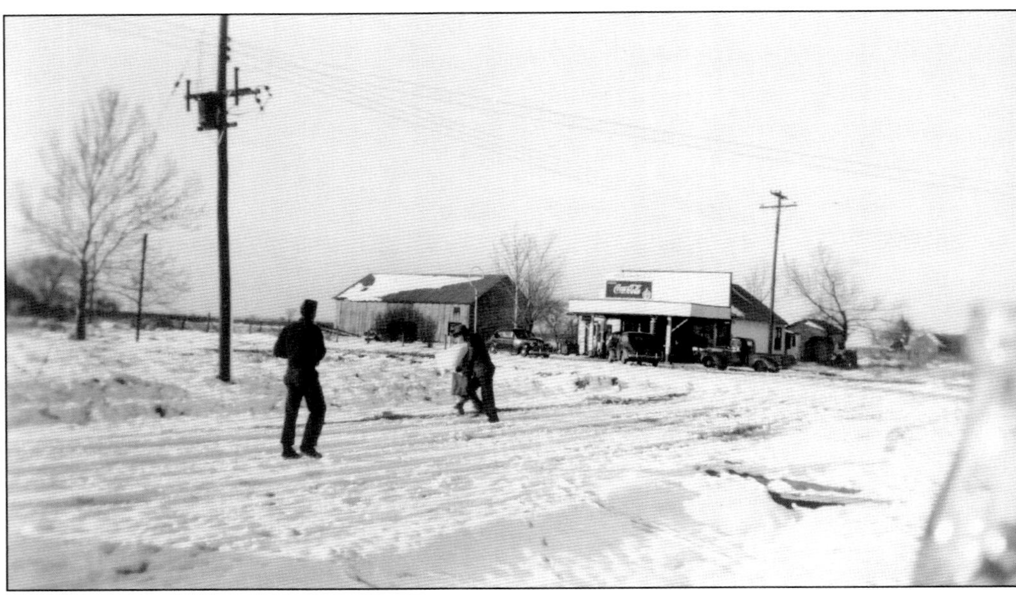

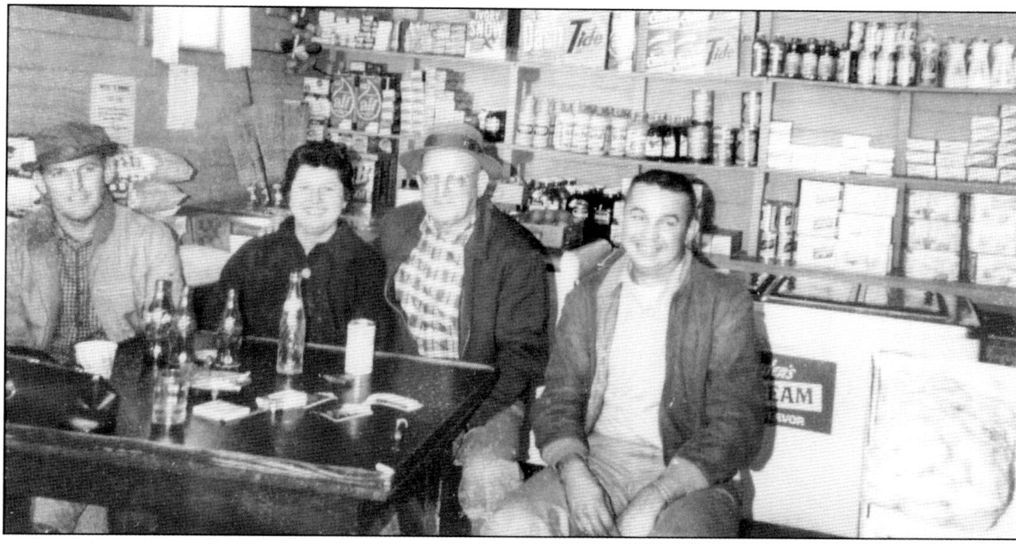

Pictured at Andrew Konecny Jr.'s store about 1950 are, from left to right, Earl Hooks, Mary Jane Hooks, John Lisko, and Charles Makovec. Although the community had a relatively small population, there were three stores (Saranie store, Minnie's, and the Konecny store). (Courtesy of Mrs. Edward D. Hooks.)

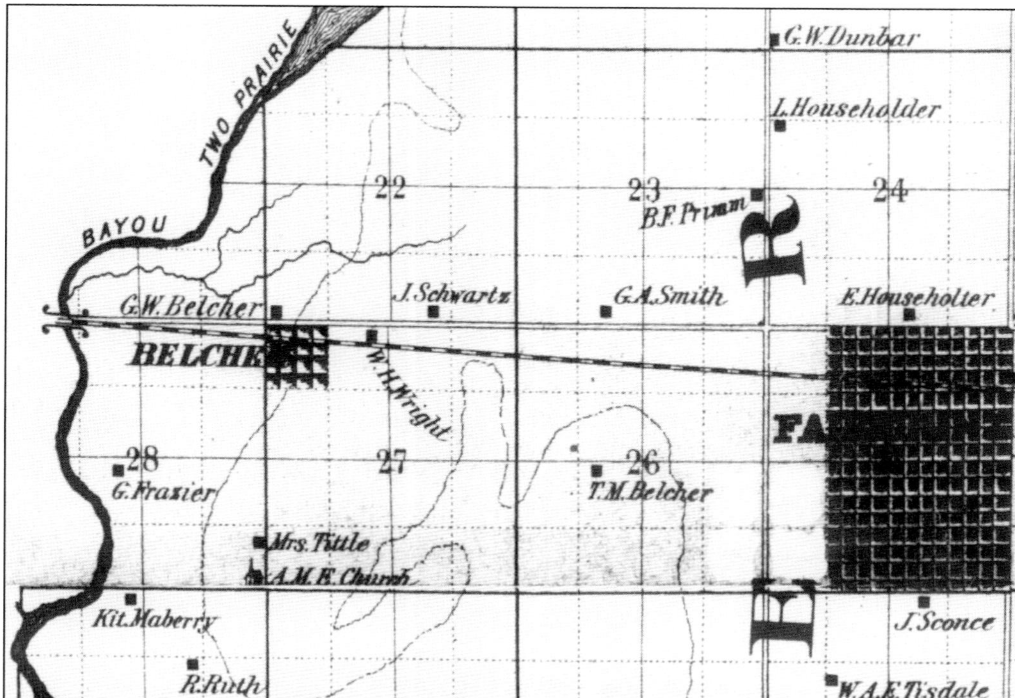

Settlement commenced about 1880 in the scattered community of Fairmount, indicated by the large dark rectangle on J.G. Thweatt's 1892 county ownership map. The Mississippi & Little Rock Railway line passed through Fairmount and Belcher, two miles to the west. After operating for several years, the rail line was abandoned in 1906, and the wood-burning locomotive no longer crossed the Grand Prairie. (Courtesy of the National Archives.)

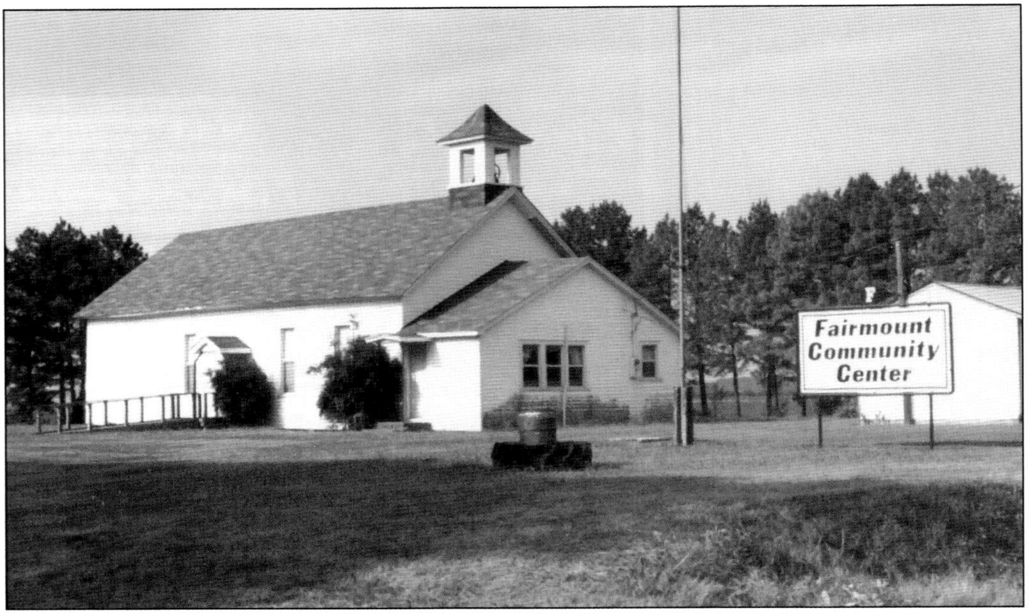

The Fairmount school district was dissolved in the 1950s. Some of the children started attending school in Stuttgart, and others transferred to the DeValls Bluff district. The former school building has been used as a gathering place for many years. (Courtesy of Bill Sayger.)

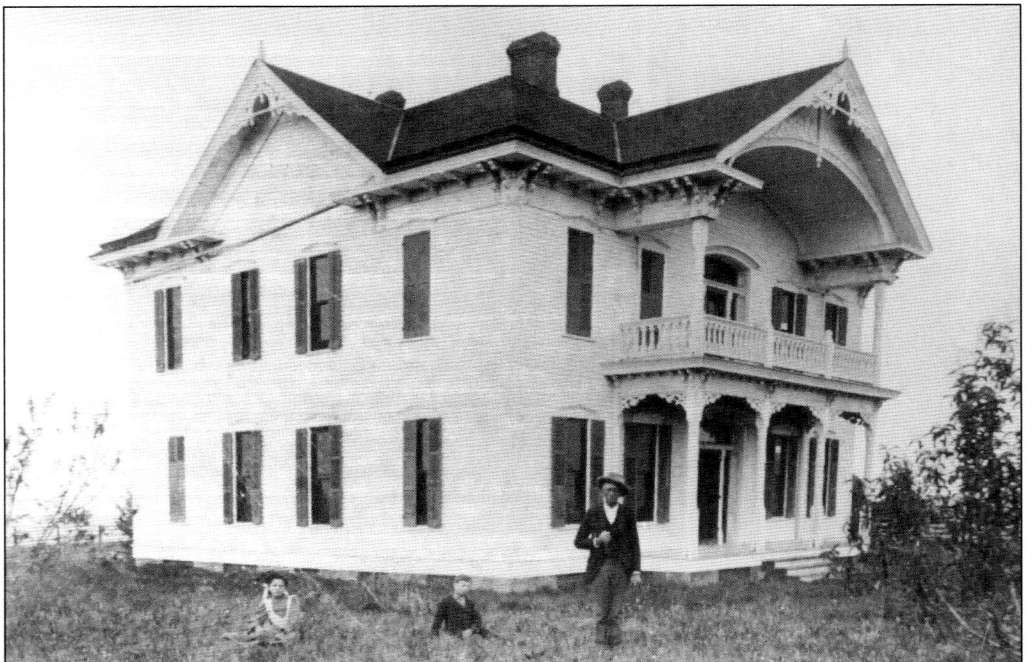

Joseph A. Harr came to Prairie County and built this home in the Fairmount community in 1886. He was a land agent, farmer, and banker and promoted the development of the community. From left to right in the undated photograph are Agnes Stipsky, Harr's housekeeper; Mike Garrich; and Joseph Harr. Agnes later became Joseph's wife. (Courtesy of Larry Harr.)

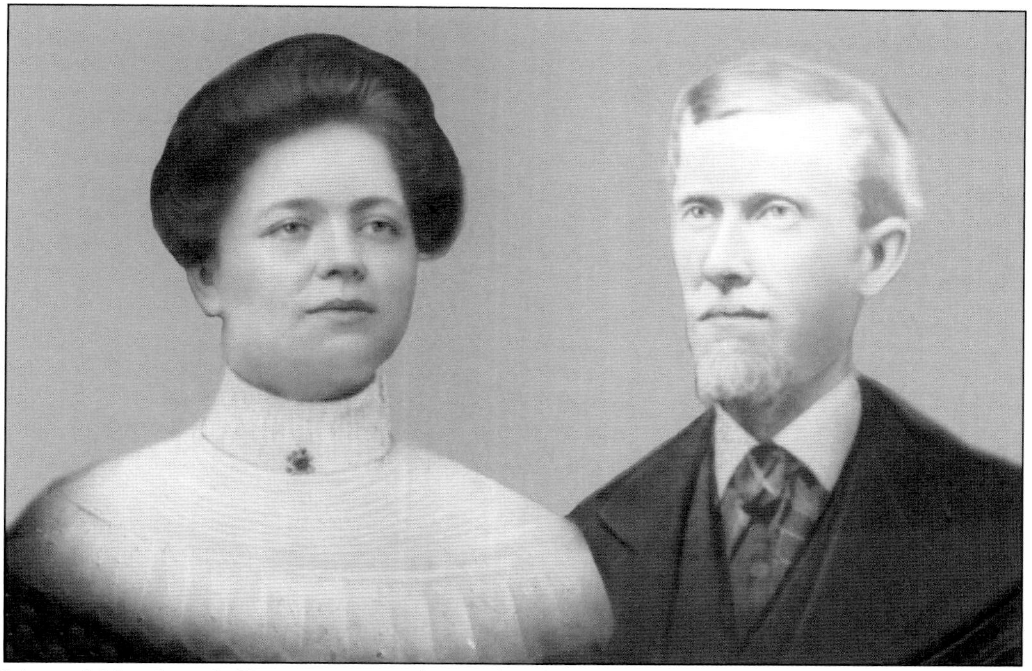

Mr. and Mrs. Joseph Harr appear in this undated photograph. Joseph was a stockholder and strong supporter of the short-lived railroad through Fairmount. Many prominent people including Arkansas governors were guests in the Harr home. (Courtesy of Larry Harr.)

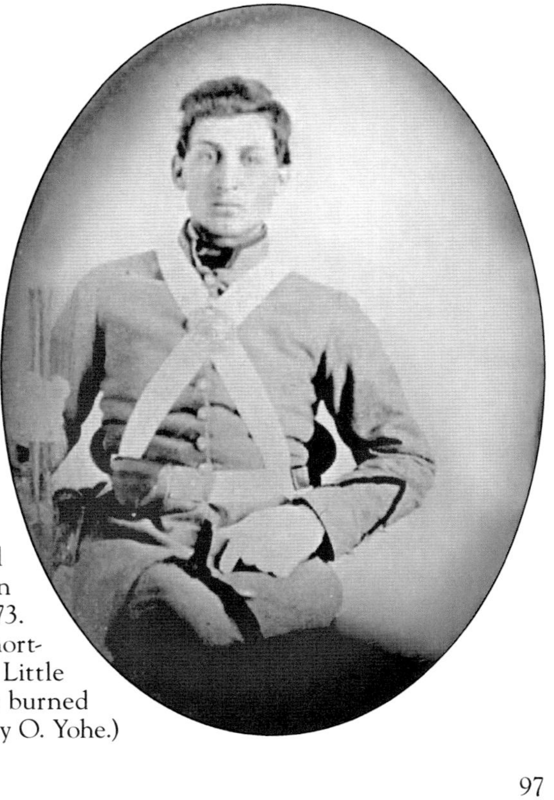

Patrick A. Yohe (born 1866) was a successful businessman in Morning Sun, Iowa, when he bought 680 acres at Fairmount in 1873. The Belcher train station, used by the short-lived and never-completed Mississippi & Little Rock Railway, stood on the property but burned shortly after the purchase. (Courtesy of Perry O. Yohe.)

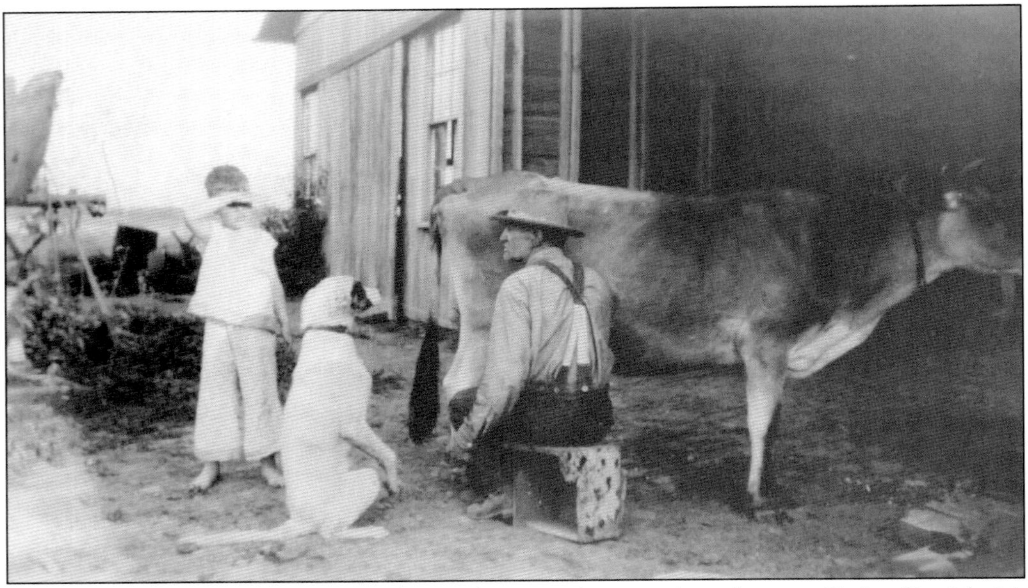

Perry O. Yohe (born 1925) and the dog are keeping close watch on his grandfather Patrick A.'s milking operation. Perry's father, Carl, was taken out of school in the ninth grade to work on the family farm; Carl farmed rice there for 66 years. (Courtesy of Perry O. Yohe.)

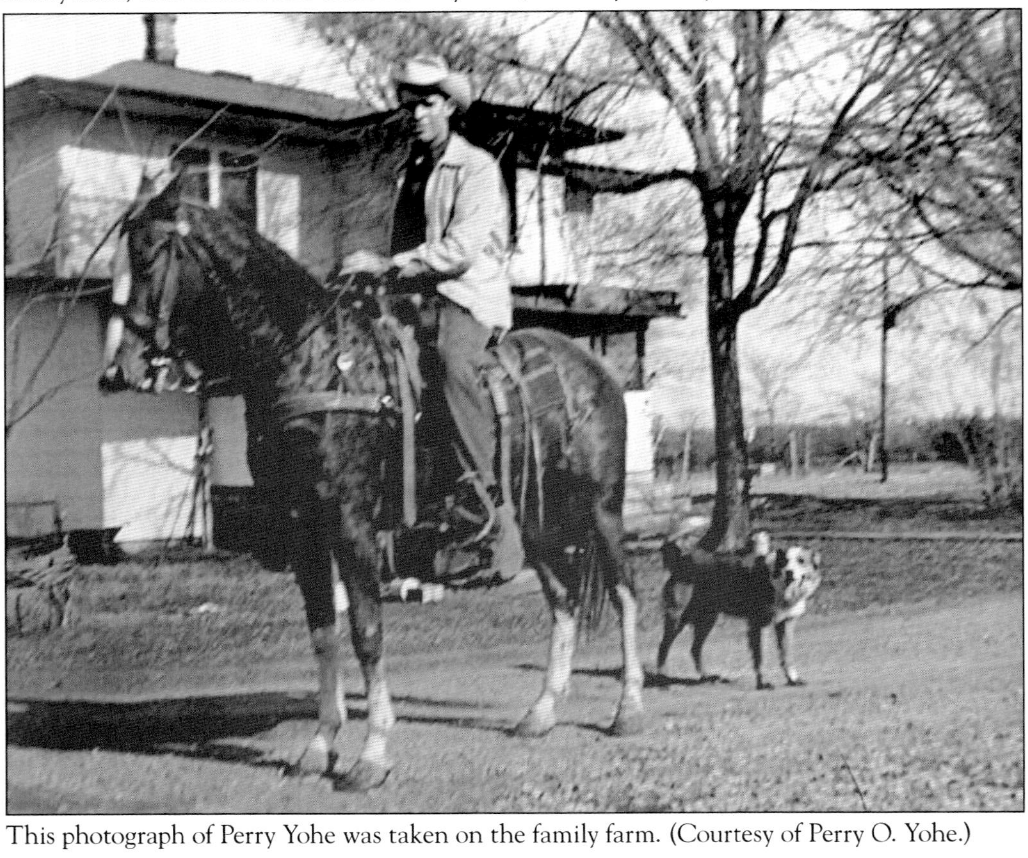

This photograph of Perry Yohe was taken on the family farm. (Courtesy of Perry O. Yohe.)

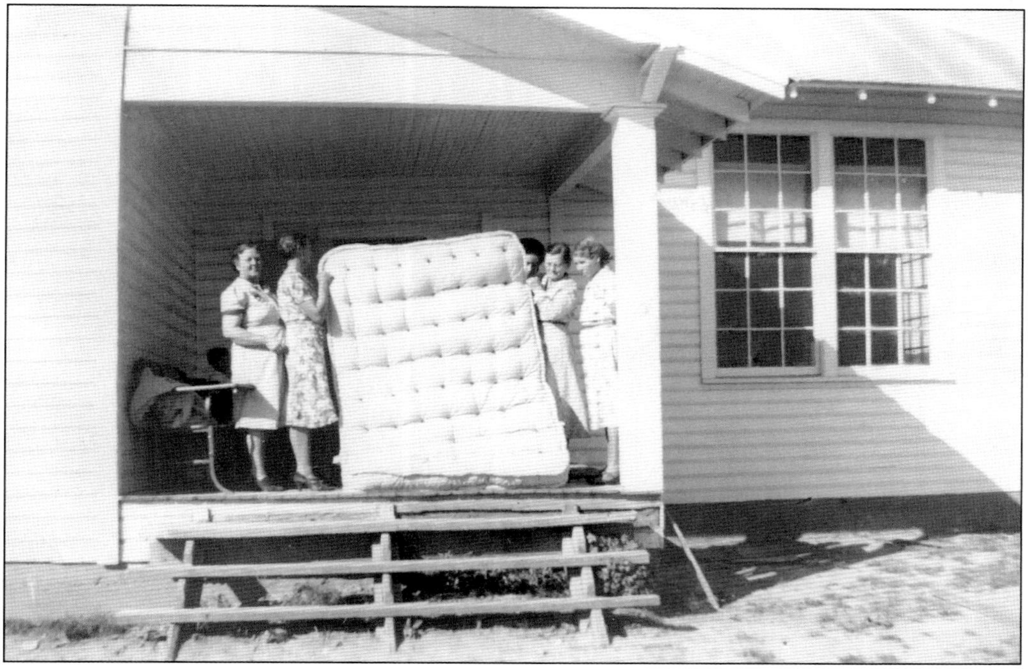

The Fairmount-Independence Home Demonstration Club was founded about 1928. Besides serving as a social outlet for women, members took on home and community improvement projects such as home canning and mattress making, as seen here in 1939. (Courtesy of the Stuttgart Public Library.)

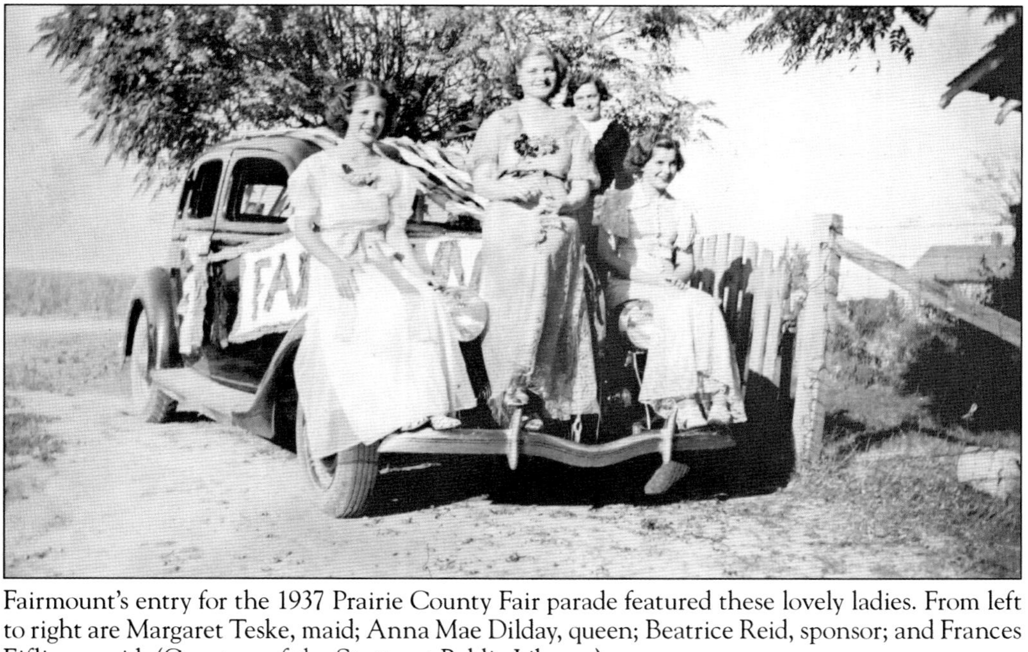

Fairmount's entry for the 1937 Prairie County Fair parade featured these lovely ladies. From left to right are Margaret Teske, maid; Anna Mae Dilday, queen; Beatrice Reid, sponsor; and Frances Eifling, maid. (Courtesy of the Stuttgart Public Library.)

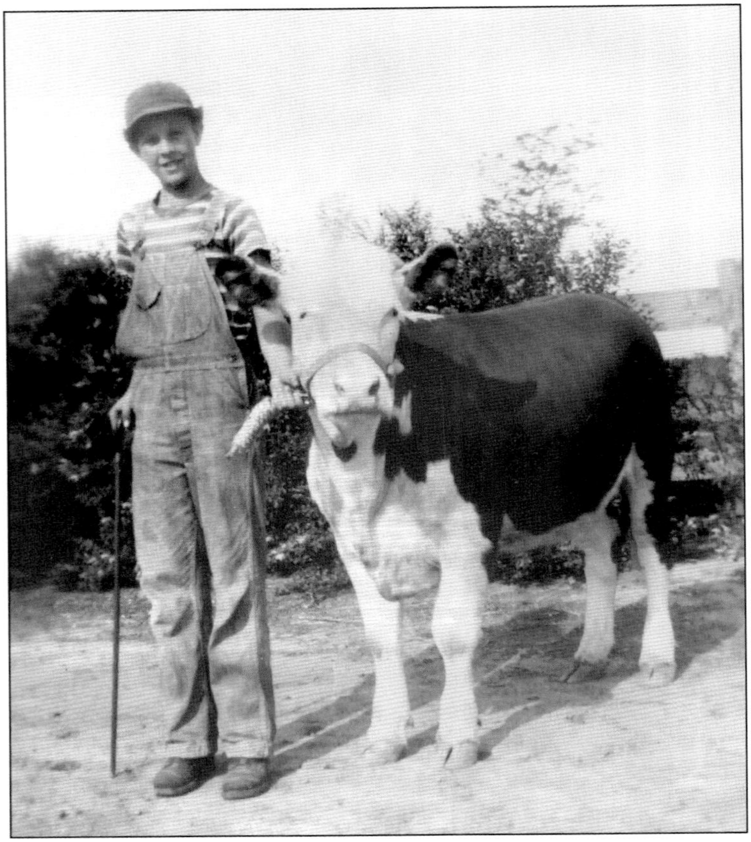

Charles Seidenschwarz of Fairmount is shown with his grand champion calf in the fat calf show in 1947. Over 2,000 people attended the Prairie County event in Des Arc in support of the youth in 4-H and Future Farmers of America clubs. The calf was auctioned to the Prairie County Bank of Hazen for 40¢ a pound. Ann Farris of Biscoe was the only girl who had an entry. (Courtesy of the Stuttgart Public Library.)

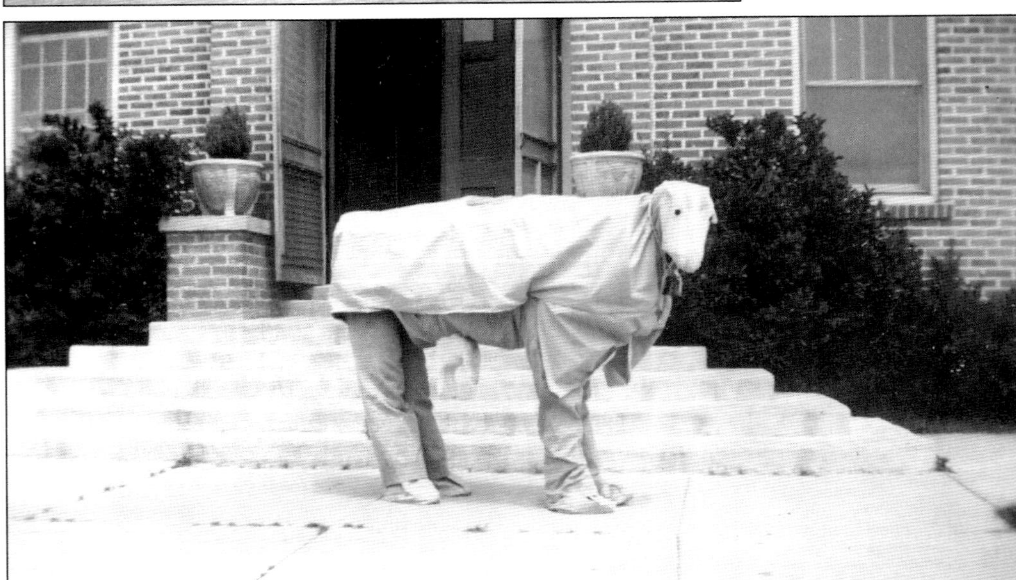

The Fairmount-Independence Home Demonstration Club won $5 for its prizewinning "cow" in a stunt night contest at Hazen in 1940. Billie Wittenauer and Rosie Seidenschwarz played the part of the cow. (Courtesy of the Stuttgart Public Library.)

Six

A German Community Is Renamed

Payer Becomes Ulm

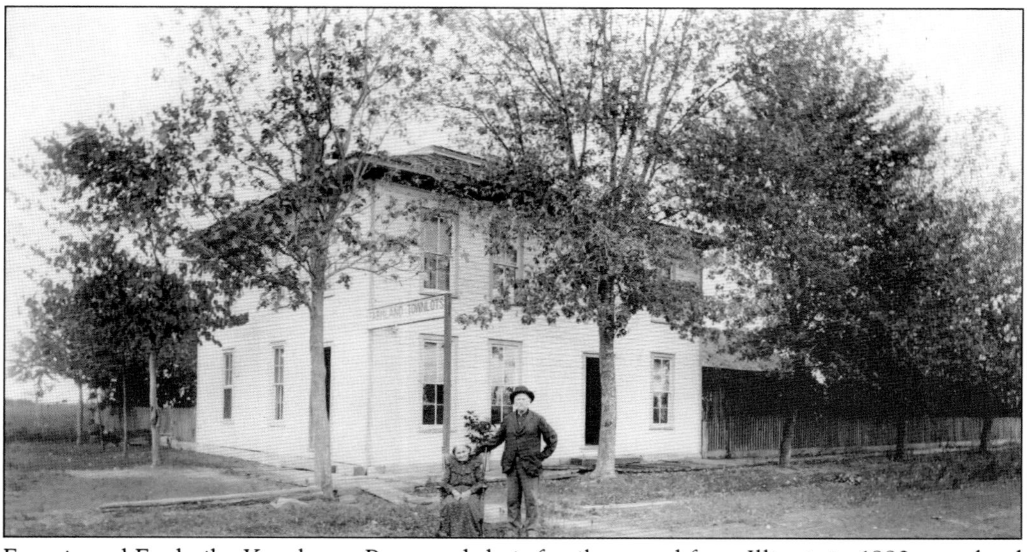

Francis and Frederika Kornbaum Payer and their family moved from Illinois in 1880 onto land they had purchased on the Arkansas–Prairie County line. In 1883, the Cotton Belt rail line was completed, which cut through their property. Other German families came and settled at what become known as Payer (later Ulm). (Courtesy of the Museum of the Arkansas Grand Prairie.)

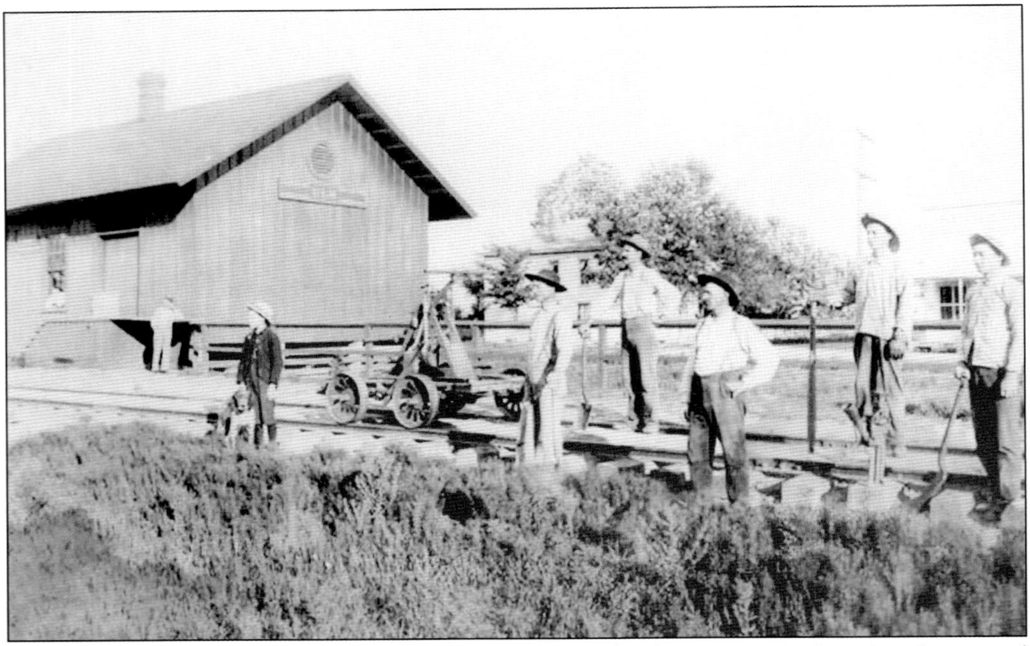

The southwest end of the Ulm depot is shown here with what appears to be a hand-operated railcar on the tracks. After the railroad came through, the Payers moved north of the tracks to take advantage of the rail transportation and subdivided the land into lots. (Courtesy of Henry Wilks.)

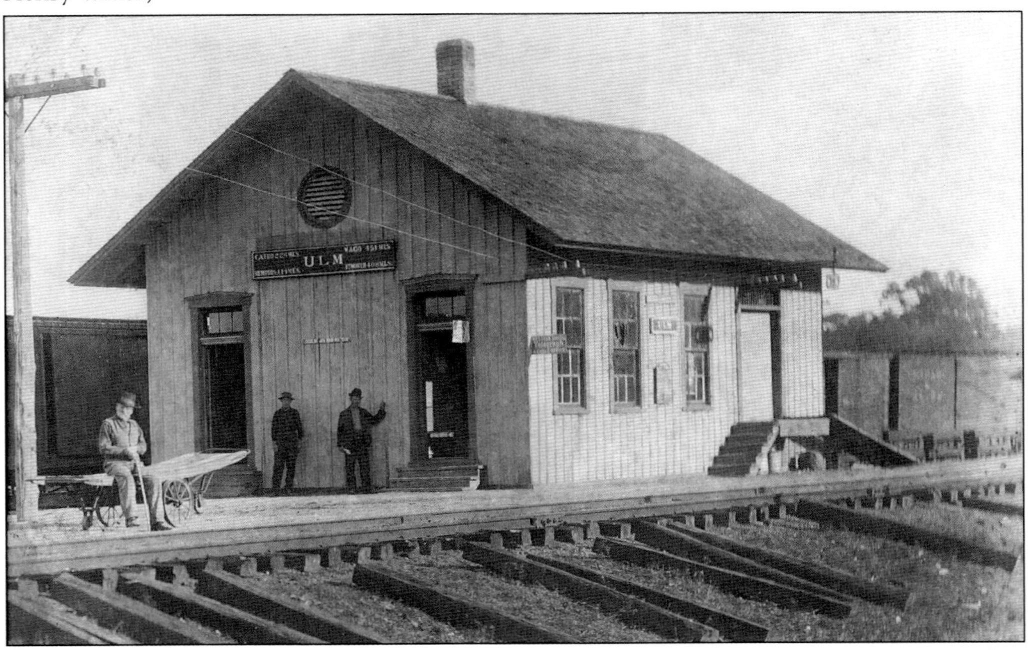

The narrow-gauge Texas & St. Louis Railroad line, which passed through Ulm, was opened in 1883 and was converted to standard gauge three years later. In 1891, the line's name was changed to St. Louis Southwestern Railway and became commonly known as the Cotton Belt. Pictured is the Ulm depot around 1910. (Courtesy of Ray Hanley.)

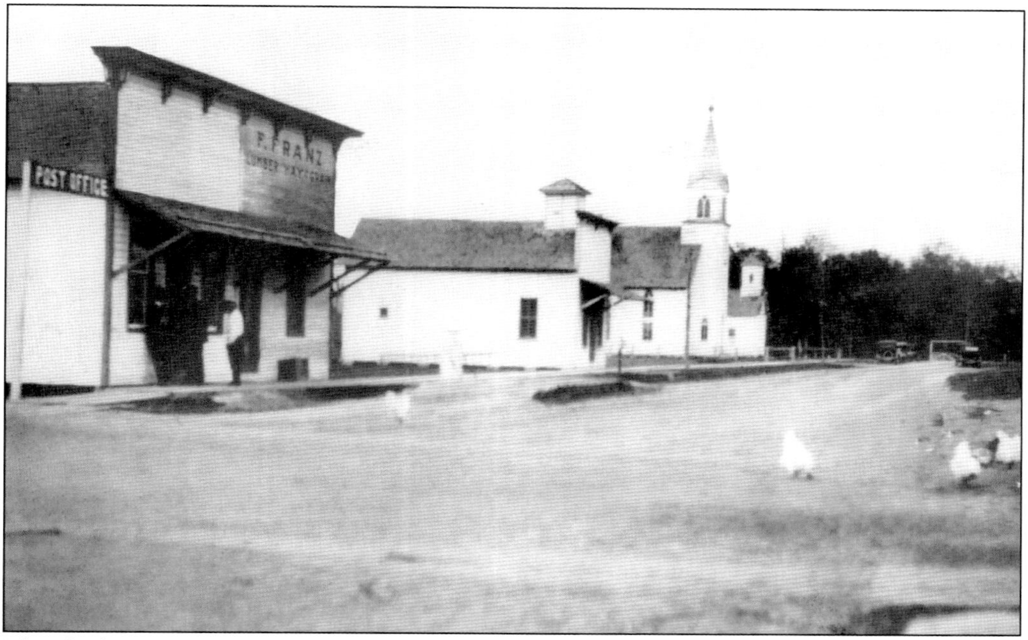

The chickens are roaming free in this c. 1915–1920 photograph of, from left to right, the post office; F. Franz's lumber, hay, and grain store; an unidentified building; the Lutheran church, constructed in 1903; and the old church, built in 1883 one mile west of Ulm, but moved to this location 10 years later. (Courtesy of Carl Renken.)

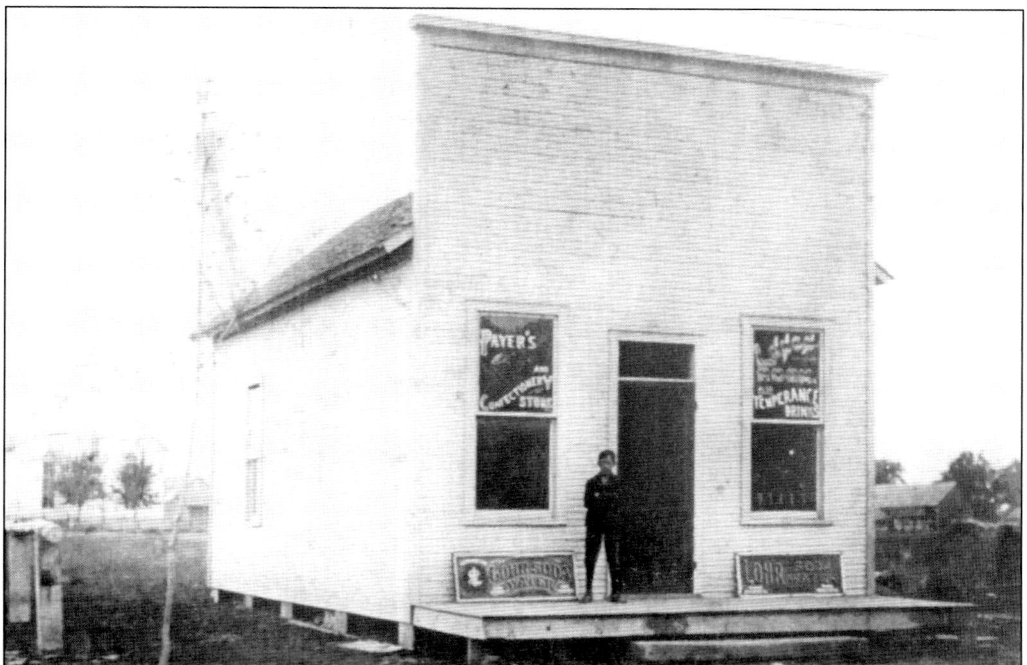

In the early 20th century Payer's Confectionery offered "temperance drinks," like Lohr Soda Water. (Courtesy of the late Irwin Seward.)

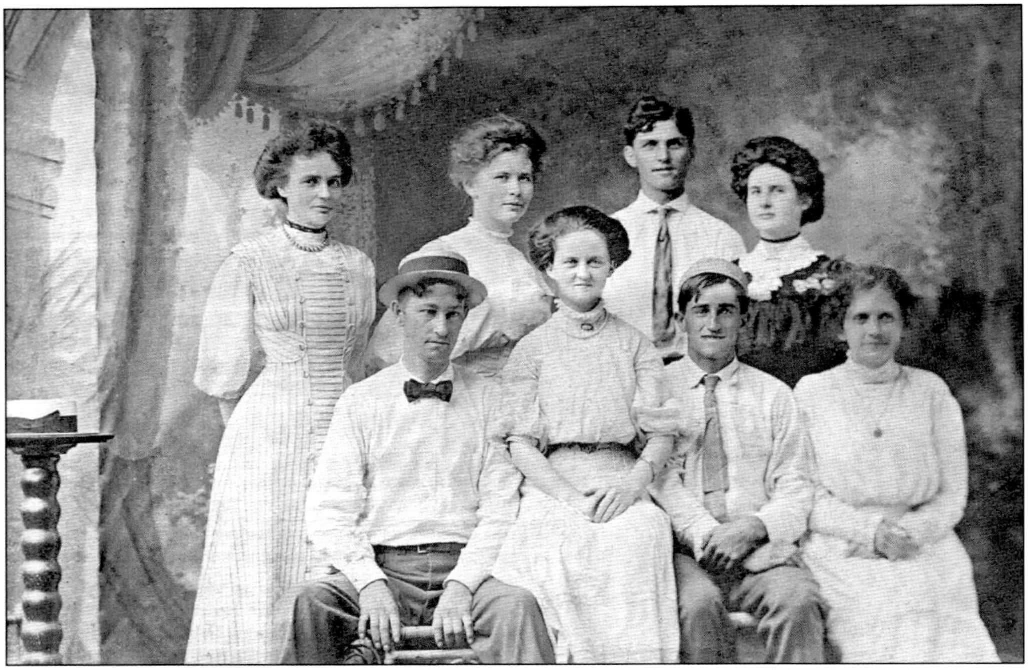

Heinrich Kerksieck (1838–1890) was born in Germany, enlisted with the Union army during the Civil War, and served with the 49th Illinois Volunteer Infantry. He saw some service in Prairie County and liked the countryside. He moved to Ulm in 1889 with his wife, Augusta Kreimier Kerksieck, and family. Their children in this c. 1912 photograph are, from left to right, (first row) Herman, Emilie, Henry (or William), and Sophie; (second row) two unidentified, William (or Henry), and unidentified. (Courtesy of Ann Kerksieck.)

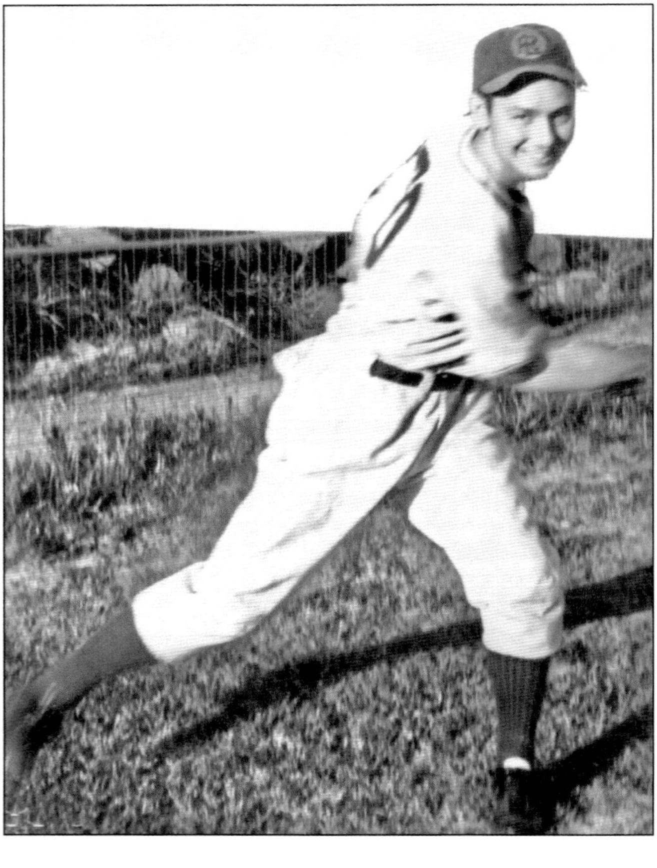

Wayman Kerksieck (1913–1970), the son of H.H. Kerksieck of Ulm, was a pitcher for the Philadelphia Phillies. (Courtesy of Henry Wilks.)

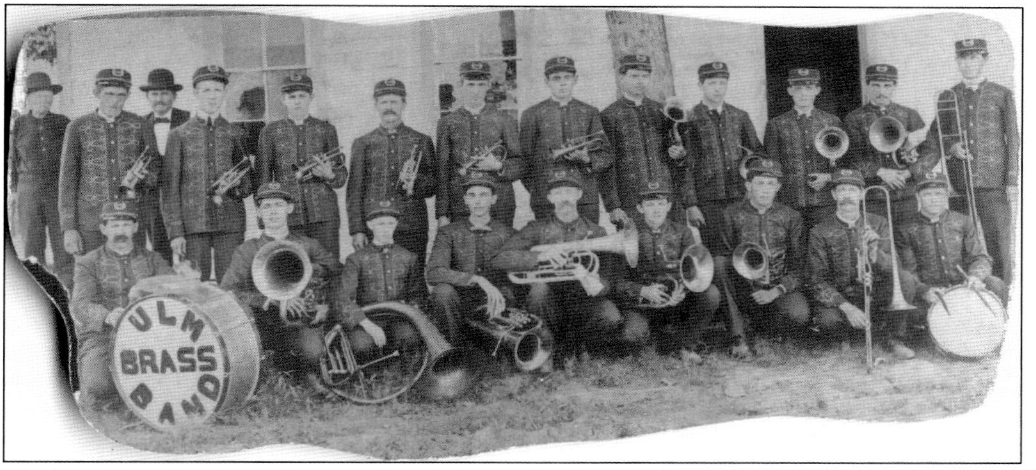

The Ulm Brass Band members are, from left to right, (first row) John Janett, George Hein, Cline Massey, Albert Clawitter, Charles Massey, Willie Moritz, Otto Moritz, Fred Kerksieck, and Charley Payer; (second row) Francis Payer, Mr. Winkler (nonuniform), Walter Bremer, Ed Reitz, Ernest Bremer, Fred Englemann, John Brands, Ed Kornbaum, John Stahl, Johnny Leder, Albert Packebush, Charley Packebush, and H.H. Kerksieck. (Courtesy of the Museum of the Arkansas Grand Prairie.)

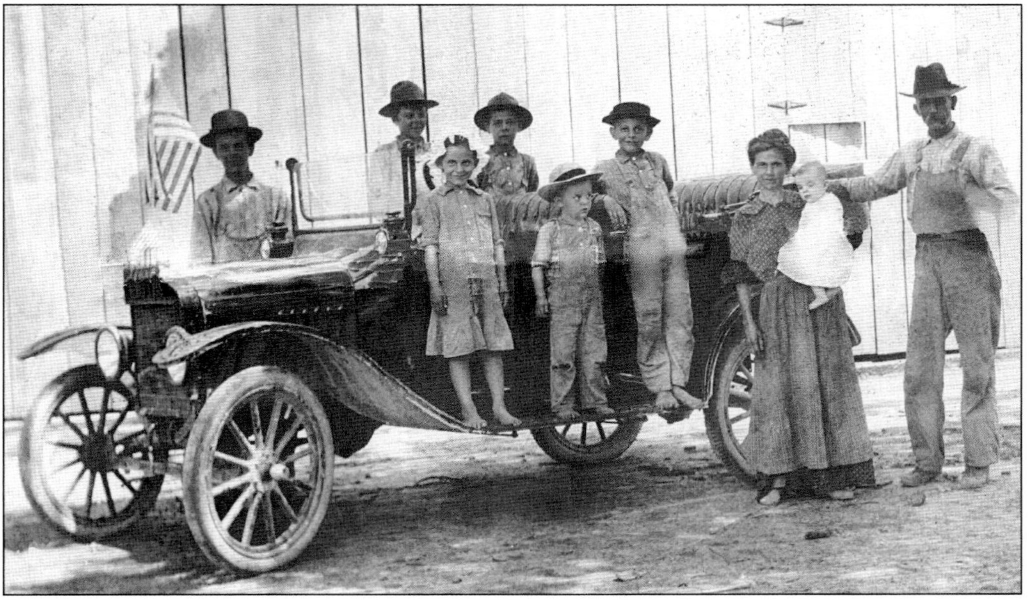

John Joseph (born 1865) and Mary Meyer Fricker moved to near Ulm about 1910. Shown in this c. 1920 photograph are, from left to right, William, Joseph, Marie, John Jr., Roy, Phillip, Mary, Elise, and John Fricker Sr. (Courtesy of Linda Uhiren.)

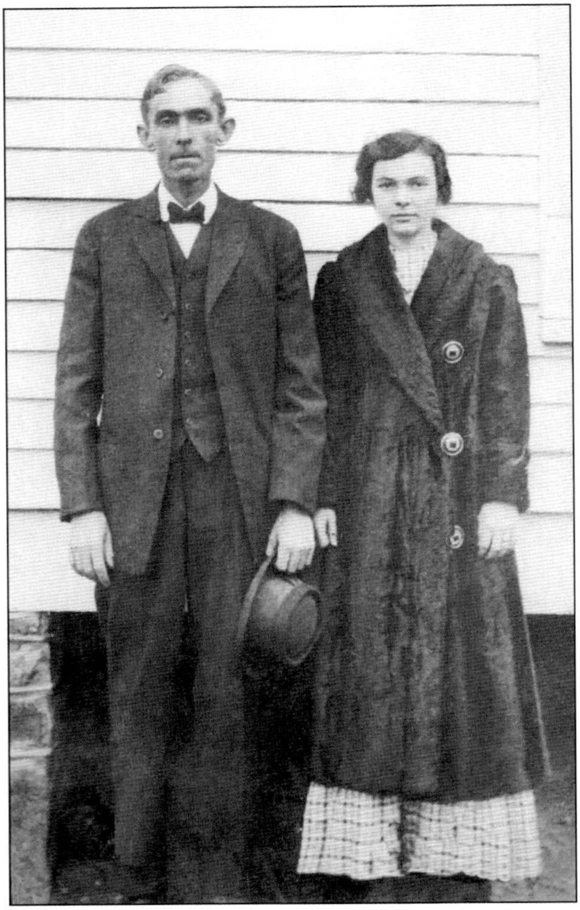

Mary Fricker's brother Mike Meyer (1884–1959) is shown here with his niece Pearl Fricker in an undated photograph. Mike and his mother moved to Heber Springs, Arkansas, in the 1920s where he operated a photographic studio until his death. In 1939, Mike had his name legally changed to Mike Disfarmer. His photographs of rural Arkansans gained national recognition, being regarded as art some years after his death. (Courtesy of Linda Uhiren.)

Shown around 1910–1912 at an Ulm gin are, from left to right, (first row) Alex Clawitter, Ernest Franz, Ted Kreimier, ? Oltman, and Eddie Kerksieck; (second row) ? Brechtl, Alvin Kerksieck, two unidentified, Willis Payer, and Adolph Oltman. (Courtesy of Henry Wilks.)

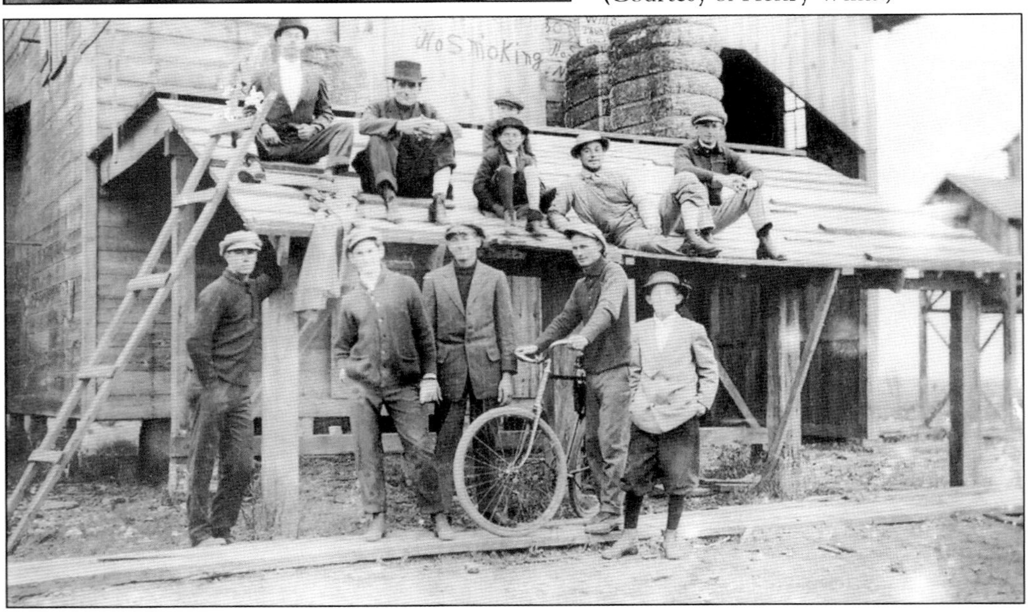

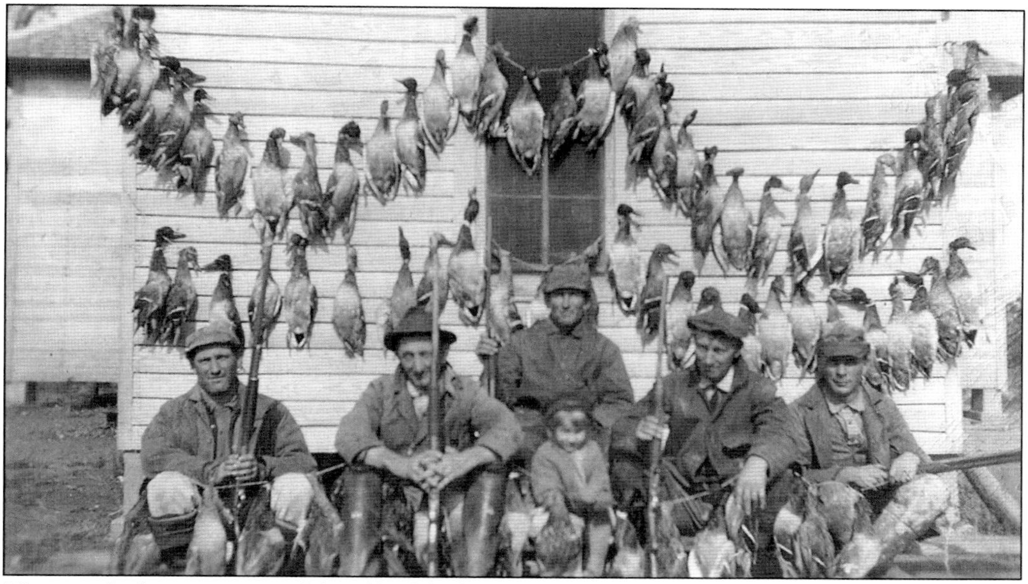

The men had a very successful mallard duck hunt on Maple Island. From left to right are Nubby Packebush, Robert Henry, Leroy Moritz with daughter Pauline, H.H. Kersieck, and William Kornbaum in 1927 or 1928 at the Leroy Moritz home near Ulm. (Courtesy of Ann Kerksieck.)

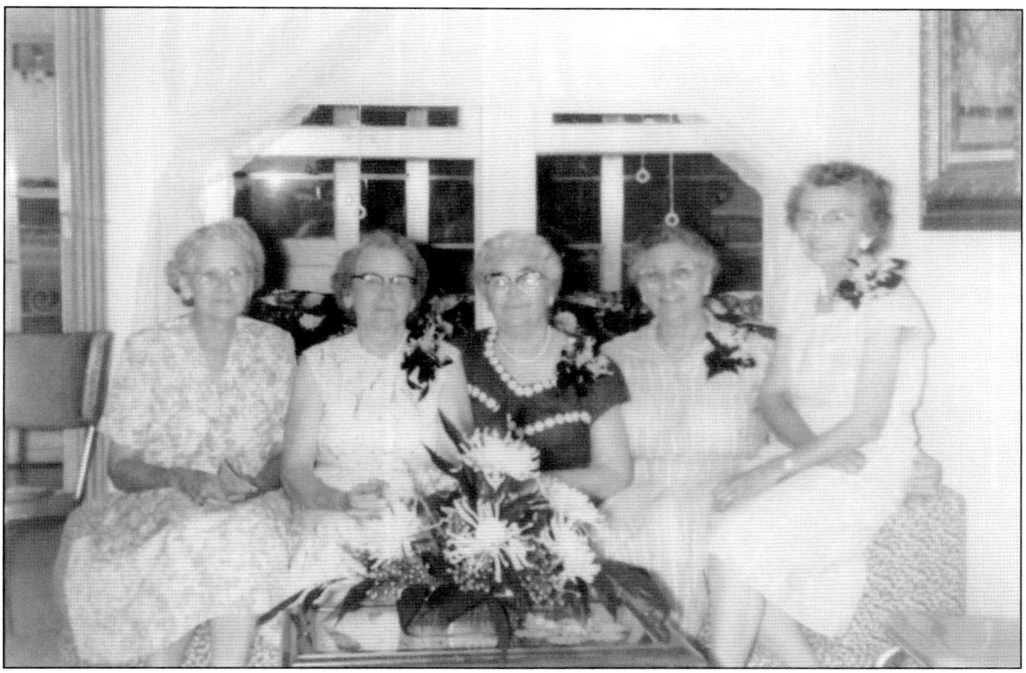

These ladies were celebrating the 32nd anniversary of their Ulm Home Demonstration Club on July 21, 1960. From left to right are Mrs. H.H. Kerksieck, Mrs. ? Strong, Mrs. Jack Bull, Mrs. Bernie Jansen, and Mrs. Henry Wilks. (Courtesy of Henry Wilks.)

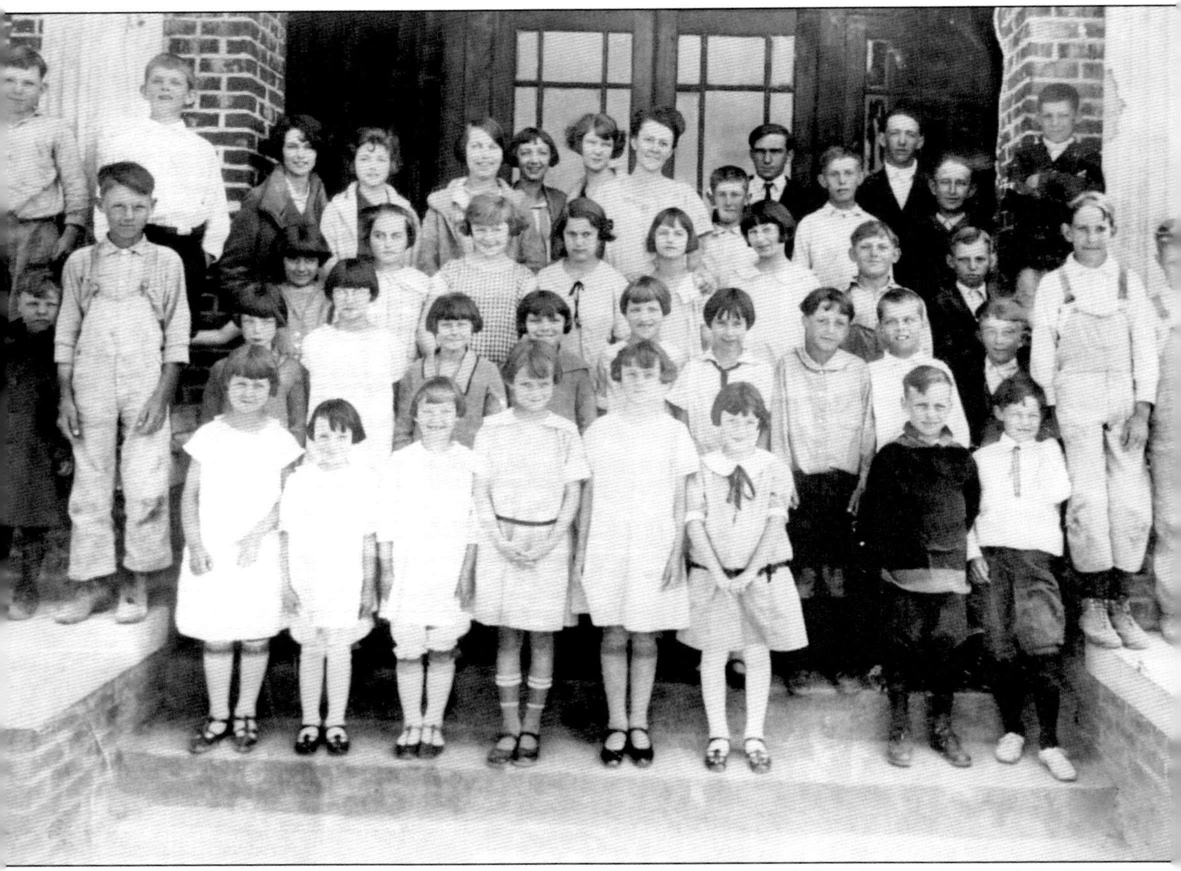

Students are seen in 1924 at the Ulm school, which was consolidated into the DeValls Bluff school system beginning in 1950. On the left cement block are, from left to right, (first row) Chester Hancock and Milton Fricker; (second row) Marvin Trotter and Louis "Binc" Miller. On the right cement block are (first row) Dick Dobbs and Paul Dobbs; (second row) Waymond Kerksieck. On the steps are (first row) Evelyn Michel (Trotter), Maylene Payer, Bernice Roenn, Elvira Roenn, Estelle Timmerman, Florence Payer, Howard Brechtel, and Irwin Seward; (second row) Alberta Kerksieck, Wanda Michel, Marguerite Kerksieck (Brown), Lucile Brechtel (Davis), Loretta Uahlenbrock, Pauline Payer, Royce Patterson, Edward Fricker, and Leo Vester; (third row) Gertrude Lytton (Martin), Minnie (?) Miller, Marie Lytton (Reitz), Emmaline Payne, Bertha Kerksieck, Thelma Wofford, Theodore Clawitter, and Sidney Timmerman; (fourth row) Ellen Feilke (Clawitter), Susanne Clawitter (cousins), Edna Fricker (Mrs Edwin Hosto), Lois Patterson (Kittle), Edna Isringhouse, Mrs. Lydia Payne (teacher), Harold Kerksieck (Dizzy), ? Whittaker (teacher), Kermit Kerksieck, Mann Patterson, and Alva V. ?. (Courtesy of the late Irwin Seward.)

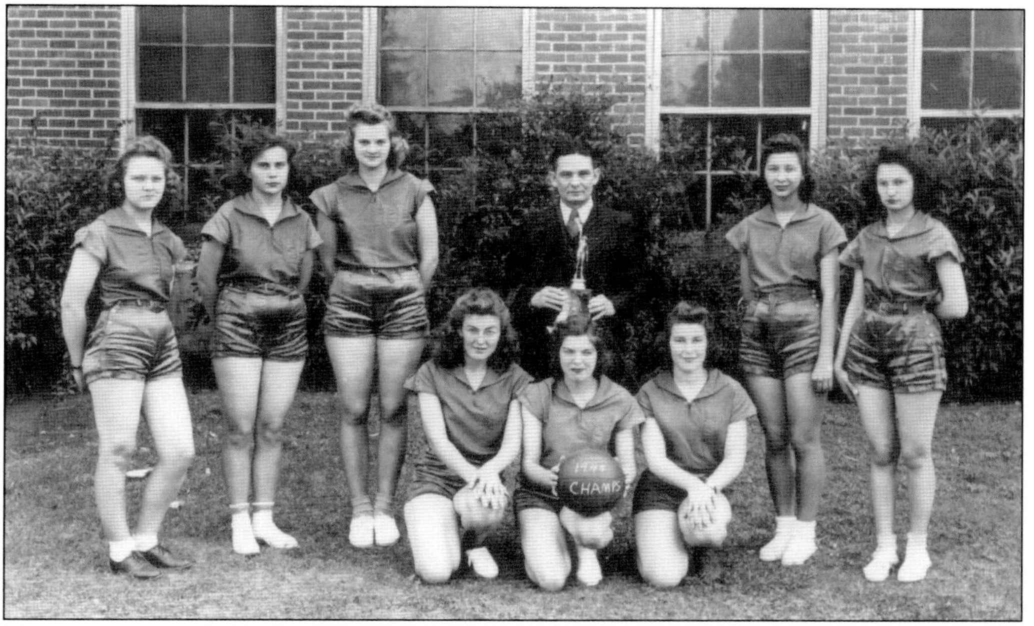

The girls' basketball team at Ulm High School made the town proud in 1944 by becoming the district champions. Pictured are, from left to right, (first row) Lucy Cruthis Brown, Nedra Kremeier Hansen, and Florence Trede Murdock; (second row) Dorothy Payor Wilks, Gracie Dobbs Eifling, Gertrude Schroeder Rabeneck, coach Forest Shumate, Betty Brands Oliphant, and Kathryn Hahn Hein. (Courtesy of Henry Wilks.)

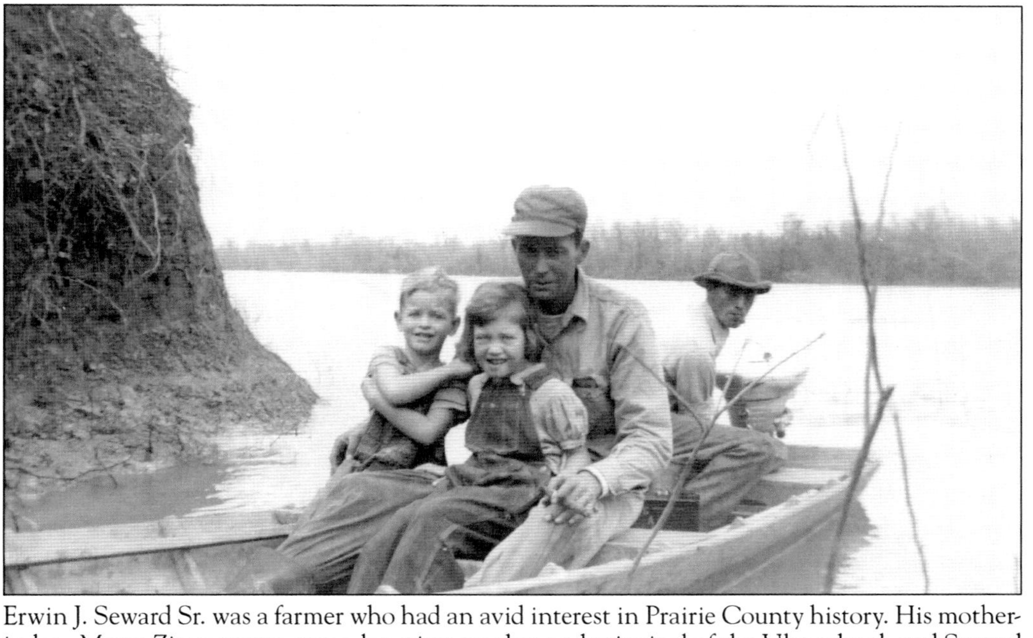

Erwin J. Seward Sr. was a farmer who had an avid interest in Prairie County history. His mother-in-law, Marea Zimmerman, was a longtime teacher and principal of the Ulm school, and Seward coached the girls' basketball team there in the 1930s. Pictured in June 1952, Seward and his children Irwin J. Jr. and Georgia, with Clifford Timmerman manning the outboard motor, are enjoying a boat ride. (Courtesy of Georgia Seward.)

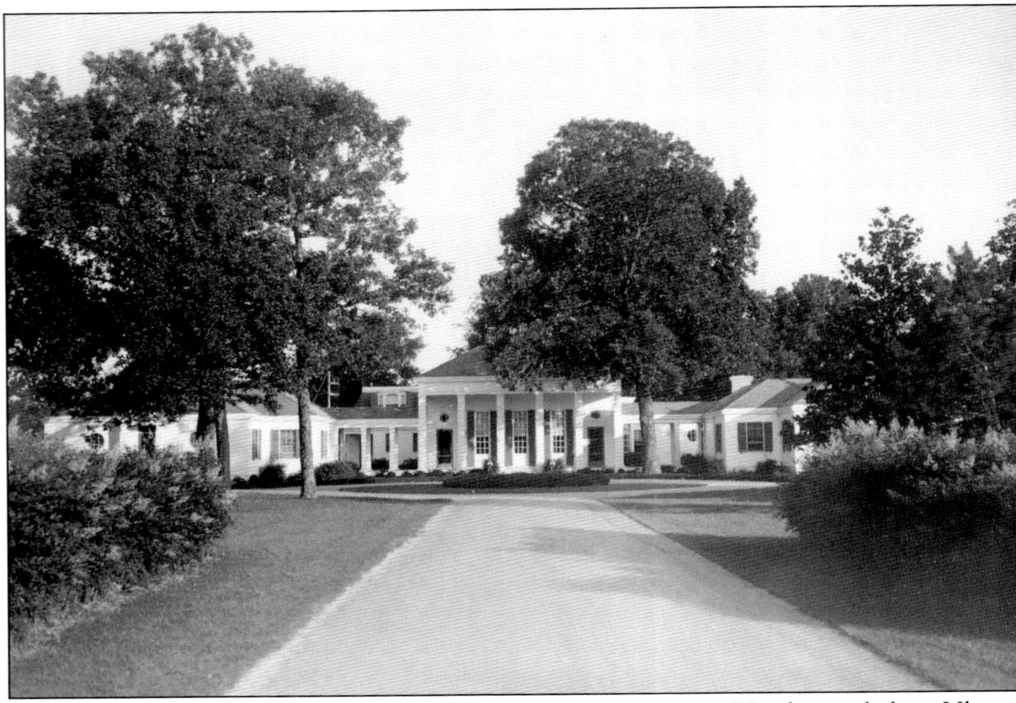

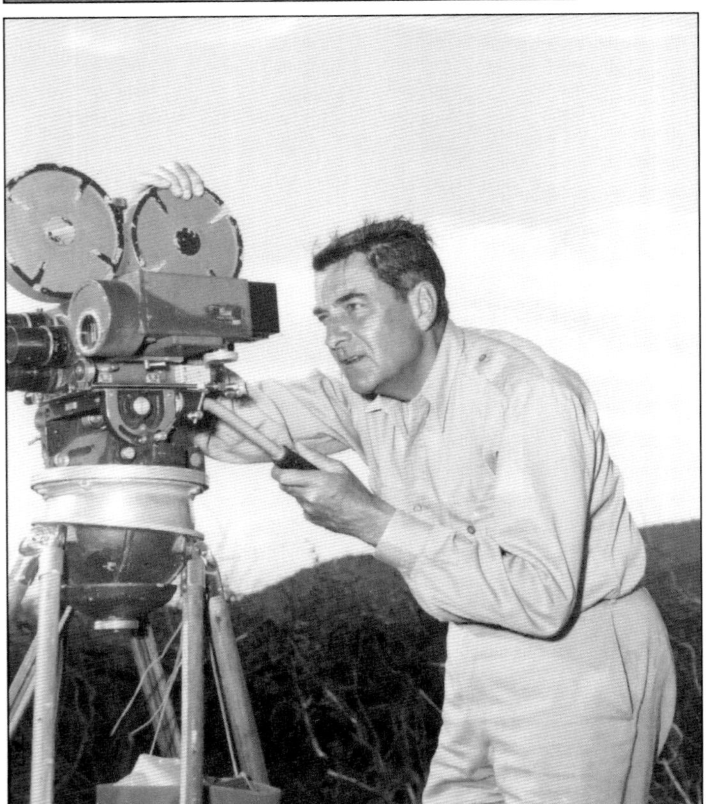

Not far north from Ulm is the duck hunting camp and retreat of the late Edgar Monsanto Queeny of St. Louis, which features buildings and landscape elements constructed between 1929 and 1968. The design of the main house is Colonial Revival. Following the death of Mrs. Queeny in 1975 the property was sold to the Frank Lyons family. The 1950s photograph of Queeny (left) was taken in Africa during the filming of *Masai*. (Courtesy of the Museum of the Arkansas Grand Prairie.)

Seven

The Land of Cotton

Biscoe, Beulah (Upper Hill), and Brasfield

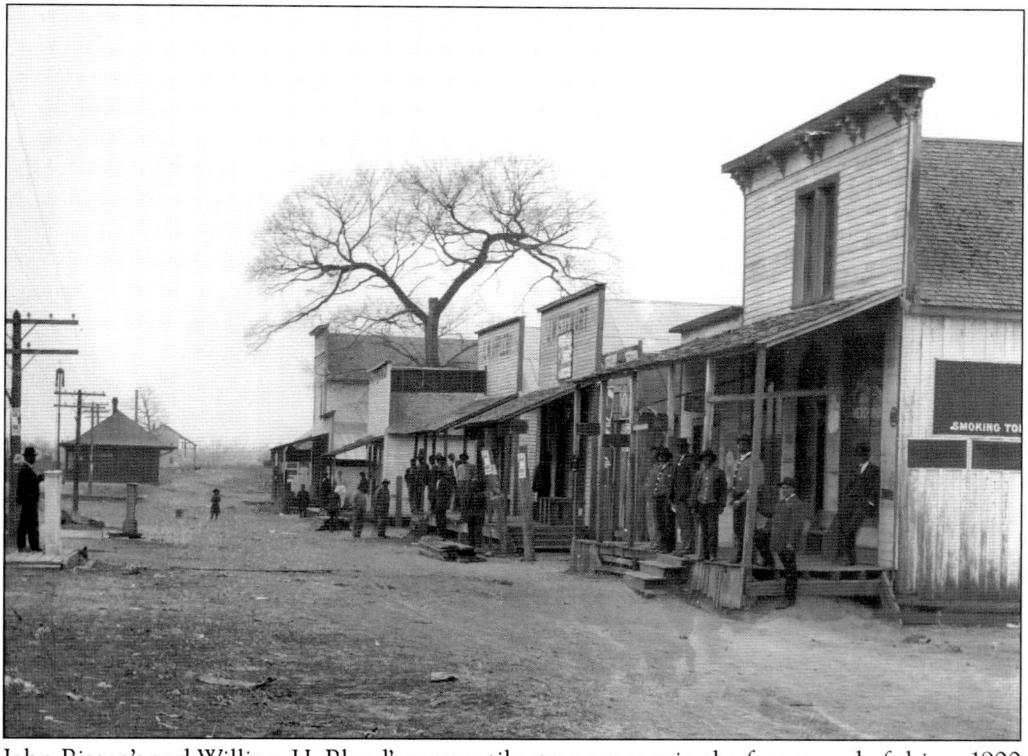

John Biscoe's and William H. Bland's mercantile store appears in the foreground of this c. 1900 photograph. It was replaced by a brick store building owned by the Scroggins and later by Brooks and Mable Betzner. At the end of the block is A.L. Aydelott's general store. To the left is the train depot, and at a distance is the cotton gin. (Courtesy of the Torrreyson Library, University of Central Arkansas.)

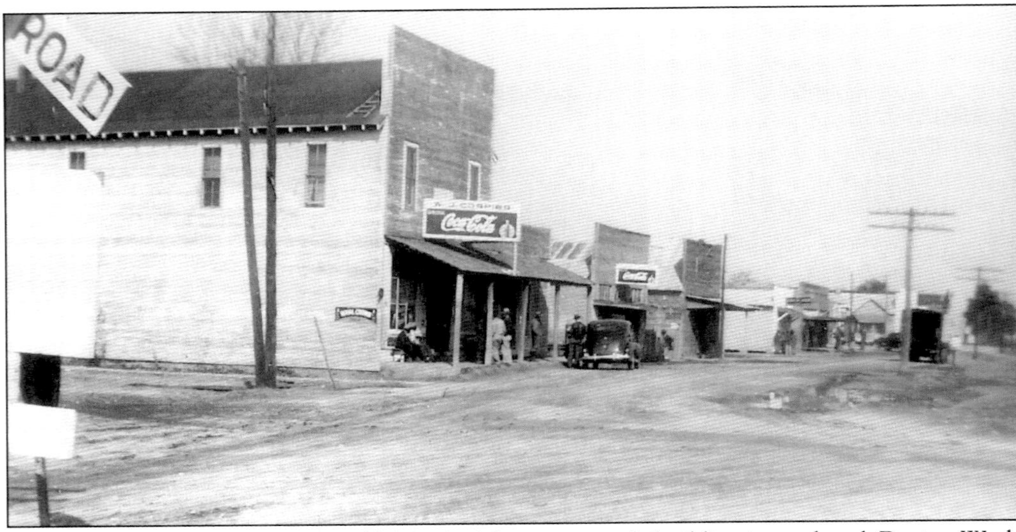

In 1933, W.J. Corpier turned the old A.L. Aydelott mercantile building into a hotel. During World War II, glider pilots received their training at Stuttgart. On weekends, some of the servicemen would come to Biscoe to drink and have a good time. One Saturday night, an inebriated Upper Hill man checked into the hotel and later fell out of a window of his second-story room, luckily receiving only minor injuries. (Courtesy of John Naill.)

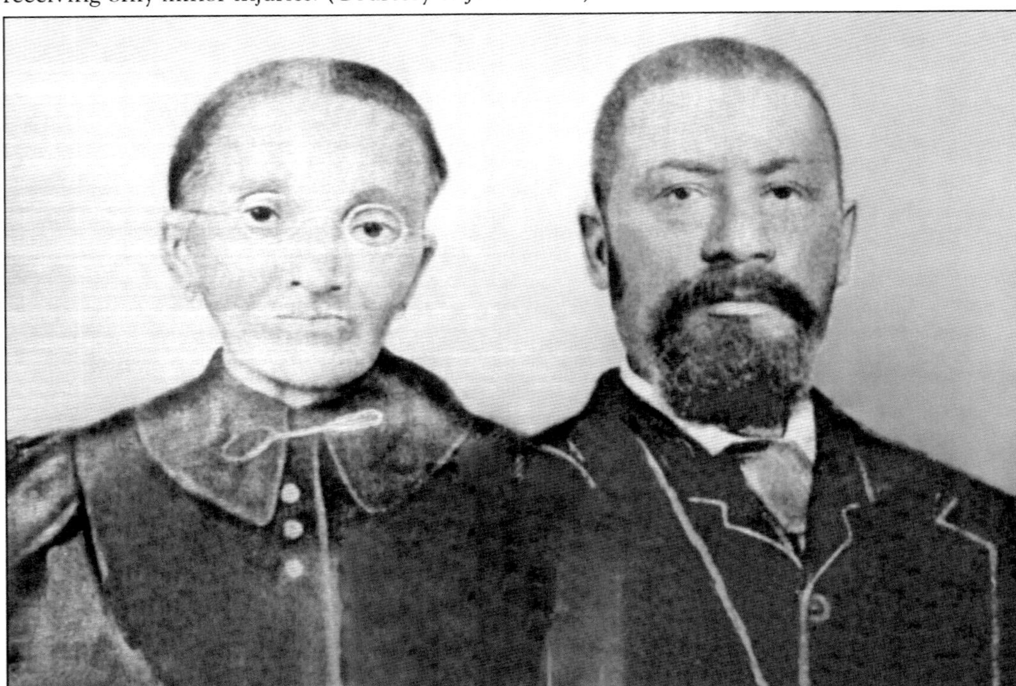

George Washington Toone was a member of Company 1 of the 54th US Colored Infantry during the Civil War and was injured during the war in a train wreck on the Memphis & Little Rock Railroad. His wife was Rachel, the daughter of a Tennessee slave owner, Charles Temple, and his slave Johanna. He settled at Biscoe and served as a minister there. (Courtesy of the late Ruth Odom Bonner.)

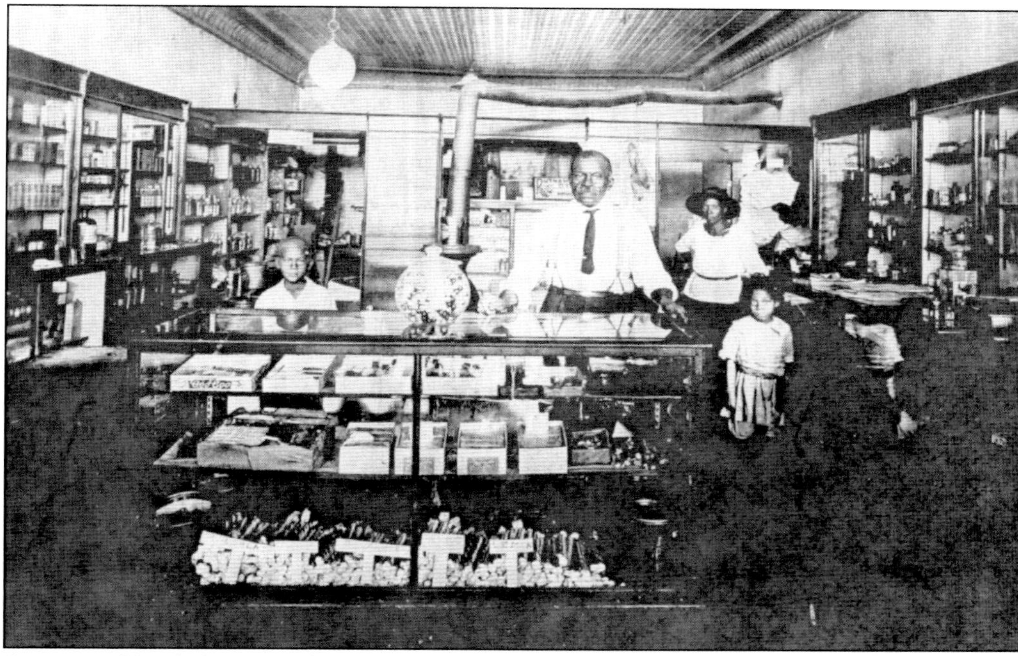

George and Rachel Toone's daughter Ada married Dr. Elijah B. Odom, who practiced medicine at Biscoe from 1899 to 1924. Odom appears in this photograph in his drugstore with two of his children and an unidentified woman. The Odoms also had a general mercantile store in Biscoe. (Courtesy of the late Ruth Odom Bonner.)

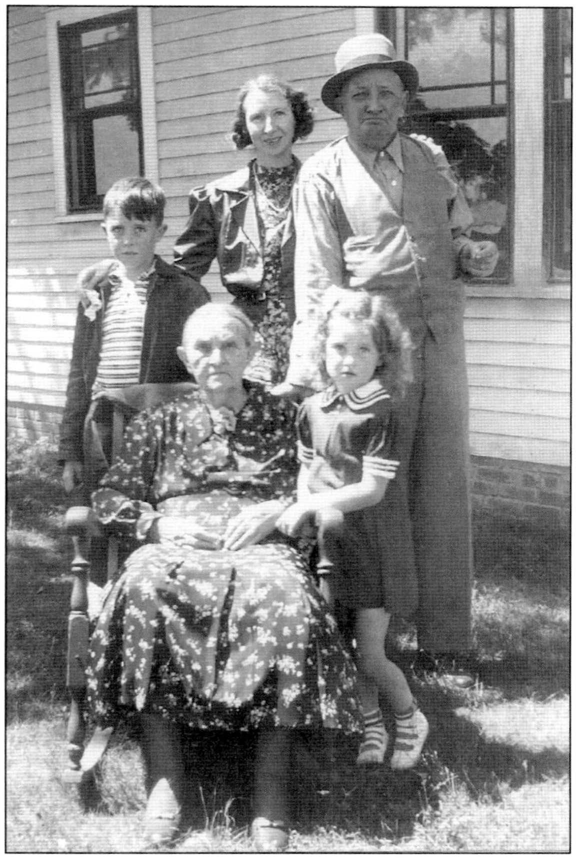

Charles and Ann Betzner moved to Biscoe in 1911 when they bought part of the George Naill farm east of Highway 11. Appearing in this 1945 photograph with them are their daughter Kathleen Betzner Farris and their grandchildren Roger and Ann Farris. (Courtesy of Rita Farris.)

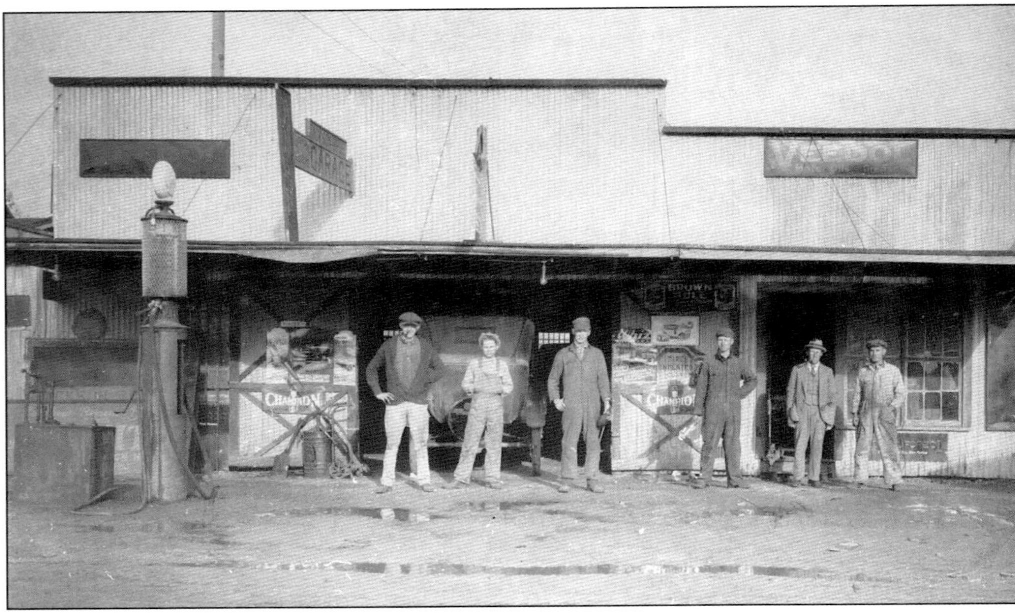

Jackson's Garage was on Madison Street at Biscoe across the street from the Scroggins general store. Pictured in 1924 are, from left to right, Raymond Farris, Jack Farris, Ed "Salty" Farris, Tom Reynolds, Ollie Reynolds, and Ted Jackson. (Courtesy of Rita Farris.)

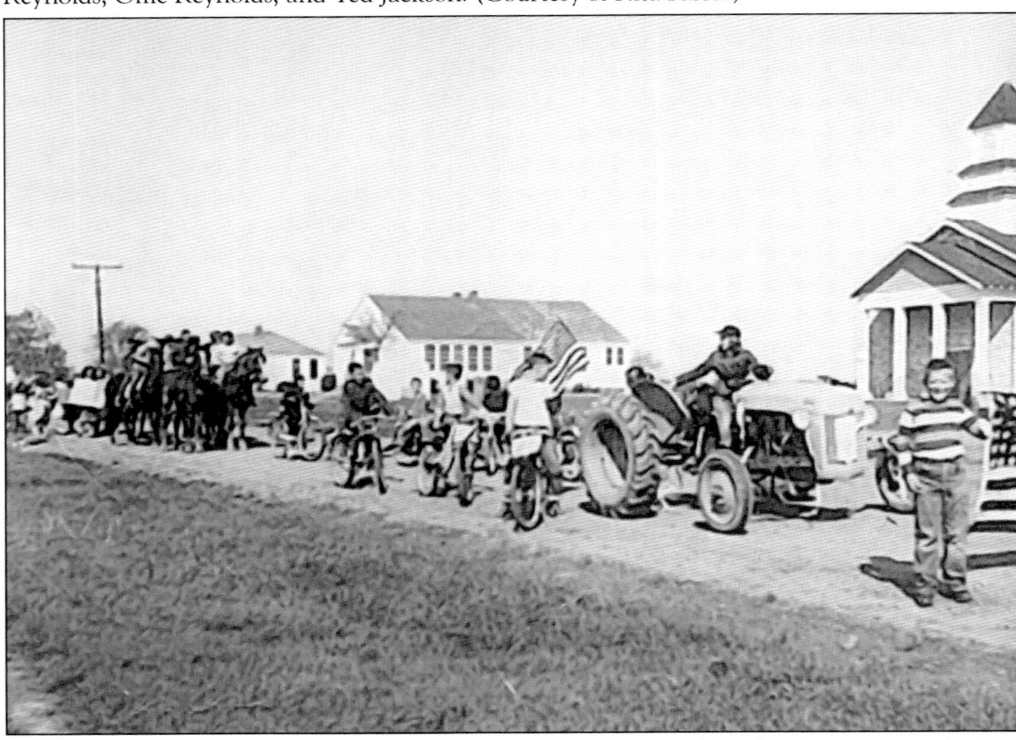

A parade winds its way through Biscoe as part of the vacation Bible school program at the First Baptist Church about 1952. Patsy Clark Prince is driving the tractor. The church appears to the right, followed by the elementary school and community building. (Courtesy of Patsy Clark Prince.)

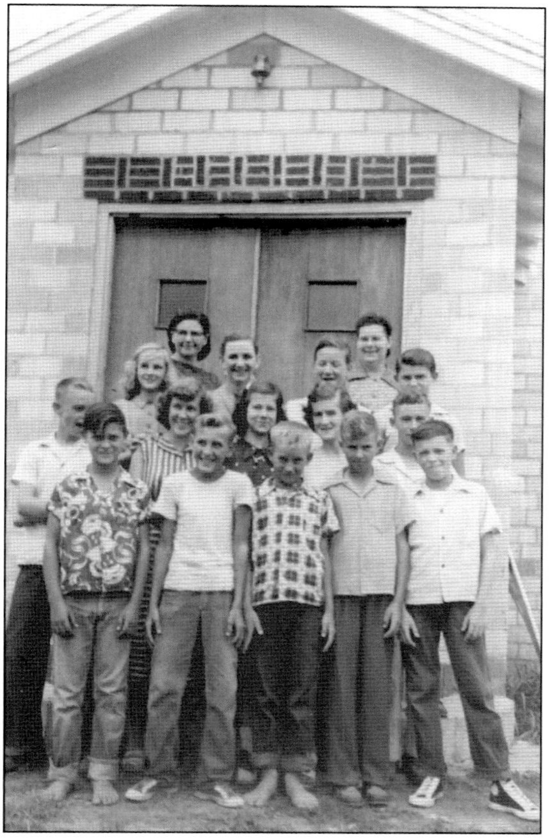

In the 1950s, the Assembly of God Church was a place where young people could meet and socialize. From left to right are (first row) Billy Jack Alberson, Jimmy Nicholas, Bronson Browning, Dewey Hall, and Richie Prine: (second row) Clifton (Pete) Castleberry, Barbara Nicholas, Betty Joe Overturf, Omega Coulson Miller, and unidentified; (third row) Patsy Browning Castleberry, Julia Mae Hall, Sharon Mross, and Roby Alton Alberson: (fourth row) Reba Dixon and Annie Alberson. (Courtesy of David Smith.)

The state's deer population was quickly disappearing by the 1920s, but the Arkansas Game and Fish Commission's restocking program was a resounding success. Biscoe area men just in from a hunt in the 1950s are, from left to right Clarence Leroy "Duke" Gurley, Joe Cook, Marvin Gurley, Burvel Mayhew, and Dallas Tipton. (Courtesy of David Smith.)

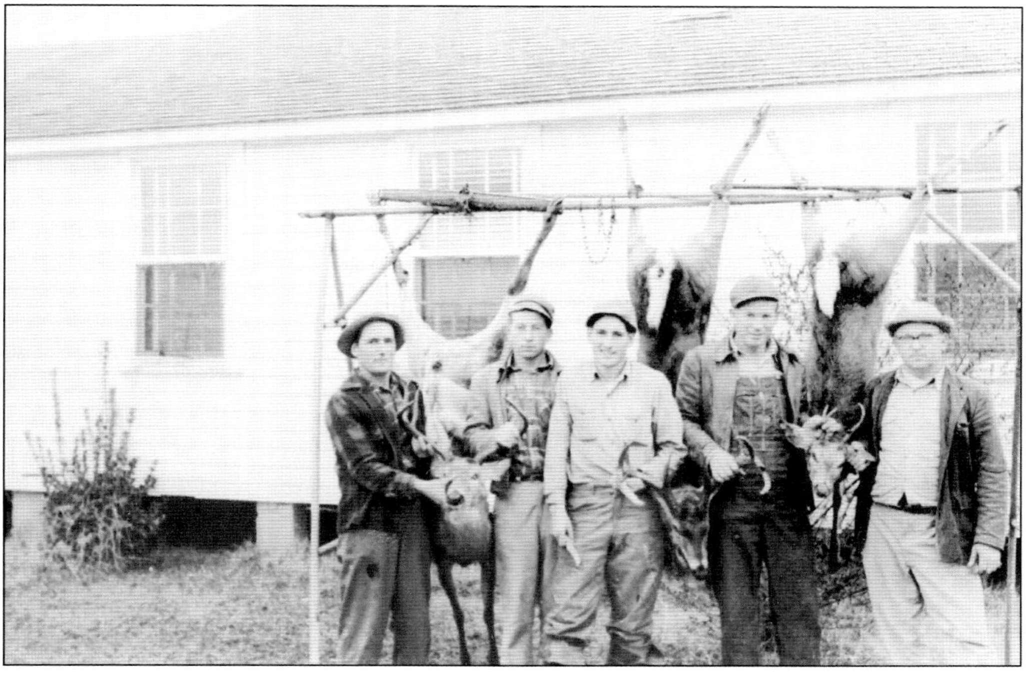

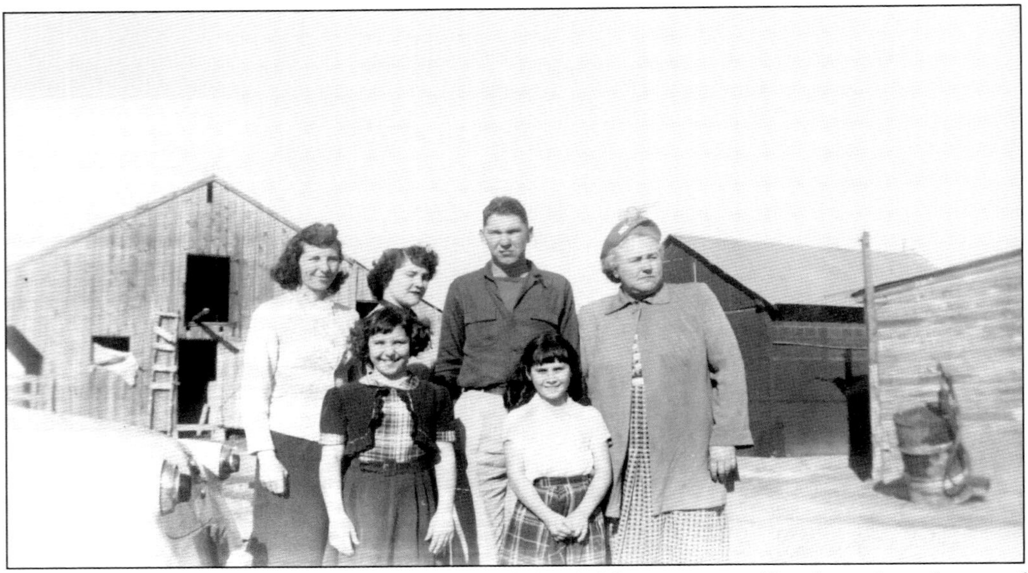

In 1938, the Farm Security Administration subdivided large tracts of land north and west of Brasfield and around Biscoe into 40-acre lots for a resettlement project for farm families needing homes. A house, barn, chicken house, smokehouse, and toilet were constructed on each unit. Henry and Ethel Wagner purchased one of the lots. Shown in this c. 1952 photograph are, from left to right, (first row) Bonnie Wagner and Phyllis Dickson; (second row) Lois, Dora Mae, Kirby, and Ethel Wagner. (Courtesy of June Pendergrass Cox.)

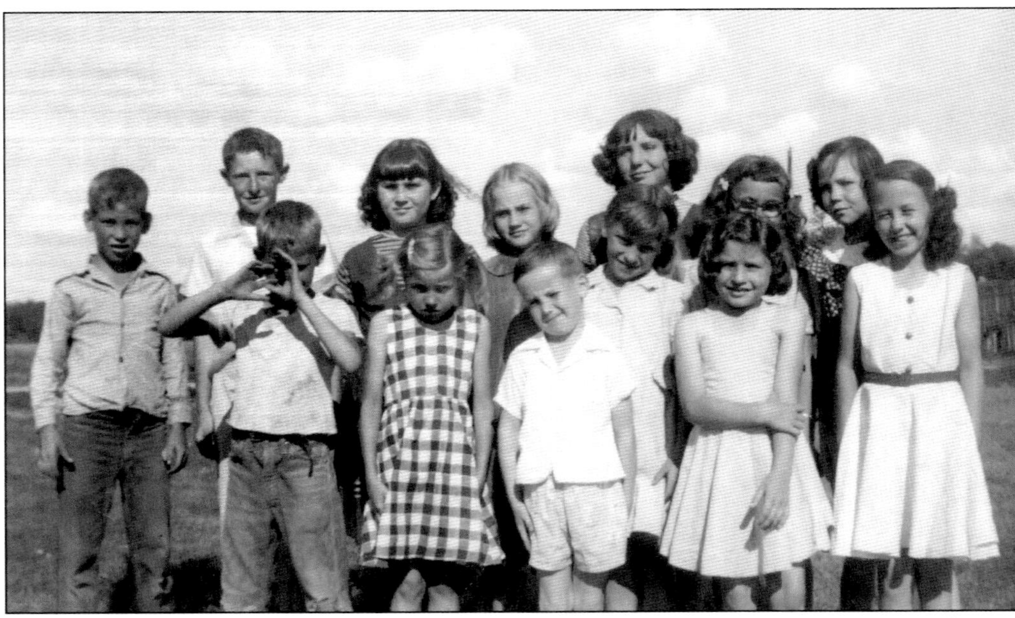

Photographed in 1953, these Biscoe farm children are, from left to right, (first row) Coy Thomas, Mary Ellen Cook, Rickey Don Cook, Margaret Thomas, Maudie Nail Robinson, and Shira Jo Rollins; (second row) James Thomas, Loran Dixon, Phyllis Dixon, Linda Cook Hall, Bonnie Wagner, Gloria Hall Strohl, and Charlene Keel. (Courtesy of June Pendergrass Cox.)

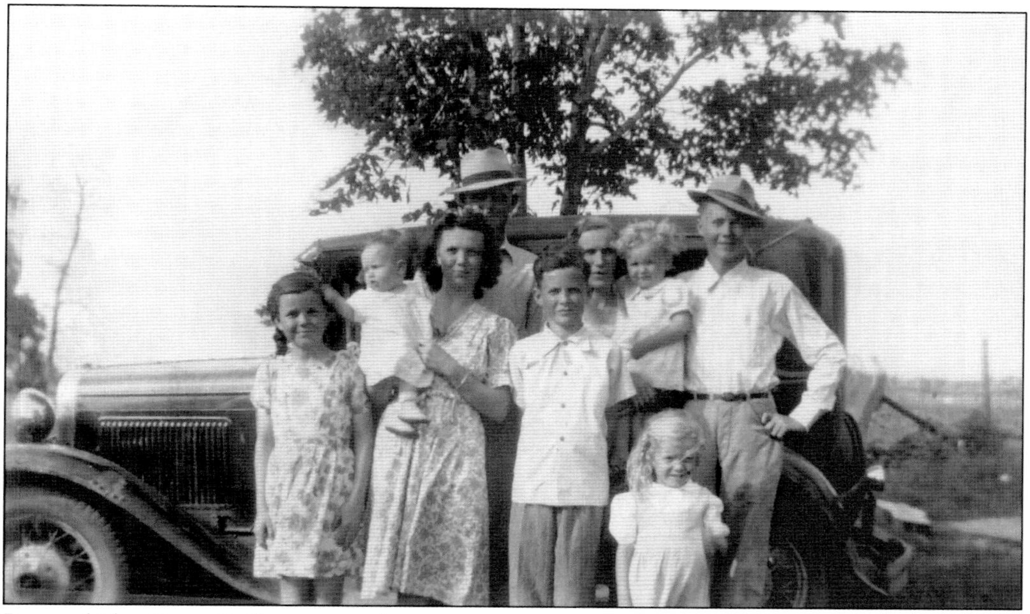

Roy and Floy Petty Coffman moved to the Biscoe Farm area in the 1920s. The Coffmans sharecropped cotton there and later at Letchworth, the Plunkett-Bond farm, Black Lake, and other places in Prairie County. In the photograph of the Coffman family are, from left to right, Lorrain Coffman; Charlotte and mother, Ina Dell Coffman Carr; Roy, Wayne, Floy, and Margaret Coffman; and Calvin Carr. Floy Sue Coffman is in the foreground. (Courtesy of June Pendergrass Cox.)

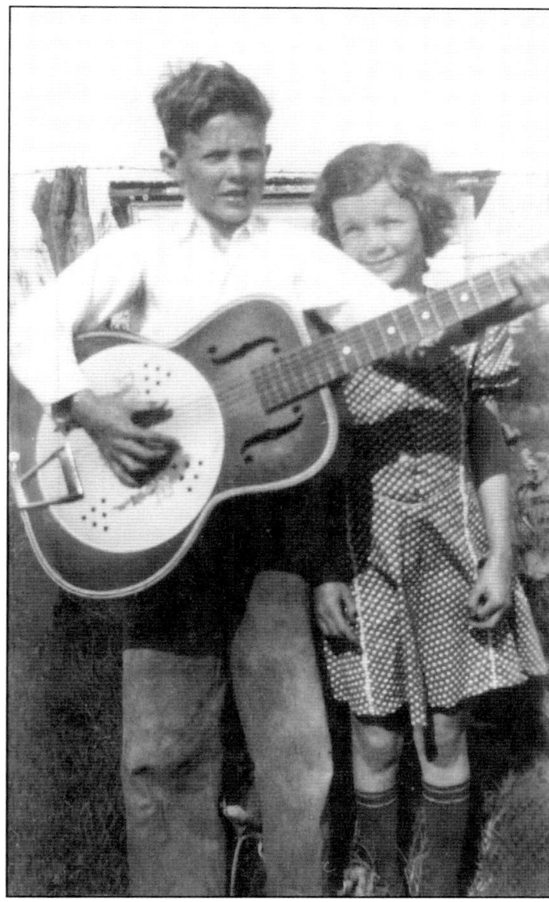

Wayne and Lorraine Coffman appear in this 1942 photograph. Wayne learned to set type at the *White River Journal* newspaper office in Des Arc and excelled as an artist. From an early age, he played guitar, and he and Lorraine played and sang for church groups and other gatherings. (Courtesy of June Pendergrass Cox.)

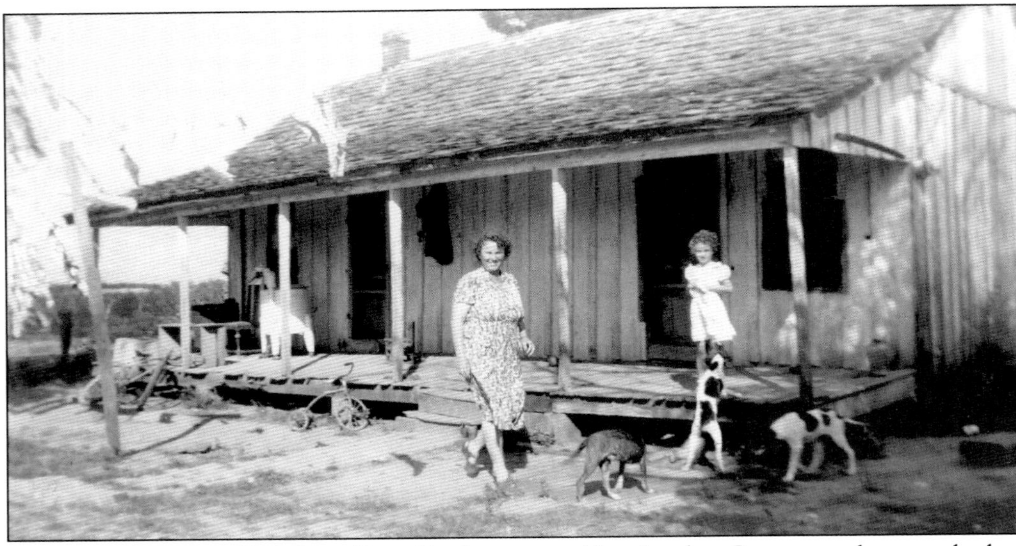

On September 30, 1953, Athena Petty Pendergrass and her daughter June were photographed on the front porch of their home on the Plunkett-Bond plantation at Beulah, three miles north of Biscoe. Athena and her husband, Bill, were tenant farmers there. Her father and mother migrated to the area from near Hector, Pope County, in the 1930s, as did many others. (Courtesy of June Pendergrass Cox.)

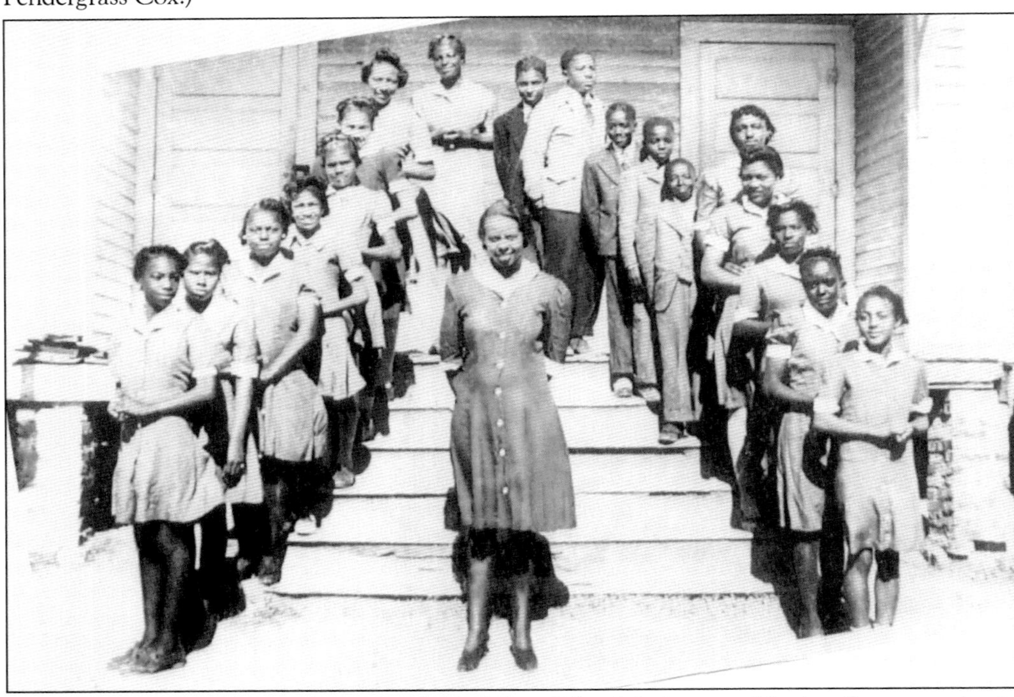

Bennie Lee Bryant, the teacher at Beulah's Aiken School (a Rosenwald school), appears in the foreground in this c. 1940 photograph. From left to right are Ella Mae Thomas, Lilly May Allen, Clara May Myles, Imogene Leachman, Deney Baily, Dorothy Mae Snow, "Rush" Jones, Ed Rycraw, Sonny Franklin, Burnis Woods, Elbert Thomas, Percy West, Lodis Williams, Ivory Franklin, Hannah Pinkney, Marie Anderson, and Lutilla Rycraw. (Courtesy of Annie Williams.)

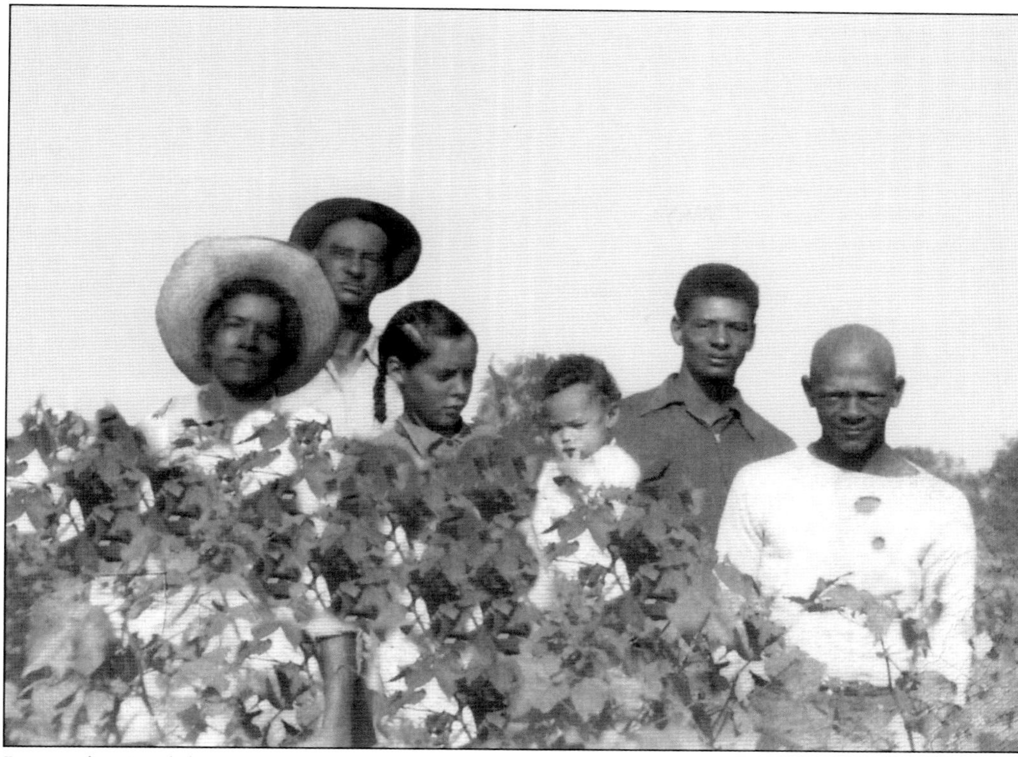

Pictured at Beulah in 1950 are, from left to right, Annie Williams and her husband, Arthur Sr.; Dolores Alexander Williams with son Marvin Lee; her husband, Arthur Jr.; and his brother Joe Lewis Williams. (Courtesy of Delores Alexander Williams.)

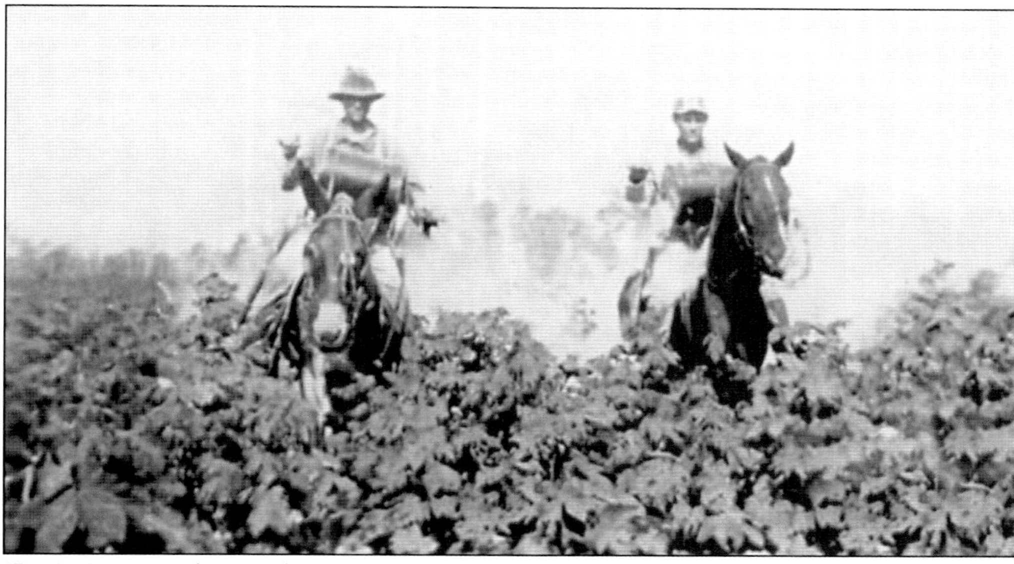

"Doc" Watson and an unidentified man are distributing a pesticide in a cotton field, probably on Upper Hill, about 1950. The poison dust used to kill army worms and grasshoppers was distributed from canisters by a hand-crank blower through tubes pointed behind the men. Purportedly, this dust was less toxic than other pesticides used on area farms. (Courtesy of June Pendergrass Cox.)

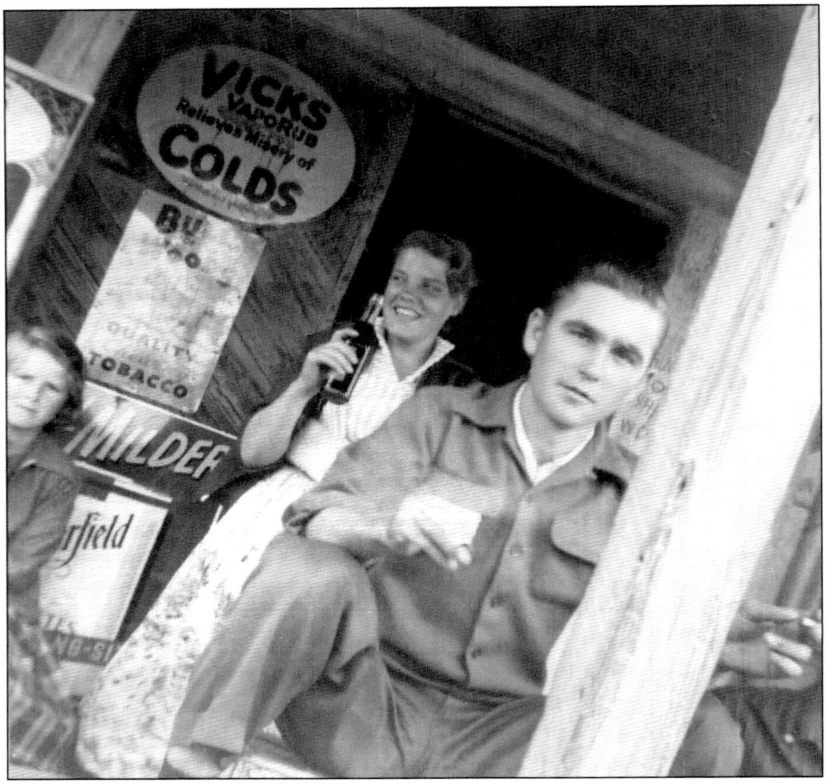

Walter Black's little store was located at Beulah, at the corner of Highway 33 and Sandy Banks Road. Relaxing on an autumn day in 1957 on the porch of the store are, from left to right, Donna Martin, Lois Young, and Scoot Hughes. Walter's brother Fred had a store in Biscoe. (Courtesy of June Cox.)

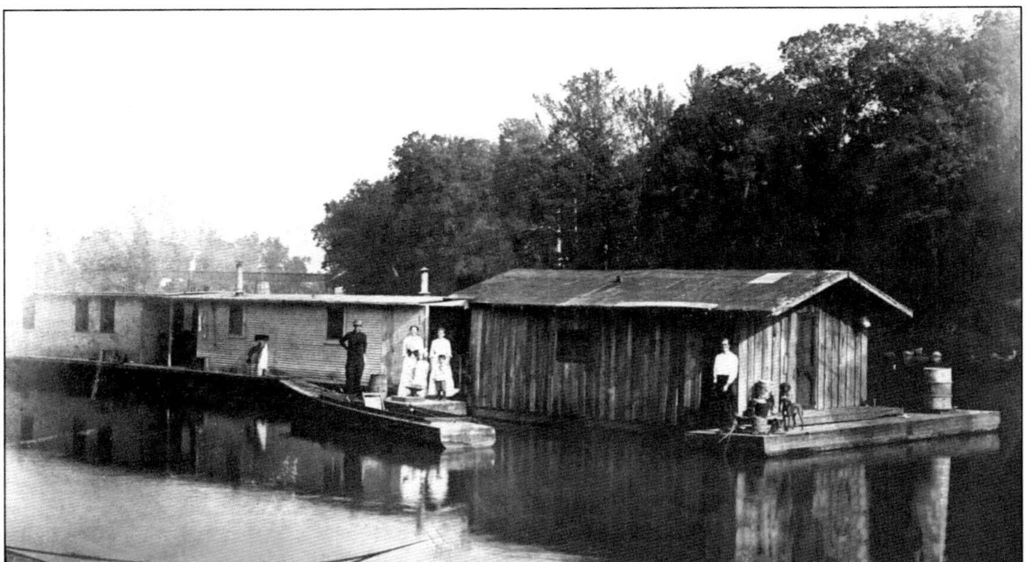

The Rock Island turn bridge is in the background of this c. 1910 photograph of the Potter houseboats on the Cache River at Brasfield. Individual identifications are not possible, but on board would be Reuben Talley Potter and his wife, Emmaline Mashburn Potter. Possibly also on board could be Emmaline's brother William Z.M. "Gum" Mashburn and his wife, Mattie. (Courtesy of Torreyson Library, University of Central Arkansas.)

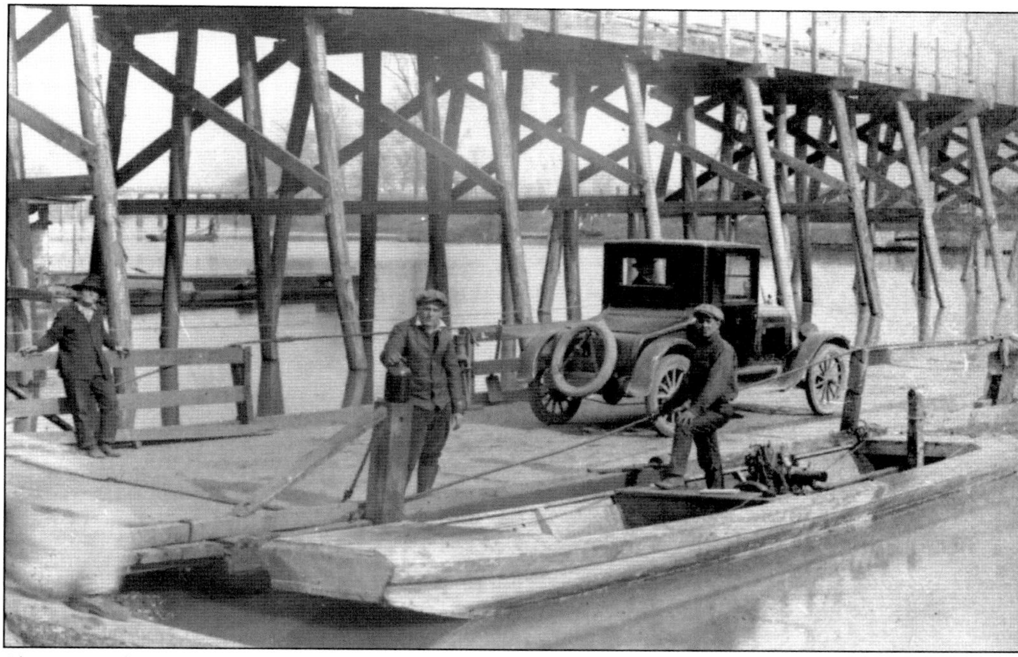

Shown in this 1924 photograph of the Brasfield ferry on the Cache River are, from left to right, Jack Harris, Joe Carmack, and Oliver Sayger. Around Christmas that year, the bridge was open for traffic on the old Highway 70 from Little Rock to Memphis. A new higher roadbed was built between DeValls Bluff and Brinkley and opened in 1934. (Courtesy of the Torreyson Library, University of Central Arkansas.)

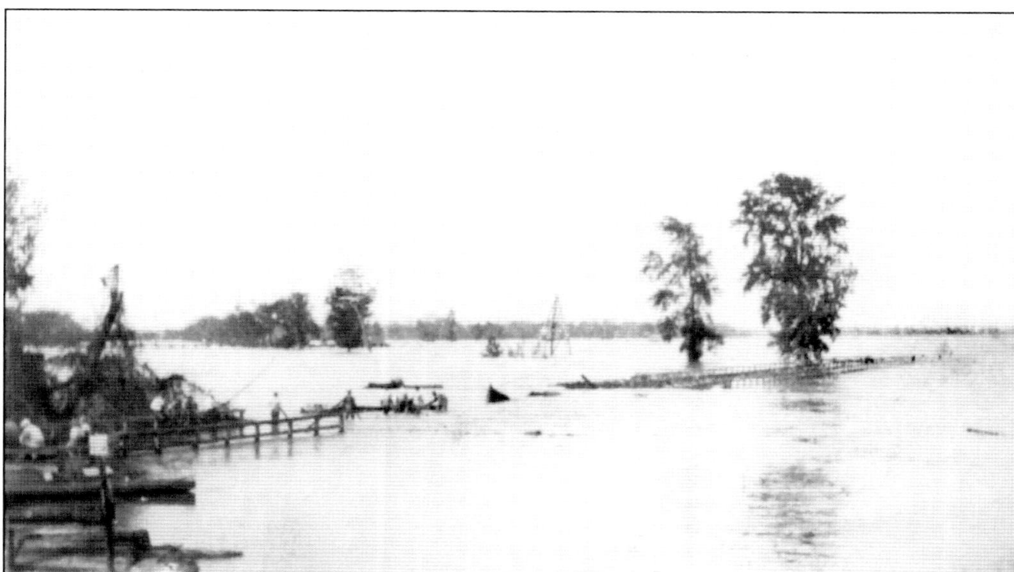

This photograph of the submerged bridge (the same one as above) dramatically illustrates the rise of the Cache River at Brasfield during the 1927 flood. (Courtesy of the Torreyson Library, University of Central Arkansas.)

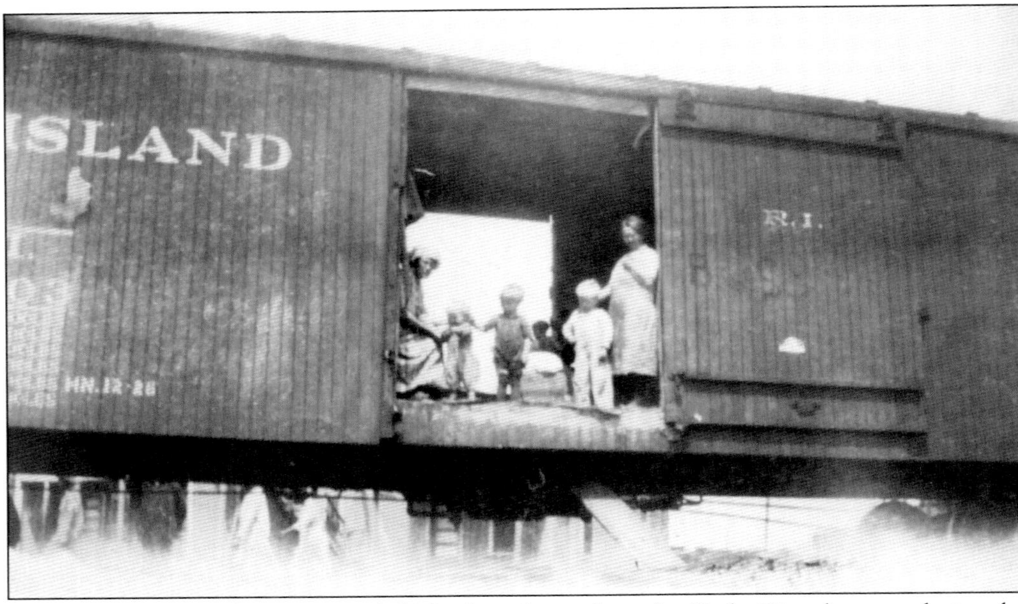

The Red Cross placed tents at Brasfield for the refugees from the Cache River bottoms during the 1927 flood. Some families were allowed to stay in Brown Lumber Company's garages and resaw shed. Others like the Roberts family, shown here, lived in boxcars placed on the railroad's side track. (Courtesy of Torreyson Library, University of Central Arkansas.)

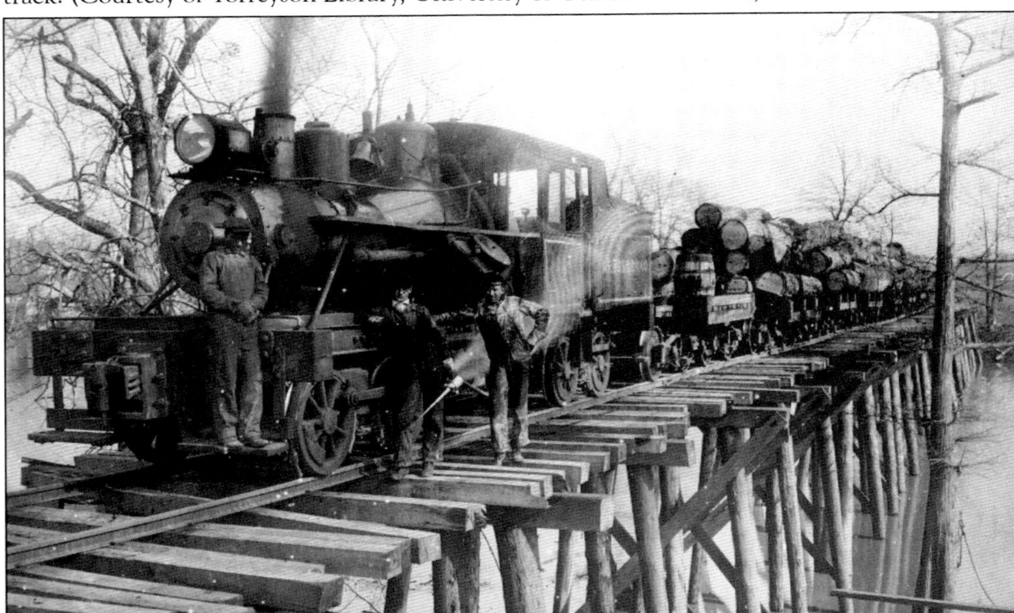

W.P. Brown and Sons Lumber Company used two Heissler locomotives to transport logs from the Cache River bottoms to its mill site at Brasfield. Shown in this 1923 photograph taken on its Cache River bridge are, from left to right, "Texas" (brakeman), Roy Mitchell (fireman), and Joe Hodge (engineer). (Courtesy of the Torreyson Library, University of Central Arkansas.)

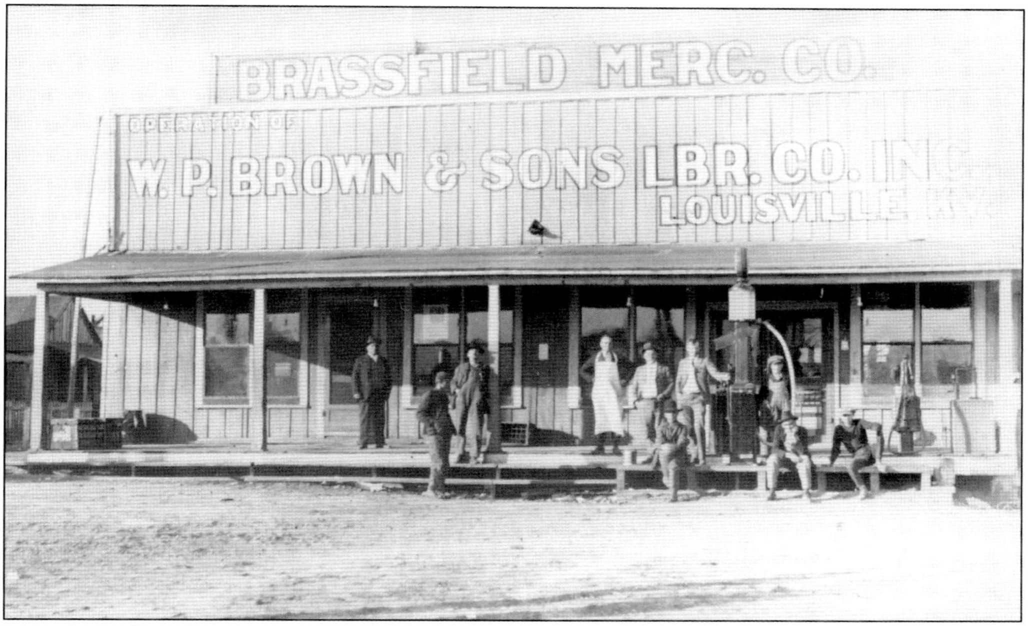

Brown Lumber Company's commissary store served the needs of the company's many workers and farm families. Pictured are, from left to right, (first row) three unidentified and Oliver Sayger; (second row) Sam Carmack, Jack Harris, Emmit Ruff, Walter Williams, John Lilley, and Joe Carmack. (Courtesy of the Torreyson Library, University of Central Arkansas.)

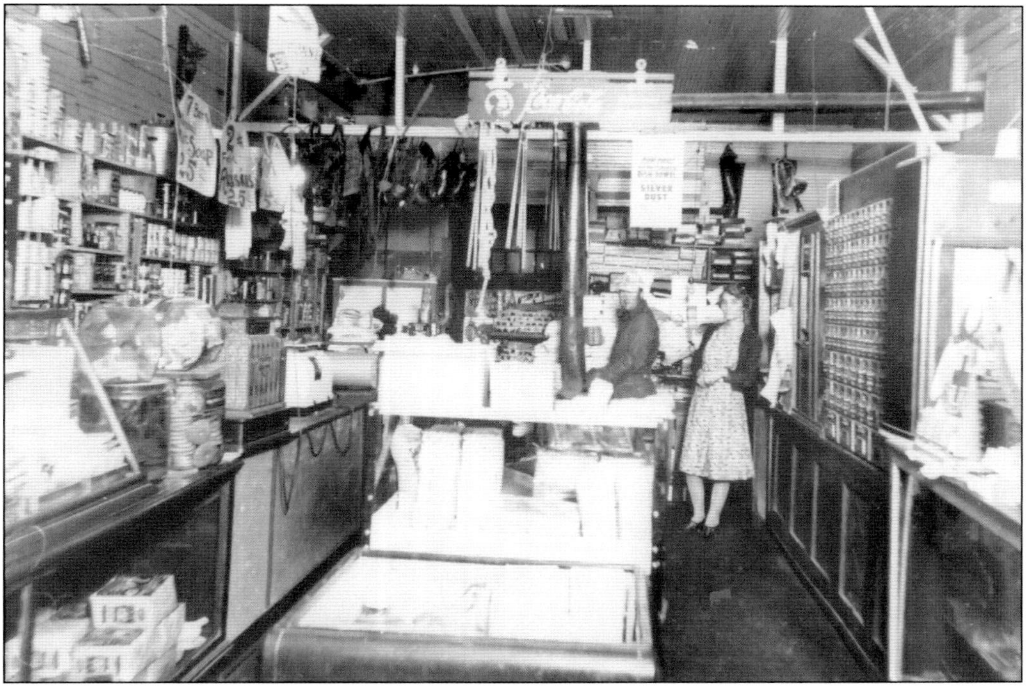

Richard Overholt and Katie Williams appear in this late 1940s photograph of Katie and husband Walter's mercantile store at Brasfield. She was the town's postmaster. Note the mailboxes to the right. (Courtesy of Torreyson Library, University of Central Arkansas.)

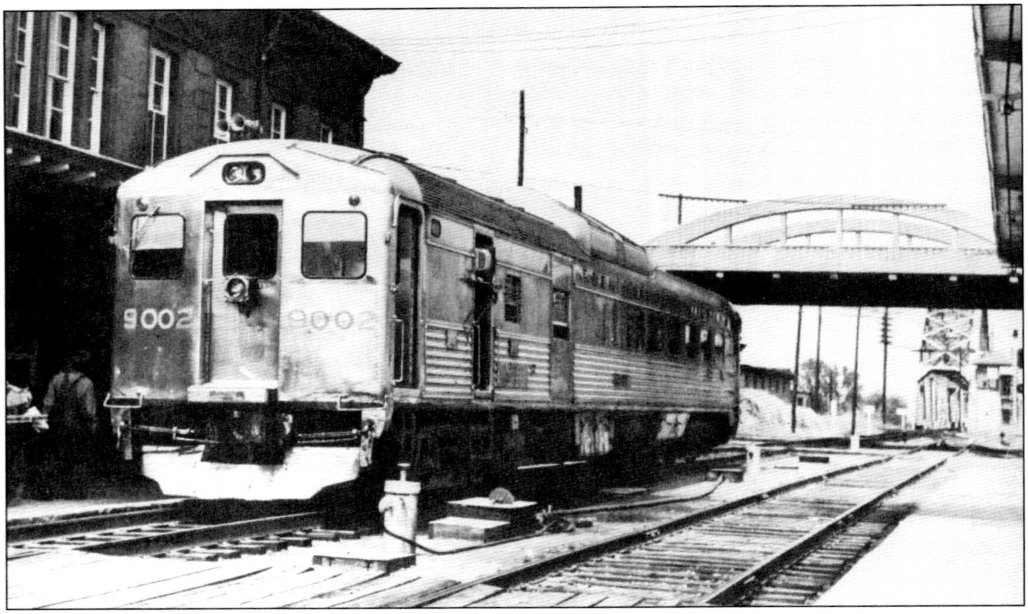

The Rock Island Railroad had two of these rail diesel cars named the *Choctaw Rockette*, commonly known as the "Doodlebug," which worked in tandem between Little Rock and Oklahoma City, making a round trip each day. In the 1950s, Katie Williams, postmaster at Brasfield, would pay a child 5¢ to deliver the mailbag that was thrown off twice a day by this train. (Courtesy of the Rock Island Archives.)

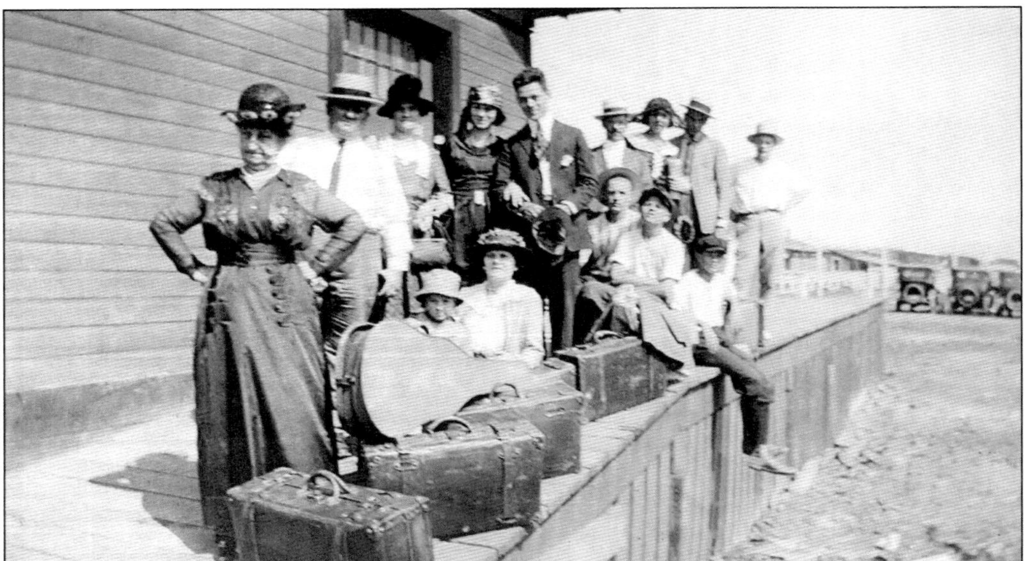

Possibly as early as 1911, several Little Rock families were coming to Brasfield by train and transported by boat to the Argenta Cache River Fishing Club, two miles upstream. In this c. 1920 photograph taken at the Brasfield depot are, from left to right, (first row) unidentified, Frieda Busse Blackburn, unidentified, Charles Blackburn, and unidentified; (second row) Frederica Schmand Schwarz, Jack Blackburn, Anna Schmand, Mary Sites, unidentified, William Schmand, Alma Schmand Stephen, Earl M. Stephen, and Albert Schmand. (Courtesy of Randy Stephen.)

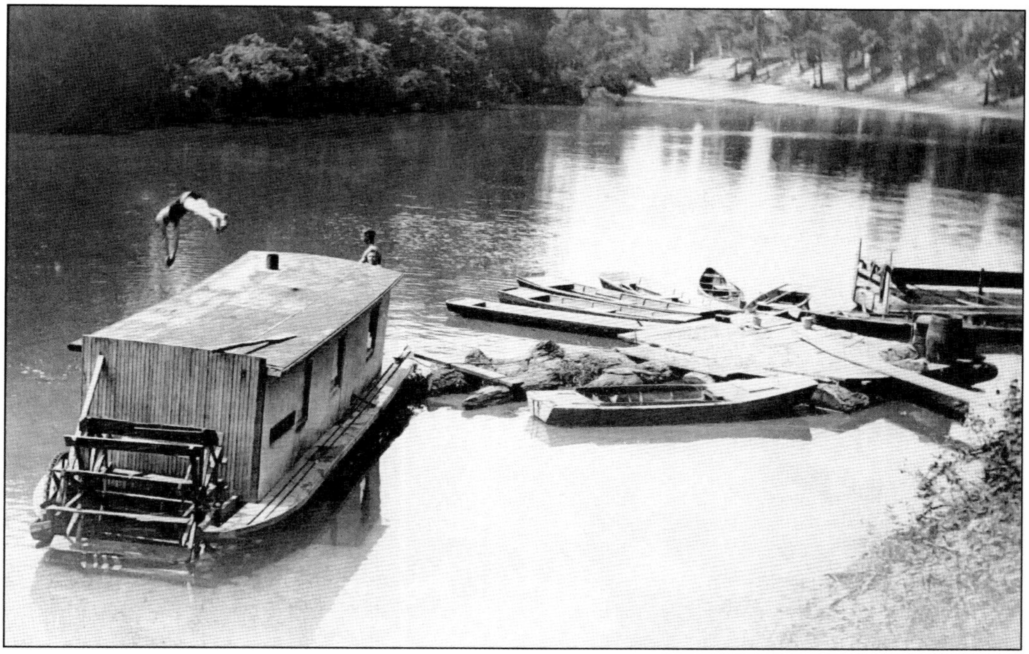

This little sternwheeler on the Cache River and inboard motorboats were used to transport Argenta Cache River Fishing Club members from Brasfield to their clubhouse. Brown Lumber Company also used a sternwheeler to house crews cutting timber and rafting logs at Culotches Bay and at other points on the river. (Courtesy of Randy Stephen.)

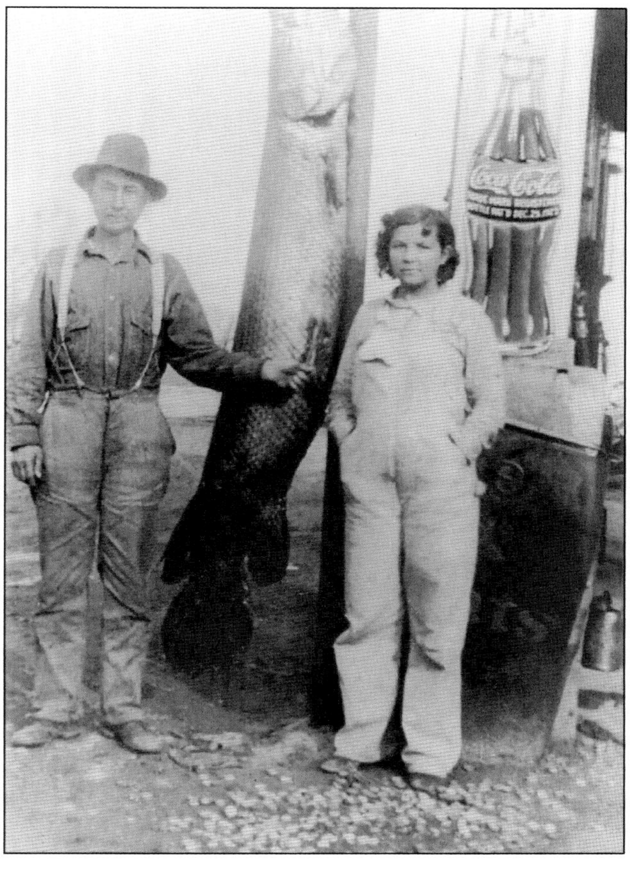

J.A. Washam (1878–1953) and his daughter Madge posed with this monstrous alligator gar in 1937. Unfortunately, the head with its pointed snout does not appear in this photograph. The Indians sometimes used the thick scales to tip their arrows when hunting for small game such as birds. (Courtesy of Edith Miller Thomas.)

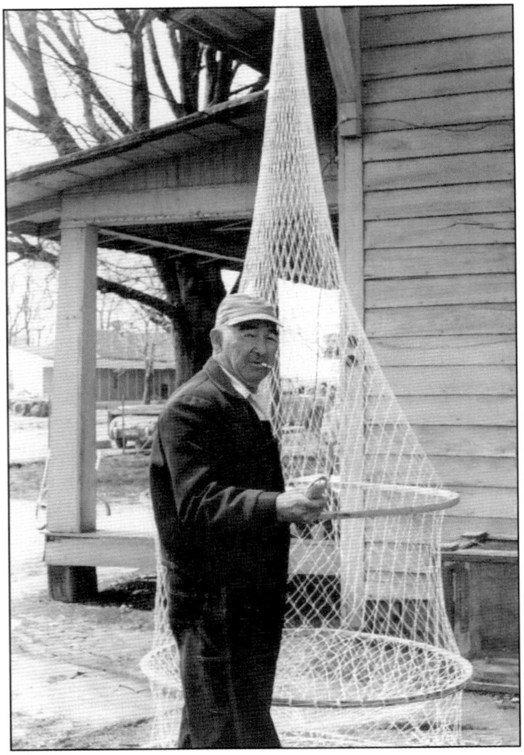

Roy Kidd "Buss" Sayger is using his knitting needle to attach hoops to a barrel fishing net. As late as the 1950s, some fishermen were still using handcrafted wooden hoops. Now, they are all made of fiberglass. (Courtesy of Bill Sayger.)

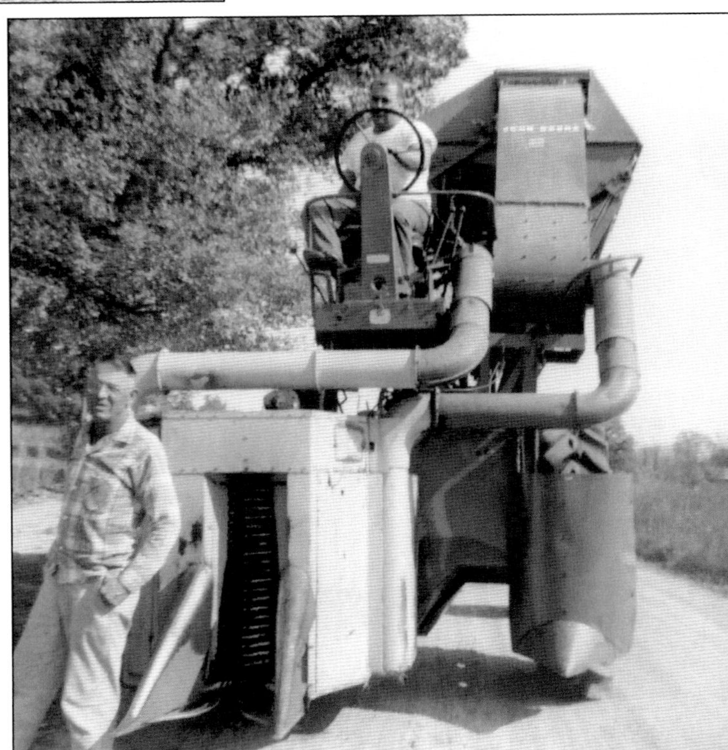

In the late 1940s and 1950s, many people left eastern Arkansas seeking better paying jobs and to escape racial discrimination. The shortage of labor forced large landowners to bring in mechanical cotton pickers to help harvest the cotton. This one-row cotton picker was photographed in Brasfield about 1960. Pictured are Oliver Sayger (left) and Bobby Dean Holloway. Today's machines can harvest six rows at a time. (Courtesy of Bill Sayger.)

John and Ruby Shegog raised cotton and sharecropped on Hester Buck Robinson's land near Brasfield. The sharecropping system came into use following the Civil War. The freed blacks and whites would farm for the landowners, who provided housing, seed, equipment, and needed items. In return, the sharecroppers received a portion of the profits after the harvest. (Courtesy of Torreyson Library, University of Central Arkansas.)

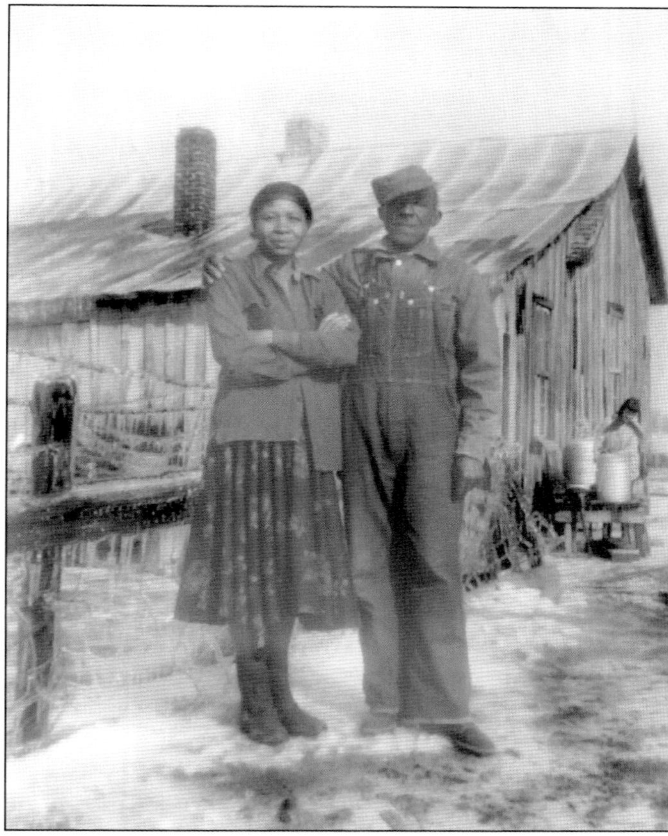

Pictured around 1950 are, from left to right, Patsy Clark Prince and Betty Sue Prince in front of Jelks's Confectionery in Brasfield. Part of the front of A.A. Moss's general store is visible in the background. (Courtesy of Patsy Clark Prince.)

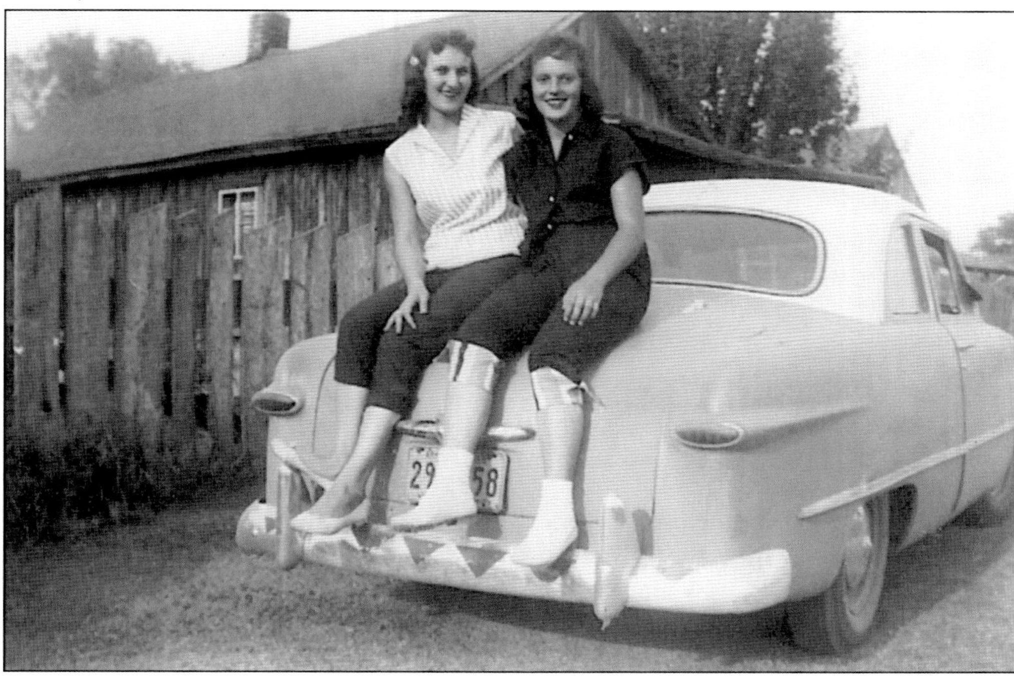